JOHN DART, news editor of the *Christian Century* magazine and a religion writer at the *Los Angeles Times* for thirty years, has written extensively about New Testament research. His books include *The Laughing Savior: The Discovery and Significance of the Nag Hammadi Gnostic Library; The Gospel of Thomas: Unearthing the Lost Words of Jesus;* and *Deities & Deadlines*. Dart has won numerous reporting awards.

DECODING MARK

DECODING
MARK

John Dart

TRINITY PRESS INTERNATIONAL
A Continuum imprint
HARRISBURG • LONDON • NEW YORK

Copyright © 2003 by John Dart

Trinity Press International, P.O. Box 1321, Harrisburg, PA 17105
Trinity Press International is a member of the Continuum International Publishing Group.

Cover design: Brenda Klinger

Library of Congress Cataloging-in-Publication Data

Dart, John, 1936–
 Decoding Mark / John Dart.
    p. cm.
Includes bibliographical references and index.
 ISBN 1-56338-374-8
 1. Bible. N.T. Mark—Criticism, interpretation, etc. 2. Secret Gospel according to Mark. I. Title.
 BS2585.52 .D37 2003
 226.3'06—dc21

                        2003010300

Printed in the United States of America
03 04 05 06 07 08   10 9 8 7 6 5 4 3 2 1

To Morton Smith (1915–1991)

Contents

Acknowledgments

I AM GRATEFUL to the many university and seminary professors who for years admitted this journalist into their conferences and confidences. By the same token, I thank *Los Angeles Times* editors who for three decades allowed me to report biblical research news along with other religion stories. Morton Smith's discovery of the Secret Mark fragment and the findings of Helmut Koester and Joanna Dewey all enabled this study to take surprising steps forward. Smith, Arthur Dewey, John Dominic Crossan, Marvin Meyer, Scott G. Brown, and Charles Hedrick gave good advice when asked. This book might not have been written had it not been for the vital support of Henry Carrigan, Trinity Press's editorial director. Amy Wagner followed up with deft manuscript guidance; Ruthann Dwyer excelled in copyediting. Two scholars did not know how important they were to my two-stage discoveries in the Gospel of Mark: My digging tools were well-worn copies of *An Analytical Concordance to the Revised Standard Version of the New Testament* by Clinton Morrison and *New Gospel Parallels, Volume One, The Synoptic Gospels* by Robert W. Funk. The Revised Standard Version was used because of its rather literal translations of the Greek. The editors of *The Christian Century*, my employers since 2000, have my gratitude for their flexibility and encouragement. Finally, I thank my wife for her love, and her tolerance of my helter-skelter piles of books, and hours in front of the computer screen.

CHAPTER 1

A Night with Jesus—the Lost Episode

TAKING TIME OFF from campus duties in 1958, the Columbia University professor of ancient history traveled to Israel to revisit one of Eastern Christianity's best-known monasteries. "I was ready for a rest and remembered the tranquility of Mar Saba," recalled Professor Morton Smith, referring to the desert retreat.

Smith had stayed at Mar Saba Monastery for two months in 1941 while pursuing graduate work at Hebrew University in Jerusalem. The twenty-six-year-old American was on a traveling fellowship from Harvard Divinity School when World War II closed the Mediterranean Sea and he "got stuck" in Jerusalem. Smith decided to work for a doctoral degree at Hebrew University, studying relationships between the Gospels and writings of the earliest rabbis. He would later earn a second doctorate in theology at Harvard.

During Smith's student days in Jerusalem, his landlord was a Greek Orthodox priest who was impressed by the American's fascination with liturgical rites at the Church of the Holy Sepulchre in Jerusalem. The priest secured an invitation for Smith to visit picturesque Mar Saba, which dated back nearly fifteen hundred years as a monastic site. Smith made the trip to the monastery by donkey, as part of a food convoy traveling the dozen miles southwest from Jerusalem. Finally descending into a steep, virtually treeless canyon, Smith saw a monastery structure built into the cliffs. Caves once used by hermit monks dotted the

1

canyon walls. Smith was struck by the silence of Mar Saba and its uncomplicated regimen, which consisted of long, postmidnight Byzantine rites, prescribed times for prayer, and the one daily meal at noon.

In the years after World War II, Smith maintained a correspondence with monastery officials. In 1958 he accepted an offer to catalog a collection of manuscripts in one of their libraries. Smith traveled by taxi this time and noted that electric lights illuminated the monastery's interior. His ardor for lengthy liturgies had dimmed by this visit. But he looked forward to a routine of handling books and musty manuscripts without distractions.[1]

Smith began each morning by climbing a long stairway, accompanied by a monk, to the library tower. There he sorted through printed books for any handwritten materials on blank pages or insertions. When he found four to five manuscripts, the two men left the tower together, and Smith went to his cell. He typically read hymns, prayer books, sermons, and lives of the saints. The next morning, again with his escort, Smith returned the previous day's manuscripts to the library and thumbed through more volumes.

"Little by little the chaos of old books was reduced to order," Smith recalled years later. "I had not expected much from the Mar Saba manuscripts," he said, knowing that writings deemed important had already been sent to Jerusalem to the library of the Greek Orthodox patriarchate. "But there was always the chance that something was missed," Smith said.[2]

While perusing some more handwritten pages, Smith observed that the covers typically were stiffened with older pages glued together. Near the end of his stay, he noticed just such a page stuck to the back leaf of a seventeenth-century book of the letters of St. Ignatius of Antioch. "I found myself . . . staring incredulously at a text written in a tiny scrawl I had not even tried to read in the tower when I picked the book containing it," he said.[3]

Before Smith was a copied fragment of a letter purportedly from Clement of Alexandria, a late-first-century C.E. churchman in Egypt's most prominent city of that day. The letter began by praising its recipient, one Theodore, for refuting the teachings of the Carpocratians, a heretical sect that by all accounts flouted sexual conventions. Smith's first rush of excitement grew from the chance that he had stumbled upon previously unknown correspondence from one of Christendom's leading church fathers.

"I hastened to photograph the text . . . three times for good measure," said Smith.[4] He felt he could not spend much time on one text and still complete the job of cataloging the library's manuscripts. Once away from the monastery and back in Jerusalem, he hoped to study the photos more carefully.

The Secret Gospel of Mark

Fortunately, the photographic prints were clear enough for Smith to write out a transcription of the Greek and translate it. He soon saw that the text's importance lay not in what it told about tensions between Clement and the Carpocratians. Instead, the significance was in a writing that Clement called the "Secret Gospel of Mark" (which I refer to hereafter as "Secret Mark") and an excerpt from that document that Clement quoted. No previously known Christian literature or letters had ever alluded to a secret version of the Gospel of Mark, much less quote from such a text.

The Gospel of Mark, the earliest of the New Testament's four gospels, had an extraordinary impact on Christianity's rise. Its story of Jesus provided the narrative core for the gospels of Matthew and Luke and may have influenced the Gospel of John. Written by most estimates thirty-five to forty-five years after Jesus' death, Mark tells an engrossing tale of the Nazarene from adult baptism and his wonder-working ministry in Galilee to his teachings on the way to Jerusalem and his dramatic arrest, crucifixion, and resurrection. Mark ends mysteriously with an unnamed "young man" in an empty tomb telling three women that the crucified Jesus had risen.

According to the letter found by Smith, Clement told his addressee that Carpocrates, the founder of the sect, had apparently obtained a copy of the Secret Gospel from the church in Alexandria. The Carpocratians, one of many gnostic groups engaged in theological battles with what became Christian orthodoxy, were mixing lies with truth in teaching from the Secret Gospel, Clement complained.

Clement recounted church tradition that Mark was a scribal associate of the apostle Peter during the latter's stay in Rome and then went to Alexandria after Peter's martyrdom. But in addition Clement wrote that Mark had expanded on his original gospel while in Egypt to include some secret material for advanced believers. "He composed a more spiritual Gospel for the use of those who were being perfected," said Clement. It was "read only to those who are being initiated into the great mysteries."[5]

As known from his other writings, Clement of Alexandria had defined the Christian as the true possessor of "gnosis," or special spiritual knowledge. That elite status was also claimed by groups such as the Carpocratians in the early centuries of Christianity. But to Clement, Christian gnosis was a treasured gift. In confiding his understanding of Mark's purpose, Clement wrote to Theodore, "[T]o the stories already written he added yet others and moreover brought in certain sayings of which he knew the interpretation would, as a mystagogue, lead the hearers into the innermost sanctuary of that truth hidden by seven [veils]."[6] Clement added that authentic Christians should never admit that the Secret Gospel was written by Mark; indeed, they should deny it under oath.

Then, answering Theodore's inquiry, Clement wrote out a section of Secret Mark that he accused the Carpocratians of altering. Unlike today's Bible readers—who can refer to chapter and verse numbers, a much later innovation in the churches—Clement could refer Theodore only to sections of Mark bordering the Secret Mark passages. After the third prediction by Jesus that the Son of Man would rise after three days (which ends at 10:34), here is what followed, "word for word," according to Clement:

And they come into Bethany, and a certain woman, whose brother had died, was there. And coming, she prostrated herself before Jesus and says to him, "Son of David, have mercy on me." But the disciples rebuked her. And Jesus, being angered, went off with her into the garden where the tomb was, and straightway a great cry was heard from the tomb. And going near Jesus rolled away the stone from the door of the tomb. And straightway, going in where the young man was, he stretched forth his hand and raised him, seizing his hand.

But the young man, looking upon him, loved him and began to beseech him that he might be with him. And going out of the tomb, they came into the house of the young man, for he was rich. And after six days, Jesus told him what to do and in the evening the young man comes to him, wearing a linen cloth over [his] naked [body]. And he remained with him that night, for Jesus taught him the secret of the kingdom of God. And thence, arising, he returned to the other side of the Jordan.[7]

Clement said that Secret Mark then resumes with an episode about James and John (10:35–45 in biblical Mark). The church leader noted that added material in the Carpocratian version reported by Theodore—about "naked man with naked man" and other things—are not found in the church's copy. Clement also said that after the words in biblical Mark, "And he comes into Jericho" (at the start of 10:46), the Secret Gospel adds only:

> And the sister of the young man whom Jesus loved and his mother and Salome were there, and Jesus did not receive them.[8]

Clement further cautioned Theodore: "But the many other [things about] which you wrote both seem to be and are falsifications. Now the true explanation and that which accords with the true philosophy . . ."[9] The text of the letter broke off here, in the middle of a page, according to Smith.

Realizing he had stumbled across a letter of possible "extraordinary importance," Smith felt conflicting instincts. "If it was a fake of some sort and I rushed into print with an announcement of a 'great discovery,' I could make myself an internationally conspicuous fool," he later recalled. "So I kept my mouth shut."[10]

The American started consulting experts. The handwriting style was identified by several as typical of the eighteenth century C.E. Smith knew that would not present problems if it could be shown that the copied letter (perhaps a many-times copied letter) resembled Clement's style, ideas, and vocabulary. "By good luck, a lot of Clement's work had been preserved—three big volumes full," Smith said.[11] Most of the fourteen scholars solicited by Smith to compare Clement's known writings with the new letter found similarities so close that it "was either written by Clement or it is a deliberate and careful imitation, not to say a forgery."[12]

Smith announced his find in 1960 at an evening session of the year-end meeting of the Society of Biblical Literature, the nation's largest group of biblical scholars. The *New York Times* reported twice on the discovery, with the second-day story focusing on the critical response by Pierson Parker of General Theological Seminary. Parker doubted that the quoted gospel passages were written by the author of Mark, even if Clement was indeed the letter's author. Instead, Parker said, the story of Jesus raising a young man from the dead and teaching him was probably written by a Christian somewhat before Clement's time.[13] A short report in the January 6, 1961, issue of *Time* emphasized not the newly found Jesus story but the first-ever evidence that some early Christians held a secret gospel reserved for use by an inner circle of Christian initiates.[14]

The Acerbic Professor Publishes

More than a decade went by before Secret Mark stirred scholars again. Smith wanted to publish simultaneously a popular account for interested laypersons and a detailed work for an expected legion of skeptics in academia. Sharp criticism was almost guaranteed, partly because of Smith's personality. The sharp-tongued professor, for one thing, usually expressed disdain for scholars he regarded as second-rate. Not only that, Smith had a penchant for publicity—a practice that irked many colleagues.

Smith finished writing both books in 1966, but the scholarly volume for Harvard University Press moved slowly through revisions. That delayed the release of *The Secret Gospel*—his Harper & Row book bearing his most sensational conclusions. The two tomes finally were published in 1973 and reaffirmed the Columbia University professor's delight in making waves.

Smith suggested that the mystery initiation in Secret Mark, together with selected hints in the New Testament, revealed the historical Jesus to be a first-century C.E. mystagogue. Through the rites of this *magus*, or magician, "the disciple was possessed by Jesus' spirit and so united with Jesus."[15] Smith further speculated that by hallucination or self-hypnosis, the disciple could ascend with Jesus to the heavens and be set free from the laws governing the lower world. "Freedom from the law may have resulted in completion of the spiritual union by physical union," Smith wrote.[16] Especially suggestive were Secret Mark's words that Jesus and the young man he raised from the dead "loved" one another. Smith contended that certain libertine, erotic strands of early Christianity, including movements branded as heresies, could have stemmed from the teachings of Jesus—shocking statements for churchgoers, to be sure, but disturbing also to learned clergy and professors.

Some reviewers who welcomed the discovery of a previously unknown episode about Jesus nevertheless felt that Smith's speculations about the historical Jesus were unwarranted. Other reviewers did not bother to consider Smith's reconstruction of Jesus' image. Instead, they raised suspicions of a forgery by an eighteenth-century scribe, or even a hoax perpetrated by Smith himself.

Notes

1. Morton Smith's account of his discovery and subsequent research is drawn entirely from his popularly written book *The Secret Gospel: The Discovery and Interpretation of the Secret Gospel according to Mark* (New York: Harper & Row, 1973). A later paperback edition by the same title and with a foreword by Elaine Pagels and a postscript by Smith was published in 1982 by the Dawn Horse Press (Clearlake, Calif.). His scholarly version is *Clement of Alexandria and a Secret Gospel of Mark* (Cambridge, Mass.: Harvard University Press, 1973).

2. Smith, *The Secret Gospel,* 11.

3. Ibid., 12.

4. Ibid., 13.

5. Ibid., 15.

6. Ibid.

7. Ibid., 16, 17.

8. Ibid., 17. Smith translated *neaniskas* as "youth" but I use "young man" as well as "secret" instead of "mystery" hereafter to conform to the RSV translation of this figure in Mark.

9. Ibid.

10. Ibid., 18.

11. Ibid., 20.

12. Ibid., 28.

13. "A New Gospel Ascribed to Mark: Copy of Greek Letter Says Saint Kept 'Mysteries' Out," *New York Times,* December 30, 1960; "Expert Disputes 'Secret' Gospel: Theologian Says Style of Excerpts Does Not Show They Were by Mark," *New York Times,* December 31, 1960.

14. "The Secret Gospel," *Time,* January 6, 1961, 48.

15. Smith, *The Secret Gospel,* 113.

16. Ibid., 114.

CHAPTER 2

Forgery, or Clue to Early Christianity?

WORDS LIKE "FAKE" AND "HOAX" were freely bandied about one December day in 1975 at a special conference of academic heavyweights in Berkeley, California.[1] Some two dozen professors and graduate students discussed Morton Smith's Secret Mark discovery in the desert nearly two decades earlier and his provocative views of its significance. The speaker lineup included three future presidents of the Society of Biblical Literature (SBL).[2]

One of those three was Paul J. Achtemeier, who declared that Smith's "major failing" was "his disregard of any attempt to carry on a sound tradition-historical analysis" of the fragment in question.[3] However, Achtemeier kept his remarks short, referring conferees to his recent review of Smith's book. But the seminary professor nevertheless echoed widespread skepticism in scholarly circles. Some pointed to the lack of an independent verification of the manuscript as photographed and described by Smith.

Two other New Testament specialists defended Smith at the Berkeley meeting. They chided those who considered any text not included in the Bible—so-called apocryphal writings—as historically suspect. They also defended Smith's theories about Jesus as a mystery teacher. "Prof. Smith's hypothesis is at least as good as any other hypothesis I know," said Harvard Divinity School's Helmut Koester. Church members in Corinth, Greece, whom the apostle Paul advised in two letters, "probably understood baptism as a mystery initiation," Koester said. "Christian teaching for [the Corinthians] was esoteric wisdom."[4]

The unusually frank debate, with Smith present, was held at a center run by the University of California (UC) at Berkeley and the multi-seminary Graduate Theological Union (GTU). The colloquy began on a relatively calm note with a keynote talk by Reginald H. Fuller, a well-regarded biblical scholar from Virginia Theological Seminary. Skipping over the question of whether Clement was the actual author of this letter, Fuller zeroed in on the quoted segment from Secret Mark, called "Longer Mark" at the meeting. He agreed with Smith that the resuscitation of a dead man resembles the "raising of Lazarus" in the Gospel of John. But the section in which Jesus stays with and instructs the young man struck Fuller as a later appendage to the resuscitation story. He agreed that the phrase "after six days" in the newly discovered story refers "to a preparatory period for sacramental initiation."[5]

As for the mutual "love" of the young initiate and Jesus, Fuller said, "There is no reason to suppose that Longer Mark intended anything homosexual in that phrase"—no more than it did when biblical Mark (also in the tenth chapter) said Jesus "looked upon and loved" a rich man unwilling to give up his wealth to follow Jesus.[6] As a result, Fuller concluded that the story of Jesus and the young man "turns out to be far less significant for the reconstruction of the historical Jesus and far less sensational than Professor Smith supposed."[7]

In his response, Smith complimented Fuller, after a fashion. Calling Fuller's paper "one of the first considered evaluations by a competent scholar," Smith said many reviews, "even in responsible journals, have been little more than expressions of hostility and often grossly inaccurate." Furthermore: "As the ludicrous performances of other scholars have shown, it is an exceptional man who can give an objective account of new evidence and new ideas."[8]

Smith disputed only a few details in Fuller's paper, including how far back in time Smith would place the origin of the new Jesus story. Some form of the resuscitation story is old, claimed Smith. The core account of Jesus raising a young man from the dead found in Secret Mark was less developed than the Gospel of John's story of Jesus raising Lazarus from the dead. Unlike the elaborate story of Lazarus and Mary in John 11, Secret Mark does not identify the youth and his sister. Smith said he was not claiming that the newfound episode was written by the author of the Gospel of Mark—despite the very vocabulary, phrasing, and writing peculiarities characteristic of biblical Mark. "There was almost nothing in it that Mark could not have written," Smith wrote in *The Secret Gospel.* "But there was one very serious objection. The text was more like Mark than a section of Mark should be. . . . This looked like the result of imitation."[9]

Summarizing in Berkeley what he thought was the literary background of the resuscitation story, Smith said it probably was written about 50 C.E. in Aramaic, a then-common language in Palestine. The author of Mark, writing around 75 C.E., did not use the account, Smith said. But after the Gospel of Mark "had won an authoritative position in the community for which it was written, someone who revered it produced an expanded edition, including at least some material translated from the Aramaic source," Smith told the colloquy. "The material thus added was cast in a style deliberately imitative of canonical Mark's," said Smith, suggesting at the Berkeley meeting that the addition might have been made about 95 C.E. It was eliminated from Mark, however, through "early censorship" of the Gospel, perhaps around 110 C.E., he said.[10] To illustrate his theory, Smith drew a diagram of overlapping circles. "Any resemblance to the Trinity is purely coincidental," said Smith in a sardonic aside on the Christian doctrine. "My theory differs from the customary account of the Trinity in a number of important respects; e.g., in being rationally comprehensible."[11]

Smith's Antagonists and Defenders

Several critics at the Berkeley conference, however, still smelled a rat. Rather than discuss the ramifications of a possible long-lost gospel episode, they asked whether the text was a hoax. "I am not concerned with an eighteenth-century forger, but with a possible twentieth-century one," said a Jesuit specialist in New Testament. "My skeptical frame of mind remains until I see the document."[12]

Two other opponents reminded conferees that scholarly evidence questions were raised in the *Catholic Biblical Quarterly* two months earlier by Quentin Quesnell, who was not at the Berkeley discussion. Edward C. Hobbs, who taught theology at the Church Divinity School of the Pacific, a seminary in the Graduate Theological Union, praised the "devastatingly on-target critique" by Quesnell, who had asked "why no scholar in the world except Morton Smith, even after seventeen years, has seen this document."[13]

Observing that Smith usually attacks views at odds with his own as "worthless," "hostile," and "muddled," Hobbs predicted that "our deliberations are unlikely to meet any different fate." He predicted that Smith would praise sympathetic responses to his work and damn those who differ. "Will we, hopefully, be allowed to choose whether we are to be labeled 'stupid,' 'ludicrous' or merely engaging in 'fantasy'?"[14]

A Smith defender in Berkeley, in addition to Koester, was Hans Dieter Betz, then of the Institute for Antiquity and Christianity in Claremont, California, and later with the University of Chicago Divinity School faculty. Betz deplored Quesnell's article for transforming Smith "into a combination of Dr. Faustus and Mephistopheles." The normally cautious Betz warned pointedly against dismissing Jesus' image as a magician and mystagogue as the invention of second-century C.E. heretics. The image of Jesus in Matthew, Mark, and Luke "does contain similar traits in spite of the fact that the gentile Christian gospel writers have done their best to reduce the element of magic and mystery," Betz said. "Whether the historical Jesus was closer to the synoptic gospels or to the apocryphal gospels is still an open question"— not a statement that Betz probably would have made if news reporters were at the Berkeley discussion.[15] This journalist's account of the meeting comes from a transcript received much later. Betz did complain to me once when I worked as a religion writer for the *Los Angeles Times* that news stories on the relatively liberal findings in biblical studies made life difficult for faculties at mainline seminaries. The church public, seldom exposed to anything more than traditional Bible interpretations, tended to get upset over alleged historical uncertainties in biblical accounts, he indicated.

At the closed meeting in Berkeley, however, Betz minced no words. On the polarized reactions to Smith's claims, Betz contended unhappily that biblical scholars fall into one of two types: "One, strangely enough, resents the discovery of new texts, and another is fascinated by them." As for himself, "I see the Mar Saba fragment as part of the numerous writings which have surfaced in the past generation and which will force us to rewrite the history of primitive Christianity," said Betz.[16]

Betz also criticized a contrast commonly drawn in New Testament research between the presumed purity of "originally simple gospel accounts" and the supposed later corruptions of the Jesus story in apocryphal gospel materials. The word *apocryphal* literally means "hidden" or "obscure." But it also has come to mean in a popular sense "false" or "unsubstantiated"—since early church authorities declined to endorse what they regarded as spurious accounts for entry into the biblical canon.

Koester seconded some of Betz's views. On the question of Jesus as a mystagogue, Koester noted that whether Jesus himself initiated or baptized anyone remained an enigma. He pointed to "indications for the existence of mystery concepts and rites at an early date in the history of Christianity."[17] And Smith's theory of how the young man's resuscitation story found its way in and out of canonical Mark is not far-fetched, according to Koester, who affirms there must have been "a great variety" of copies and editions of the four gospels: "During the period from circa A.D. 50 to the end of the second century, there was also no protection against alteration for any of this literature.What finally came to be the canonical version may not have been the original at all."[18] Mark and John very probably fall into this category.

The two New Testament gospels of Mark and John contain apparent additions, some cherished by churches, some not. The longer endings to the Gospel of Mark (16:9–20), absent from the oldest manuscripts, are largely ignored, except by snake-handling churches in Appalachia who accept the risen Jesus' prediction that baptized believers will pick up snakes and drink poison without harm. The Gospel of John comes to an apparent close at the end of the twentieth chapter. The twenty-first chapter, which some scholars think was added later, describes the risen Jesus urging Peter to "feed my sheep," a line still heard in churches. In another case, the earliest manuscripts of John lack the story of the woman accused of adultery (7:53–8:11). Jesus rescues her when he tells anyone without sin to cast the first stone. While it's possible that the story went back to the historical Jesus, it conceivably was inserted into John, however belatedly, because of the exquisite lesson in judgment and forgiveness. Apparently, none of the other gospel writers knew of it.

Despite the opinions of Koester, Betz, and Fuller that the new Jesus anecdote was plausibly ancient, most of the conferees were suspicious of one or more aspects of Smith's claims. A GTU doctoral student who attended the proceedings, Joanna Dewey, recalled twenty-five years later while serving as academic dean at the Episcopal Divinity School in Cambridge, Massachusetts, that she was impressed by the skeptical assessments of professors from the UC Berkeley classics department. "They tore into it," she told me in a telephone interview. "They thoroughly convinced me that it was a late forgery."[19] Dewey, who had already published an important article on Mark two years earlier, was influenced greatly in studies of that gospel by Hobbs at the Episcopal seminary in the GTU consortium.

The Balance Sheet on Secret Mark

Seven years later, in 1982, Smith tallied up "the score" for and against his discovery.[20] Since his two books were published in 1973, Smith counted eleven scholars who thought that the new Jesus story of resuscitation and initiation of the young man had existed in some form prior to the writing of the Gospel of Mark. However, fifteen others thought "the secret material [was] composed entirely from scraps of the canonical gospels and free invention"—and dismissed it as apocryphal and relatively insignificant.[21] On the question of forgery or fake, Smith fared better: Twenty-five scholars said Clement wrote it, six suspended judgment or did not discuss it, and four felt that Clement did not compose the letter.

Smith also pointed out a boost for the credibility of Clement's letter from another source. In January 1980, Thomas Talley of New York's General Theological Seminary had asked about the Clement letter when he was in Jerusalem. The archimandrite Melito told Talley that he had brought the manuscript from the Mar Saba Monastery to the Greek Orthodox patriarchate's library. The librarian there said it was removed from the printed volume but was unavailable for inspection because it was being studied. Two decades later, Talley confirmed to me in a phone conversation that what Smith wrote was accurate. The retired seminary professor could not add any details, however, and he had not pursued the matter further.

My own contact with Smith was mostly through the mail.[22] I wrote to him in 1977, a year after my book was published on the Nag Hammadi Library, a discovery in Egypt in 1945 that was as important for Christian studies as the Dead Scrolls were for Judaism. I had cited some parallels between quasi-gnostic, apocryphal Christian writings and the Secret Mark episode quoted by Clement.

"I'm happy that you've noticed the many similarities between my picture of Jesus and the traditions of early gnosticism," Smith replied. He said that he purposely left out gnostic-like parallels because "they would have given aid and comfort to the obscurantists who were sure to try to dismiss the new material as 'gnostic and apocrypal.'"[23] Smith said that those parallels and material from so-called magical papyri of that era would appear in his next book, provocatively titled *Jesus the Magician.* Shortly after it was published in 1978, he thanked me for sending him my review in the *Los Angeles Times,* noting he had received no other review except "a snide advance notice that appeared in *Kirkus*—the defensive objections of some pious Christian determined to keep as many people as possible from considering the facts."[24] Nevertheless, the book won Columbia University's Lionel Trilling Book Award, and Smith himself was honored in 1980 by the Society of Biblical Literature for his historical work supporting biblical studies.

The disparate reactions Smith drew from others were captured a couple years later by Elaine Pagels, a New Testament scholar who taught at Barnard College, a neighboring campus to Smith's Columbia University. "Professor Smith is that rarity among scholars, an excellent writer," wrote Pagels, author of *The Gnostic Gospels* and other books enjoyed by the public. In a foreword to a paperback reprint of Smith's *Secret Gospel,* Pagels observed, "While his scholarly credentials are impeccable, Professor Smith's theory—as he himself anticipated—has proven to be explosively controversial."[25]

Some colleagues praised Smith's wide-ranging expertise but disdained his manner and imagined that he had devious motives. One such scholar, hardly a traditionalist and not without controversial theories of his own, told me in 1987 in private correspondence that he regarded *The Secret Gospel* by Smith to be "a marvelous hoax, one that only someone with his skills and temperament could pull off." An emphasis on the esoteric "has long been a Morton Smith way of tweaking the noses of Christian scholars, people he essentially dislikes," said the critic, who did not wish to be identified. Smith dedicated the popular edition of *The Secret Gospel* to "The one who knows"—a line that struck that critic and others as a hint of conspiracy to deceive.

Smith retired as professor emeritus in 1985 and died on July 11, 1991, at his Manhattan home at age seventy-six. He died of heart failure and had no immediate survivors, according to a *New York Times* obituary.[26]

By then, most gospel studies, even those solely dealing with Mark, made little or no mention of the fragment from Secret Mark, because virtually no one, not even Smith, believed it was composed by the original gospel author. "My conclusion from its style, that the writer imitated canonical Mark and therefore was later, has generally been accepted," Smith wrote in a postscript to the 1982 reprint of his popular book.[27] If the original composition should be dated at 75 C.E., then the earliest possible date for the "secret" edition of Mark "would be sometime in the 80s," he said. "Many scholars reject on principle all conjectures except their own," Smith added. Smith fully anticipated that his conjectures would be generally rejected because he introduced notions that were "unfashionable (Jesus practiced baptism) or shocking (and magic!)."[28] Yet, he admitted being surprised that a few scholars, including Koester, accepted the possibility that Jesus had some secret doctrines or initiatory ceremonies.

When Koester wrote about Secret Mark, however, he usually emphasized that it was evidence for Mark's unstable beginnings—that the Gospel developed in stages during the first century. At a Southern Baptist seminary in 1980, several years before a fundamentalist movement assumed the denomination's leadership, the Harvard professor gave a lecture with a subtitle that described what he thought was the Gospel's evolutionary stages: "From Mark to Secret Mark to 'Canonical' Mark."[29] He had broached the subject five years earlier in the Berkeley conference discussing Smith's work. In effect, Koester was asking, "Which edition of Mark did Luke use?" It surely was not the same one Matthew did because Luke leaves out a big, miracle-filled section of Mark that Matthew "borrows" almost completely for his gospel. By 1980, Koester was elaborating on the possibility that Luke may have used a more original version of Mark than Matthew possessed. Koester's ideas would soon spur my own inquiry.

Notes

1. For the transcript of the conference on December 7, 1975, see William Wuellner, ed., *Longer Mark: Forgery, Interpolation, or Old Tradition?* (Colloquy 18; Berkeley, Calif.: Center for Hermeneutical Studies, 1976).

2. Future SBL presidents participating: Paul J. Achtemeier, 1989; Helmut Koester, 1991; Hans Dieter Betz, 1997.

3. Wuellner, *Longer Mark,* 16.

4. Ibid., 30.

5. Ibid., 9.

6. Ibid., 8.

7. Ibid., 11.

8. Ibid., 12.

9. Morton Smith, *The Secret Gospel: The Discovery and Interpretation of the Secret Gospel according to Mark* (New York: Harper & Row, 1973), 42–43.

10. Smith in Wuellner, *Longer Mark,* 12.

11. Ibid., 13.

12. Stanley B. Marrow, J.J., in Wuellner, *Longer Mark,* 59.

13. Hobbs in Wuellner, *Longer Mark,* 48–67. See Quentin Quesnell, "The Mar Saba Clementine: A Question of Evidence," *The Catholic Biblical Quarterly* 37, no. 1 (January 1975): 48–67.

14. Hobbs in Wuellner, *Longer Mark,* 20.

15. Betz in Wuellner, *Longer Mark,* 17.

16. Ibid., 18.

17. Koester in Wuellner, *Longer Mark,* 29.

18. Ibid., 30.

19. Telephone conversation with Joanna Dewey, date unknown.

20. Morton Smith, "Clement of Alexandria and Secret Mark: The Score at the End of the First Decade," *Harvard Theological Review* 75, no. 4 (1982): 449–61.

21. Ibid., 455.

22. Morton Smith, letters to author, September 24, 1977; May 24, 1978.

23. Morton Smith, letter to author, September 9, 1977.

24. Morton Smith, letter to author, May 5, 1978.

25. Elaine Pagels, foreword to *The Secret Gospel: The Discovery and Interpretation of the Secret Gospel according to Mark,* by Morton Smith (Clearlake, Calif.: Dawn Horse Press, 1982), xi.

26. Morton Smith, Columbia Professor and Ancient-Religion Scholar, 76," *New York Times,* July 13, 1991.

27. Smith, "Postscript," *The Secret Gospel* (1982), 151–53.

28. Ibid., 153.

29. Southwestern Baptist Theological Seminary in Fort Worth, Texas, which sponsored the November 5–6, 1980 conference, "A Time for Reappraisal and Fresh Approaches," brought many mainstream and evangelical New Testament scholars together.

CHAPTER 3

The "Big Omission" in Luke

A GOSPEL, LITERALLY "GOOD NEWS" in Greek, is not a journalistic report. Though the Gospel of Mark in particular carries the sense of a fresh eyewitness account full of dialogues and descriptive details, the accounts of Jesus in the New Testament were written in the last third of the first century, more than three decades after the crucifixion of Jesus. And in tone and purpose, all four biblical gospels were what we understand today as "evangelistic,"—which is from the same Greek word for "gospel"/"good news."

Most scholars and pastors say those writers, also called "the evangelists," drew upon oral and written traditions for what Jesus taught and did, how all that could be understood in light of the Hebrew Bible, and what his relationship to God meant for humankind. The authors also are said to have portrayed Jesus' ministry in ways that would address the concerns of believers in the 70s, 80s, or 90s of the first century. Aside from recognizing the evangelists' attempts to inspire, persuade, and defend, experts in the gospels have sought to understand the likeliest literary relationship among the three Synoptic (side-by-side similarity) Gospels of Mark, Luke, and Matthew.

Despite my opening disclaimer, I want to compare the most-favored theory of synoptic relationship to the hard-driving journalism of the mid-twentieth century when several newspapers competed in big cities with several editions for street sales. My scenario squeezes into days what happened over decades in the late first century. That is, Mark's Gospel appeared first; then Luke and Matthew liberally borrowed from Mark and added material, including the Q sayings source.

In this analogy, Luke is a talented rewrite staffer on deadline. This time, he had to rework a major story about a savior figure who deserved full-scale news treatment from a variety of sources. The main reporter, Mark, had returned to the office after days in the field, armed with interviews of people who had surprisingly good recall of long-ago conversations. Mark was admired for his storytelling ability, but there were drawbacks. His prose was inelegant, often repetitious, and he wrote in a breathless tabloid style. He inexplicably depicted the principal followers and family members of Jesus as dreadful losers. Mark turned in his tightly written story, which was rushed into the first edition. A carbon copy of Mark's original version was handed to Luke in the newsroom. The star rewrite man was redoing it for later editions of the *New Testament Times,* hoping to smooth out the narrative and fill in some gaps.

There was nothing in Mark's story, for example, about Jesus' life before his adult baptism and nothing on what happened after he was reported to have left his burial cave. Mark's story lacked many pithy maxims and clever parables attributed to Jesus, such as those in a collection of quotes like "Blessed are the peacemakers. . . ." Luke decided to soften Mark's rough description of Jesus' followers and family, finding ways to spare them abuse. Luke's longer, polished, "complete" story ran in all later editions.

The next day, the competing *New Testament Herald* published its own "good news" story about Jesus. This one, credited to a Matthew, looked suspiciously like a rewrite of Mark's piece in the *Times* first edition. But like Luke, Matthew began the story with Jesus' birth and inserted copious quotes from the sayings source Luke used. Alas, the story was out. The *New Testament Beacon* also published a profile on Jesus, by one John, who had quite different contacts yet apparently had seen Mark's story too.

One caveat to the comparison. The Gospels were originally anonymous—no bylines. To this day, scholars do not know for certain who wrote "Mark" and "Luke," or "Matthew" and "John." Later Christians assigned the Gospels, rightly or wrongly, to names in early church history. (Following a custom of convenience, I will refer to Mark, Matthew, Luke, and John as the authors but for variety will also use reminders such as "Mark's author.")

My analogy was pursued partly to say that the rewriting "Luke" of both eras saves much of the story, people, terms, and sequence written by Mark. While Luke rewrites for clarity, shortens Mark's long segments, inserts special material, and omits episodes that strike him as odd or unsuitable, he unmistakably borrows Mark's narrative matrix.

Curious Gap

In that light, a surprisingly large gap appears in Luke's ninth chapter. A long stretch of narrative in Mark, the equivalent of two chapters in length, is missing in Luke. The so-called Big Omission has long stumped students of the Synoptic Gospels. After condensing the "feeding of the five thousand" (Mark 6:33–44) for his own gospel, Luke moves directly to the scene where Jesus asks his disciples who people think he is (Mark 8:27–33) and continues to be guided by Mark's sequence for several episodes after that. Matthew, by contrast, borrows and reworks nearly everything from Mark 6:47 onward except for the section's last episode (Mark 8:22–26).

No one has offered the student's time-honored excuse that Luke's dog ate those pages in his version of Mark. Some speculate that the more than seventy verses in Mark were simply missing from Luke's copy. More commonly, gospel specialists have tried to suggest that Luke deliberately snubbed that part. Did Luke skip over that portion simply to reduce the volume of material in his gospel? That seems unlikely because Luke retains so much from other parts of Mark. Some commentaries suggest that the second fishes-and-loaves story (Mark 8:1–10) is so similar to the first that Luke balked at the repetition. But if that's the case, Luke leaves out other miracle stories and other encounters in that section of Mark as well.

At least two scholars of Luke, Christopher M. Tuckett and Joseph Fitzmyer, have leaned toward the idea that Luke did not want Jesus taking his message so far into non-Jewish territory. Indeed, in this section Jesus travels almost exclusively in non-Jewish regions. "Luke may have wished to avoid such an impression quite deliberately," wrote Tuckett, "because in his somewhat schematic version of history, the Gospel only goes to the Gentiles in the era of the church under the guidance of the Spirit and (to a certain extent) when the Jews have rejected the offer."[1] But Luke had no earlier objection to Mark's story of a visit by Jesus to a Gentile region on the eastern side of the Sea of Galilee when he sent demons possessing a man into a herd of swine (Mark 5:1–20; Luke 8:26–39). Nobody would be keeping pigs in Jewish country.

An entirely different solution to the question of the Big Omission is rarely treated seriously—namely, that the author of Luke worked from an unrevised copy of the Gospel of Mark, one that did not contain the part stretching from Jesus walking on water to the healing of a blind man in Bethsaida. Helmut Koester posed that question at the 1975 conference in Berkeley, California. He raised this possibility in print again, notably in a book that published proceedings of a 1980 conference at Southwestern Baptist Theological Seminary, Fort Worth, Texas.[2]

Peculiarities in a Section of Mark

Koester cited several peculiar traits in the section he said started at Mark 6:45 with the first mention of Bethsaida and ended with 8:26. First, this section contains what scholars call "doublets." The feeding of the four thousand found there, he said, "is obviously a secondary elaboration of Mark 6:34–44 (the feeding of the five thousand)." Koester termed the story of Jesus walking on the water (6:47–52) a variation on the "stilling of the stormy sea" (4:35–41). A blind man healed (8:22–26) is one of two stories healing a sightless person, the other one appearing at the end of Mark's tenth chapter.[3]

Only in this section does Jesus perform healings with "elaborate manipulations" of the kind found in Hellenistic miracle stories, said Koester. In curing a deaf man with a speech impediment, Jesus put his fingers into the deaf man's ears, spat, and touched the man's tongue. Then looking upward to heaven, Jesus uttered in Aramaic, "Be opened" (7:33–34). In healing the blind man, Jesus spat on the man's eyes and laid hands on him. Asking the man if he now sees, the man indicated he did, but in a blurry way: "I see men; but they look like trees, walking." So Jesus laid his hands on the man's eyes, and the healing took. Koester said these two miracle cures differ from wonder-working accounts elsewhere in Mark, Matthew, and Luke, which report "healing through Jesus' word, gesture or touching with the hand." Also, Koester pointed out the section's favored vocabulary, including four uses of one word for "understand" (6:52; 7:14; 8:17; 8:21). That word occurs elsewhere only once in Mark (4:10), alluding to a phrase in the book of Isaiah. "One other peculiarity should be mentioned," Koester said. "The section begins and ends with the mention of Bethsaida (6:45 and 8:22), a place which does not occur anywhere else in Mark."[4]

In questioning the theory that Luke saw but deliberately "omitted" this sequence of episodes, Koester was by no means adamant. Koester conceded during the 1980 colloquy in Texas that he had "no major interest" in claiming that Luke used an unedited version of Mark. "I will be glad to be persuaded that the Mark that Luke used contains the same materials as the Mark that Matthew used," he said.[5]

His ambivalence then notwithstanding, Koester's suggestion caught my interest in the mid-1980s. In those years, I tried to keep up with research and new ideas in biblical studies both for my own research and for news stories. That's why I knew that Robert Funk and like-minded scholars in 1985 had just begun a controversial, public approach to announcing their votes on what the Jesus of history most likely said and what were most likely words put on his lips by gospel writers and the early church. After attending one such meeting in late 1985, I wrote for the *Los Angeles Times* the first major story on the group's plans and unusual device of voting with colored balls, such as red for yes and black for no.[6] The so-called Jesus Seminar, which hoped to counterbalance TV preachers who taught the Bible in fundamentalist fashion, generally reflected liberal-to-moderate critical scholarship that otherwise rarely made news. Thus, the Seminar's twice-annual meetings gave the news media, who routinely cited critics of the seminar, many chances to visit the usually obscured world of biblical interpretation.

My other reporting since joining the *Times* in 1967 included advances in interfaith relations and women's ordination; religious-political disputes over civil rights, homosexuality, and abortion; and the usual gamut of national and local religious events and trends making news. In my off-duty hours, I was reacquainting myself with the latest studies in Christian origins and gnostic sects fought by the early church as heretics. My first book, *The Laughing Savior* (1976), dealt with the 1945 discovery of the Nag Hammadi Library, which contained many decidedly gnostic writings but also its now-famous *Gospel of Thomas,* a sayings collection vital for New Testament research.[7] The "laughing savior"—a disembodied Jesus figure laughing at his persecutors from above the cross—appeared in only a few of some four dozen Nag Hammadi texts, so the book became *The Jesus of Heresy and History* in an updated, revised edition out in 1988. Now abreast of New Testament studies, I returned to Koester's theory about Mark.

I must jump ahead in time here. Years later, I found strong evidence that Koester began the proposed editor's insertion too soon. Instead of at 6:45, the added section starts at 6:47. Mark's author had Jesus dispatch the disciples to Bethsaida ahead of him as he dismissed the well-fed crowd and went up a mountain to pray (Mark 6:45–46). Thus, Luke *did* see Bethsaida in his copy of Mark, but Luke moves it ahead as the site of the mass feeding (Luke 9:10–17)—not as the next destination. I mention this now (and explain later) in order to cite 6:47 hereafter as an editor's starting point.

More Oddities from an Interloper

What follows in Mark after the feeding of the five thousand is "a perplexing story," said Paul Achtemeier (who does not advocate an editor). It was "late" in the day (6:35) when Jesus got the disciples to take out the five loaves and two fish, have people sit in groups, and feed them all miraculously with twelve baskets of leftovers gathered up. The disciples are told in 6:45–46 to get in a boat to Bethsaida while Jesus goes up a mountain to pray. Much time has passed, but when the editor's insertion (6:47–48) begins, it opens with "when evening came." Jesus saw that the disciples' "boat was out on the sea" and that they were "making headway painfully." Achtemeier observed: "Again, though Jesus sees the boat in difficulty 'when evening came' (verse 47), he does not go to them until the 'fourth watch'—i.e., between 3:00 and 6:00 a.m. And when he does reach them, it is not to help after all; he 'was going to pass them by' (verse 48)."[8]

Nevertheless, Jesus does calm the stormy sea. Yet the group arrives, not in Bethsaida, but at Gennesaret. If being blown off course was the unstated reason, Jesus still makes a major side trip (7:24) to Tyre (in present-day Lebanon). Intending later to return to the Sea of Galilee, Jesus then goes, not south from Tyre, but northward up the Mediterranean coast to Sidon, then "to the Sea of Galilee, through the region of the Decapolis." That itinerary "would be roughly comparable to Philadelphia to Washington, D.C., by way of New York City and central Pennsylvania," said Achtemeier.[9] "It is impossible to trace accurately the movements to and fro across the Sea of Galilee," said British scholar Ernest Best, adding that a visit to Dalmanutha (8:10) is questionable because that place-name does not appear in ancient references.[10]

Arguments for an editor's hand must concede that some traits in Mark 6:47–8:26 blend with the rest of Mark. The adverb "immediately" appears three times here and thirty times elsewhere in the Gospel. Mark's frequent switching from past to present tense, common to storytelling even today ("he went down the street, and this guy comes up . . ."), is found here. A bit of Mark's two-step redundancy appears here as well as elsewhere in the Gospel, such as in the widow who gave "everything she had, her whole living" (12:44). The Gospel of Mark's denigrating portrayal of disciples is also carried through vigorously in this section.

Koester rightly pointed out, however, that common sense says an editor would attempt to mimic the tenor of the original writing.[11] Unlike Luke and Matthew, who created new literary works, the editor—"redactor" in academic jargon—wanted to fit the material into the existing text. The attempt failed, I ultimately concluded, because the literary intruder betrayed his hand by trying too hard. In the editor's grasp, Jesus is portrayed with exaggerated emotions and earthy language not echoed elsewhere in the Gospel.

The editor's Jesus, for instance, subjects the disciples to a dressing-down that starkly contrasts with his surprisingly patient treatment of the disciples in the rest of the Gospel. Elsewhere, Jesus issues short rebukes or admonitions then usually drops the matter. But in the editor's section, when the disciples forget to bring with them a loaf they had in the boat, Jesus warns them cryptically about the leaven of the Pharisees and Herod. Then he pummels his followers with questions (8:17–21), often not waiting for an answer:

"Why do you discuss the fact that you have no bread?"
"Do you not yet perceive or understand?"
"Are your hearts hardened?"
"Having eyes do you not see, and having ears do you not hear?"
"And do you not remember?"
"When I broke the five loaves for the five thousand, how many baskets full of broken pieces did you take up?" They said to him, "Twelve."
"And the seven for the four thousand, how many baskets full of broken pieces did you take up?" And they said to him, "Seven."

And he said to them, "Do you not understand?"

Not only is this sustained grilling of the disciples unparalleled in Mark, but Jesus also asked if their "hearts are hardened"—a deadly serious charge, said Werner Kelber. "In Jewish literature the hardening of the heart indicates disobedience, loss of redemption, and even death," he wrote.[12] In fact, the editor had already flatly told readers that the disciples' "hearts were hardened" (6:52) as an explanation for the disciples being "utterly astounded" by Jesus walking on water and not understanding the significance of the first miracle of the loaves. Previously in Mark, "hardness of heart" was a charge reserved for Jewish opponents, such as those who questioned whether Jesus should heal a man's hand on the sabbath (3:5).

The editor's Jesus stands out as an earthy showboat, a man of coarse language. Not only does he spit and use other "magical" healing techniques on two occasions; he also *groans* twice. Found only in this section of Mark and usually translated "sigh," the word's primary meaning is "groan." In healing the deaf mute (7:34), Jesus groaned as he looked heavenward. When the Pharisees challenged Jesus, demanding a sign from heaven to demonstrate his authority, Jesus groaned deeply (8:12) as he asked aloud, "Why does this generation seek a sign?"

This Jesus also speaks about defecating, though that isn't the way the verb is usually translated. The editor used a traditional Jesus saying— found in both Matthew (15:10–11) and the apocryphal *Gospel of Thomas* (14)—that what goes into the mouth of humans does not defile them; only what comes out of humans will defile them. Mark's editor rewords this saying slightly, then proceeds to explain the parable to the puzzled disciples: "Do you not see that whatever goes into a man from outside cannot defile him, since it enters, not his heart but his stomach, and so *passes on?*" (7:18–19). A footnote in the Revised Standard Version offers an alternative translation, "is evacuated." Among plain-spoken translations is the rendering "comes out in the outhouse."[13]

The editor's Jesus refers to Gentiles as "dogs" in the story of a Syrophoenician woman, a Gentile, who asked Jesus to cast a demon out of her daughter (7:24–30). Jesus eventually complied but had responded obliquely to the woman's plea: "Let the children first be fed, for it is not right to take the children's bread and throw it to the dogs." Scholars say that the "children" represent the Israelites and "dogs" was a Judean slur against Gentiles. Analysts disagree over the meaning of this episode, but Kathleen Corley has pointed out that

Jesus "calls the woman and her daughter 'little bitches' albeit indi-rectly."[14] The editor again portrays Jesus as foulmouthed, at least in his initial response. But as John R. Donahue observed, the woman turned the saying back on Jesus, who then healed her daughter because of her mother's "courageous faith." Earlier in Mark, Jesus told the brave, truthful woman afflicted with bleeding that "your faith has made you well" (5:34). The editor mimics the original author's approaches at times but errs when it comes to Jesus' personality and blows his cover with geographical mistakes.

The editor's actions require us to take a closer look at the 1940s–50s newspaper analogy. We overlooked someone. When Luke was assigned to rewrite Mark's story, he received a copy of Mark's typed story intended for the first edition. But at any paper the copy desk makes needed corrections. Apparently a crass, cigar-chomping copy editor, without consulting anyone, inserted several new paragraphs—maybe to spice it up with more miracles. At a rival paper, Matthew saw that edited version in the *Times* first edition and built upon it for his story. The first-edition version of Mark's story, bearing his byline, was one that many readers clipped and saved for years—giving it a life of its own. Luke did not work from that altered version of Mark. The managing editor, greatly impressed with Luke's rewrite and perhaps unhappy with Mark's rough prose and tough treatment of the disciples, gave Luke the byline for the story in later editions.

Back in the first century, what could have prompted someone to insert this long segment into the original Gospel of Mark? Perhaps the editor wanted to send Jesus deeper and longer into Gentile territory than Original Mark did. Still, maybe our first-century editor wasn't so different from the twentieth-century sensationalist, for the section pre-ceding Mark 8:26 is packed with six miracle-making occasions. But then I remembered a 1983 magazine article in which a seminary profes-sor counted the miracles that Jesus performs in Mark and compared them to the biblical feats of two Hebrew prophets. Suddenly, the motive for altering Mark's Gospel was clear.

Notes

1. Christopher M. Tuckett, *Luke* (Sheffield: Sheffield Academic Press, 1996), 52–53; Joseph A. Fitzmyer, *The Gospel according to Luke I–IX* (AB 28; Garden City, N.Y.: Doubleday, 1981), 770–71.

2. Helmut Koester, "History and Development of Mark's Gospel," in *Colloquy on New Testament Studies: A Time for Reappraisal and Fresh Approaches* (ed. Bruce C. Corley; Macon, Ga.: Mercer University Press, 1983), 35–85. For Koester's discussion of 6:45–8:26's peculiar features, see esp. 38–39. For Koester's reluctance to defend his idea that Luke saw an unedited version of Mark, see p. 75 in the seminar dialogue with Koester. He raises the question briefly in his *History and Literature of Early Christianity* (vol. 2 of *Introduction to the New Testament*; Philadelphia: Fortress, 1982), 168. See also Koester's longer discussion of Secret Mark in *Ancient Christian Gospels: Their History and Development* (Harrisburg, Pa.: Trinity Press International, 1990), 293–303.

3. Koester, "History and Development," 38.

4. Ibid., 38, 39.

5. Ibid., 75.

6. John Dart, "Bible Scholars Vote: What Did Jesus Say or Not Say?" *Los Angeles Times,* November 11, 1985, 1F; repr. in *Readings on Religion as News* (ed. Judith M. Buddenbaum and Debra L. Mason; Ames, Iowa: Iowa University Press, 2000), 447–52.

7. John Dart, *The Laughing Savior: The Discovery and Significance of the Nag Hammadi Gnostic Library* (New York: Harper & Row, 1976); rev. exp. ed.: *The Jesus of Heresy and History: The Discovery and Meaning of the Nag Hammadi Gnostic Library* (San Francisco: Harper & Row, 1988).

8. Paul J. Achtemeier, *Invitation to Mark: A Commentary on the Gospel of Mark with Complete Text from the Jerusalem Bible* (Garden City, N.Y.: Image Books, 1978), 103.

9. Ibid., 27.

10. Ernest Best, *Mark: The Gospel as Story* (Edinburgh: T&T Clark, 1983), 26. Also, Eduard Schweizer, *The Good News according to Mark* (trans. Donald H. Madvig; Atlanta: John Knox, 1970), 154.

11. For Koester's comments on an editor's mimicking the original author's style, see "History and Development," in Corley, *Colloquy,* 39 n.15.

12. Werner H. Kelber, *Mark's Story of Jesus* (Philadelphia: Fortress, 1979), 36–37.

13. For the translation "comes out in the outhouse" in Mark 7:19, see Darryl D. Schmidt, *The Gospel of Mark* (Scholar's Bible; Sonoma, Calif.: Polebridge, 1990), 89.

14. The Greek word for "little dog" (*kunarion*) was both "gendered and derogatory in antiquity," said Kathleen Corley, in "Feminist Myths of Christian Origins," *Reimagining Christian Origins: A Colloquium Honoring Burton L. Mack* (ed. Elizabeth A. Castelli and Hal Taussig; Valley Forge, Pa.: Trinity Press International, 1996), 59, 65 n. 66.

CHAPTER 4

Better than Elijah, Greater than Elisha

TWO OF ISRAEL'S GREATEST MIRACLE WORKERS were Elijah and his successor Elisha. They lived in the ninth century B.C.E., well after the storied reigns of David and Solomon, and a century or two before the thundering prophets Isaiah and Jeremiah—kings and prophets of renown in Israelite lore and Scripture. Yet, the nomadic, primitively garbed Elijah and his ambitious protégé Elisha were hardly obscure figures in the history of the Jews.

As depicted by biblical accounts in 1 Kings and 2 Kings, the two held a prophetic fire to the feet of Israelite rulers by repeatedly summoning the awesome power of God. And Elijah, who ascended to heaven instead of dying a mortal death, remained a symbol for future godly retribution and salvation. "Behold, I will send you Elijah the prophet before the great and terrible day of the LORD comes," says the voice of God through the last Hebrew prophet, Malachi (Mal 4:5; 3:23 in Hebrew Bible).

The Gospel of Mark played on that expectation more than once. As Mark's Jesus acquires a growing reputation as a wonder-worker, King Herod worries whether this man is a resuscitated John the Baptist, whom he had beheaded. Others in Herod's court suggested the mighty newcomer was Elijah or another returning prophet (Mark 6:14–15). Later, when Jesus asked his disciples who ordinary people say he is, the disciples offered the same three opinions heard at Herod's court—John the Baptist, Elijah, or "one of the prophets" (Mark 8:28).

Mark's Gospel aims to demonstrate that Jesus was much more than a prophet; in fact, the Christ and Son of God. But early in the Gospel, Jesus' mighty works did help to stir the populace to recall other holy men in history with heavenly connections. Elijah and his protégé were celebrated examples.

In his battles against the worship of Baal, the Canaanite god favored by Queen Jezebel, Elijah called down fire from heaven once to consume a sacrificial offering, altar and all, and twice to destroy fifty royal messengers at a time. Elijah also showed compassion. He raised a woman's son from the dead and multiplied her meager supply of meal and oil. On other occasions, he predicted a long drought, a great rain, and the death of a king. Elijah and Elisha were neither handsome nor even-tempered in biblical accounts. The cave-dwelling Elijah was "a hairy man with a leather belt around his waist" (2 Kgs 1:8). Elisha was bald. When some boys taunted him by calling him "Baldy," Elisha cursed them, and two bears emerged from the woods to maul the youngsters (2 Kgs 2:23).

When shaggy Elijah knew his earthly days were drawing to an end, he borrowed a page from Moses' saga. With Elisha at his side, Elijah parts the Jordan River, striking the water with his rolled-up cloak. Mentor and student cross to the other side where they talk:

> "Ask what I shall do for you, before I am taken away from you," said Elijah. "I pray you, let me inherit a double share of your spirit," asked Elisha. (2 Kgs 2:9)

It was not a simple request, but Elijah indicated that if his partner were able to witness his fiery ascension to heaven, then Elisha's wish was likely to be granted. A whirlwind swept Elijah into heaven. The younger man marveled at the chariots in the sky. Tearing up his own garments, Elisha grabbed Elijah's mantle, used it to part the Jordan River again, and returned to the other side. Like his teacher, Elisha used his power harshly at times, such as turning a greedy man into a leper. But he also cleansed the drinking water of Jericho, repeatedly filled a widow's empty oil vessels, multiplied loaves for a bountiful meal, and restored a dead boy to life, among other feats. He caused a sinking ax head to float in another demonstration.

Elijah's promise to bestow a double portion of his wondrous spirit upon his disciple was realized, wrote Louis Ginzberg in *The Legends of the Jews*. "During his life Elisha performed sixteen miracles, and eight was all his master had performed," he said. Neither Elijah's eight nor Elisha's sixteen miracles are listed in surviving rabbinical commentaries, though Ginzberg thought they had been at one time.[1]

Comparing Jesus' Numbers with Elisha's

That Jewish lore was cited in a *Christian Century* article by Old Testament professor Wolfgang Roth, then dean at Garrett-Evangelical Theological Seminary near Chicago. Roth asserted that one secret to understanding the Gospel of Mark was to see Elijah and Elisha as exemplars, especially through their supernatural feats. Roth began listing the number of miracle-making occasions credited to Jesus by Mark.

Jesus' sixteenth wonder-working event, according to Roth's count, was when he healed a deaf man with a speech impediment, upon which witnesses declared: "He has done all things well; he even makes the deaf hear and the dumb speak" (Mark 7:37). Jesus' miracles "were now equal in number to those of Elisha," Roth said. "Moreover, Jesus had done them 'well' because they were greater than those of Elisha and benefited more people than Elisha's," Roth continued.[2]

"For instance, the prophet of bygone times had miraculously fed 100, but Jesus fed 5,000." In other words, Elisha fed one hundred people with twenty loaves and some garden produce (2 Kgs 4:42–44), whereas Jesus, in the first instance, fed five thousand people with five loaves and two fishes. Later, the Nazarene proceeded to feed a crowd of four thousand people seven loaves and a few fishes (Mark 8:1–10). "And while Elisha fed a multitude of people once, Jesus did so twice," said Roth. "Thus he surpassed Elisha in the manner in which the latter had surpassed his predecessor."[3]

Roth expanded upon his thesis, and his list of Jesus miracles, in his book *Hebrew Gospel: Cracking the Code of Mark,* which was published in 1988.[4] Starting with the second feeding story, Roth counts eight more miracles of Jesus in the Gospel. Roth's point was this: Just as Elisha extended Elijah's total by eight, so Jesus extended Elisha's sixteen feats by eight more—yielding a total of twenty-four in Mark.

The numerical procession was appealing, but not without its problems. To reach twenty-four miracles, the last being Jesus' resurrection, Roth includes one that is questionable—the cleansing of the Jerusalem temple. Even some of Jesus' first sixteen wonder-working *occasions*— some of which were summary lines about healings and/or exorcisms—

could be counted differently, depending on one's criteria. For example, Roth wants the sixteenth miracle (equaling Elisha) to occur just before Mark 7:37 ("He has done all things well"). But in doing so, he counted the healing of a woman's bleeding and raising of a dead girl as one miracle occasion (5:21–43), as if it were on a par with the healing "of a few sick persons" in Nazareth, where he could do "no mighty work" (Mark 6:5). Oddly, Roth left out one healing occasion—at 1:39 when Jesus went throughout all Galilee casting out demons.

I wondered, for a moment, whether Roth's miracle counting was as pointless as the proverbial question of how many angels can dance on the head of a pin. Yet it seemed to be a clue to understanding my proposed editor. First, ignoring temporarily the six miracles inserted between Mark 6:47 and 8:26, the specific miracles in biblical Mark (not vague summaries of a series of healings, etc.) would be only sixteen, and even then the torn temple curtain and the resurrection were counted in the total. That sum would merely equal, not exceed, Elisha's feats. I suspected that the editor wanted to establish at an earlier point in Jesus' ministry his credentials as the greatest wonder-worker. It was imperative for the editor to have Jesus not only outdo Elisha in total miracles but also do some twice over. That would explain why the Gospel was "supplemented" with a half-dozen miracles, including "doublets." The feeding of the four thousand (8:1–10) unimaginatively duplicates the earlier feeding of the five thousand. Walking on water (6:47–54) is a one-upmanship variation on Jesus' stilling of the storm-tossed sea. With the healing of the blind man at Bethsaida (8:22–26), the expanded Gospel of Mark has two such cases.

No Editor, Please

Roth categorically rejected the notion of an editor or an altered text. He treated the New Testament's Gospel of Mark as a literary whole composed by one author. Roth asserted that past studies ran into inconclusive dead ends whenever stages of editing were proposed for biblical texts. In a nutshell, that was what he told me in an Anaheim hotel hallway at the Society of Biblical Literature's annual meeting. I admit I was crestfallen when he would not even consider the possibility. Responding later by letter in 1985, Roth said that he did not accept the idea of "literary evolution" of biblical texts, which he said was an "18th and 19th century phenomenon" in scholarship no longer useful for analysis.[5] "I proceed from the assumption that a literary work is what it is due to its conceptual unity," he wrote. "I do find that my approach accounts in a striking way for the literary nature and integrity of a work such as Mark, and that it locates the gospel squarely in that matrix which one expects to be the primary one: The Hebrew Scriptures."

I couldn't dispute his final observation. All the gospel writers, no less Mark, drew prophetic passages and imagery from the Hebrew Bible for some of Jesus' words as well as what happened to him. But I disagreed on the notion that distinguishing between original material and editorial additions was a fruitless exercise. Roth's miracle-tally theory unintentionally provided the primary motive for editing changes in the original Gospel of Mark. The editor may have admired the original gospel. But adding six more miracles to push Jesus' total clearly above Elisha's sixteen feats, he must have thought, would enhance Jesus' stature as a man of God higher than Israel's greatest wonder-workers.

John the Baptist as Another Elijah

Another part of Roth's thesis deserved attention. Roth argued that Mark wanted readers to identify John the Baptist with Elijah in addition to comparing Jesus with Elisha. John the Baptist was the forerunner to Jesus; Elijah likewise preceded Elisha. Certainly, the opening of Mark's story suggests a parallel. The Holy Spirit comes upon Jesus at the Jordan River, where John had baptized him. It was near that same river that Elisha received a double portion of Elijah's spirit. The word picture of John the Baptist also elicits a comparison to Elijah: "Now John was clothed with camel's hair, and had a leather girdle around his waist, and ate locusts and wild honey" (Mark 1:6).

Also, following the mountaintop transfiguration vision, when three disciples see Moses and Elijah standing beside a Jesus garbed in glowing garments, the befuddled disciples engage in a discussion with Jesus at Mark 9:11–13. The disciples query Jesus on the idea that "first Elijah must come." Jesus responds, "I tell you that Elijah has come." New Testament scholars say the reference is to John the Baptist. The Gospel of Matthew also saw it that way, using Mark 9:11–13 and adding pointedly: "Then the disciples understood that he was speaking to them of John the Baptist" (Matt 17:13).

Lastly, when Jesus utters his final cries from the cross, bystanders think they hear him "calling Elijah" (Mark 15:35). Coming near the end of the Gospel, this might have been intended as a plaintive reminder of Jesus' forerunner who helped launch the ministry of Jesus at the Jordan River.

At this point, I counted three circumstances pointing to the work of an editor: (1) Luke mysteriously "omits" the material from Mark 6:47 to 8:26; (2) the exaggerated mimicry, gross depictions of Jesus, and geographical peculiarities in that section tend to distinguish the editor's writing from Original Mark; and (3) the six added miracles served to boost Jesus' score much higher than Elisha's.

How did the narrative of Mark's Gospel flow without that added section? It seemed to me that the multiplication of loaves and fishes led naturally to Mark 8:27. Apparently Luke thought likewise, for that gospel does not interrupt the story line here to insert other material. In Mark's narrative design, Jesus' mighty works and authoritative teaching had spread his fame so rapidly in Galilee that people traveled from Jerusalem in the south and the Mediterranean coastal cities to challenge him or admire him. The crowd size is greatest when he miraculously feeds five thousand people (Mark 6:35–46 = Luke 9:12–17). At the next stop, in Original Mark and in Luke (Mark 8:27 = Luke 9:18), his reputation was such that Jesus could reasonably ask his disciples, "Who do men say that I am?" And thus begins the decisive middle of Mark's Gospel, in which Jesus explains that for all his power, he will suffer much, as will those who follow him on the way.

The inserted section, however, contains an anticlimactic episode—the second multiplying of fishes and loaves fed only four thousand people. And the tirade by Jesus against his disciples in 8:17–23 presents Jesus out of character. Without that ugly scene, Original Mark has the disciples acquiring an ever-worsening reputation that culminates with their desertions at Jesus' arrest and their absence at his crucifixion and burial.

I was fairly confident about an editor's insertion, but a grander thesis remained in the back of my mind. I was reserving the possibility that the Secret Mark episode was once a part of the original gospel. That could be a problem to prove. Plausible reasons were needed to account for Luke's seeing the story and ignoring it and for the editor's removing episodes as well as inserting material. I shelved that double-pronged problem of motives for the time being.

Turning next to studying the bulk of Mark's Gospel rather than confining myself to profiling the editor, I found the research frankly more fun. The Gospel of Mark, once regarded as a poorly written assemblage of incidents, was now being lauded by growing numbers of scholars for its writing technique. Little did anyone know how remarkably good it was.

Notes

1. Louis Ginzberg, ed., *The Legends of the Jews* (Philadelphia: Jewish Publication Society, 1956), 4:239, 6:343–44.

2. Wolfgang Roth, "The Secret of the Kingdom," *Christian Century,* March 2, 1983, 179–82.

3. Ibid., 181–82.

4. Wolfgang Roth, *Hebrew Gospel: Cracking the Code of Mark* (Oak Park, Ill.: Meyer, Stone, 1988).

5. Wolfgang Roth, letter to author, December 29, 1985.

CHAPTER 5

Bracketing and Bashing

ONE VERY NOTICEABLE storytelling tactic in Mark makes some scholars think of the movies. That is the Gospel's practice of bracketing one story around another. "In film, a scene will change in the middle of the action, leaving the viewer in suspense, while the camera cuts to another scene," wrote coauthors David Rhoads, Joanna Dewey, and Donald Michie in *Mark as Story.* "The camera will return to resolve the action begun in the initial scene, thus creating a frame around the middle story."[1] These paired episodes tend to have related themes, nudging an alert audience to compare the two developments. Gospel specialists also call the literary device by such names as "sandwiching" or "intercalation," but the latter is a synonym I will avoid.

Some count more examples, but I will describe what one scholar has called "six classic cases" of sandwich stories spread about the Gospel of Mark.[2] These consensus sandwiches are at 3:20–25; 5:21–43; 6:7–32; 11:12–25; 14:1–11; and 14:53–72. Three other proposed sandwiches are in chapters 4, 14, and 15.[3] But *none* are usually proposed in the inserted section from 6:47 to 8:26, which is another clue that someone other than the original author composed that part of the Gospel. But also notice that no bracketed story is found in an even longer stretch—8:27–11:1. My answer is that no sandwiched story is *now* visible in that part of Mark. More on the "missing" bracket will appear later in this chapter.

By wrapping one story around another, Mark typically invited the reader or listener to look for irony in the juxtaposition. If Mark's irony were of a kindly, sentimental sort, then Mark perhaps would be praised for literary grace in the service of divine grace. However, Mark's bracketing often carries a stinging irony ranging from subtle digs to embarrassing contrasts. In the six bracketed pairs described below, Mark usually brandishes them as literary instruments—sometimes to critique the Jewish religious authorities but especially to write off Jesus' blood relations and defame Jesus' best-known followers.

First Bracket: Rejecting the Family of Jesus

Mark's first bracket appears in 3:20–35. The longer, middle story has Jesus countering accusations by scribes from Jerusalem that he is possessed by demonic spirits. The opening and closing segments are about Jesus' "family"—both his real one and a redefined, spiritual family.[4] The bracketed stories start with his natural family encountering a pressing crowd around Jesus. The family "went out to seize him, for people were saying, 'He is beside himself'" (v. 21). Some translate the crowd's assessment sharply, "He's out of his mind," as did the authors of *Mark as Story*.[5]

The middle section (3:22–28) brings in the scribes, who said that Jesus was possessed by a foreign spirit and that he casts out demons by the prince of demons. Asking how Satan can cast out Satan, Jesus adds that neither a kingdom nor a house divided against itself can stand. Two more teachings follow, including Jesus' warning that blasphemy against the Holy Spirit is an unforgivable sin.

Then, "his mother and his brothers came" and sent for him while still standing outside the densely packed crowd (3:31–35). Told that, Jesus posed a question: "Who are my mother and my brothers?" Looking at "those who sat about him," he pronounced, "Here are my mother and my brothers! Whoever does the will of God is my brother, and sister, and mother."

Although many scholars concede that Mark paints a very critical picture of the twelve disciples, some overlook the strong critique of Jesus' natural family members. In this first glimpse of Jesus' family, Mark makes it clear that his mother and brothers wanted to pull him away because they thought the rumors were right that Jesus was out of his mind, if not possessed. One specialist who notes the animosity toward Jesus' family, Werner Kelber of Rice University, said the family and scribes in these combined stories are outsiders, while those closely attentive to Jesus are the insiders. "After he is informed of his family's arrival, Jesus identifies those around him as the true family of God," Kelber has written.[6] Mark's Gospel does not identify members of Jesus' family until the sixth chapter. Then, when Jesus visits his hometown and astonishes people in the local synagogue, worshipers ask in an offended manner, "Is not this the carpenter, the son of Mary and brother of James and Joses and Judas and Simon, and are not his sisters here with us?" (6:3). Jesus laments in his response that no prophet is honored in his own hometown, not even "among his own kin, and in his own house" (6:4).

The Gospel of Luke disagreed with Mark's sequence in introducing the family. Luke reversed the order of these stories, putting Jesus' hometown rejection at Nazareth first and the episode defining the new spiritual family second. As is his wont, Luke treats Jesus' family with more respect, even while generally embracing Mark's account of events. In the hometown scene, Luke dropped references to family members. In the scene where his mother and brothers seek to reach Jesus through the crowd, Luke breaks up Mark's framework, scattering pieces of the sequence to different places in his gospel. Also, Luke depicted Jesus as less critical of family members so that his blood relatives could conceivably join the new spiritual family of Jesus, too (Luke 8:19–21).

Though Mark's Jesus quickly dismissed his siblings and mother, Jesus was patient with his disciples—at least in the beginning. Already identified as the Son of God (Mark 1:1), he surely knew who around him would fail him. But commissioned as a message-bearing teacher seeking followers, Jesus kept urging the increasingly confused disciples to trust in God. While apparently hoping the Twelve would be role models, Jesus instead found unidentified others around him as more worthy. And Jesus would encounter responsive individuals—like Simon the tax collector and the once-blind Bartimaeus—who became followers though not among the appointed twelve. Gutsy, unnamed souls such as an initially skeptical scribe and an awed centurion at the cross would express admiration for him at the risk of shocking nearby colleagues. All were quick to recognize Jesus' special qualities and mission.

Second Bracket: Healings of Two Females

The disciples displayed some disrespect in the second bracket (5:21–43), which wraps one healing story around another. A synagogue leader whose twelve-year-old daughter was near death appealed to Jesus for help in the opening scene. Before Jesus could get through a pressing crowd to the girl's house, however, a new story unfolds: A woman suffering from twelve years of internal hemorrhaging touched Jesus' garment. Perceiving a loss of power, Jesus turned to ask who had done that. The question struck the disciples as ridiculous: "You see the crowd pressing around you, and yet you say, 'Who touched me?'" (v. 31). Jesus did not answer. As he scanned the crowd, the woman approached him and told him it was she. "Daughter, your faith has made you well," said Jesus (v. 34).

When Jesus turned his attention to the case of the dying daughter, some said it was too late; she was dead. Allowing no one to follow him to the house except his three top disciples—Simon Peter and brothers James and John—he came upon people wailing. Upon entering, Jesus asked them why they were distressed since "the child is not dead but sleeping" (5:39). Then, the wailers "laughed at him." Jesus "put them all outside, and took the child's father and mother and *those who were with him* [the three disciples], and went in where the child was" (v. 40). With the parents and Peter, James, and John as witnesses, Jesus utters something in Aramaic and takes the girl's hand, whereupon she rises from her bed and walks. The trio of disciples has no excuse thereafter for doubting Jesus' power.

Third Bracket: Disciples on a Mission/John the Baptist Beheaded

The Twelve frame Mark's third bracketed story (6:7–32). Jesus, in the first scene, sent the disciples on a mission to preach repentance, cast out demons, and anoint the sick with oil. They were told to take no bread, no money, and only the simplest clothing on their mendicant journey (vv. 7–13)—a stark contrast to the lavish feast coming next.

The middle episode is a birthday party in Herod's court that reaches a climax with John the Baptist's beheading. Herod, so pleased with a young woman's dancing that he promised her anything, reluctantly complied with the girl's demand of John's head on a platter. In popular lore, the story is known as "Salome and the dance of the seven veils," but there are no such details in the long story of John the Baptist's fate in 6:14–29.

At the bracket's end (6:30–32), the mission has ended for the weary disciples, and they told Jesus what they accomplished. Jesus responded by telling them to go off to a lonely place "and rest a while." This bracket, at first glance, gave the Twelve its finest collective moment in Mark's Gospel—an arduous trek that went well, evidently drawing a thoughtful "welcome back" from Jesus.

But Mark administered a slap to the disciples. He ended the Baptist's beheading episode in a seemingly straightforward way, noting that when John's disciples heard of their master's execution, "they came and took his body, and laid it in a tomb" (6:29). For the audience familiar with Mark's Gospel, that act by John's disciples stood in sharp contrast to the future failure of Jesus' disciples when their master is executed. John's disciples sought their teacher's body and buried it; but when Jesus died on the cross, Peter and others had already fled. It would be a courageous outsider, Joseph of Arimathea, who requested Jesus' body from Roman authorities and placed it into a tomb. The irony comes through the juxtaposition. Verse 29 says John's disciples bury him in a tomb. Verses 30–31 have Jesus' disciples recount their recent accomplishments, yet the reader knows they will fail in the end.

At least three more framed stories are found in the New Testament's Gospel of Mark—one that primarily denigrated Jewish religious authorities and two that gave devastating pictures of disciples.

Fourth Bracket: Cursing and Cleansing?

The cursing of the fig tree brackets the story of Jesus upsetting the tables of merchants at the Jerusalem temple and saying they had made it a den of robbers (11:12–25). The two incidents, arranged and combined in this way, "illuminate each other and strengthen their effect on the audience," said scholar Bas M. F. van Iersel, who called this pairing "one of the most recognizable examples of a sandwich construction."[7] The fig tree, thriving or withering, had been a metaphor for the health or decay of the Israelites' relations with God. "Jesus' action in the Temple makes clear that the story of the fig tree is not really about the tree but what is about to happen to the Temple," Van Iersel said.[8]

Aside from criticizing religious authorities in Jerusalem, the framing story also reminded Mark's audience how slow of mind the disciples are. Mark said all the disciples heard Jesus curse the fig tree (11:14). After the temple cleansing episode, the next morning when the disciples pass a dead fig tree, Peter, the leading disciple in the Twelve, seems startled: "Master, look! The fig tree which you cursed has withered" (v. 21). Answering "them," as if addressing a dozen skeptics, Jesus said, "Have faith in God," declaring that faith can move mountains (vv. 21–23). The only other time Peter addressed Jesus as "Master," or "Rabbi," was when he blurted out the feeble idea of building booths for Moses, Elijah, and Jesus when the trio stood together before Peter, James, and John during the mountaintop transfiguration (9:5). Peter acknowledged Jesus as his teacher but was always at a loss when witnessing Jesus' demonstrations of divinity.

Fifth Bracket: Contrasts

Then there was Judas Iscariot, the betrayer, according to Mark. This story sandwich has a brief start (14:1–2) with the chief priests and scribes wondering how to arrest Jesus stealthily and kill him without stirring up a crowd. (Judas does not enter the scene yet, but readers know from Mark 3:19, when Jesus picked his twelve disciples, that Iscariot was identified beforehand as the one "who betrayed him.")

Before getting to Judas, Mark tells the story (14:3–9) of an unidentified woman who pours a flask of "very costly" ointment over the head of Jesus as he sat at a table. Some onlookers grumbled that the money used to buy the ointment was wasted. It could have been used to help the poor, they said. Jesus reproached the critics, saying that it is good to help the poor when you can but that "she has done a beautiful thing to me." "She has anointed my body beforehand for burying," Jesus said. "And truly, I say to you, wherever the gospel is preached in the whole world, what she has done will be told in memory of her."

Mark's film camera, if you will, then swept back to the chief priests and scribes (14:10–11). Judas Iscariot went to them, offering to betray Jesus. They gladly accepted, promising a reward.

Death hangs over these combined stories: The woman who somehow knew that Jesus was a marked man performed her symbolic act while elsewhere the chief priests and scribes were scheming to kill him, only to be approached by a willing snitch from Jesus' ranks. The linked scenes invite comparison. "Judas betraying Jesus for money contrasts with the woman anointing Jesus with expensive ointment," wrote the authors of *Mark as Story*.[9] In addition, this marked the last happy moment for Jesus, who showers praise on the woman's insight. Two verses later, the religious authorities, repeatedly frustrated by Jesus in the past, were buoyed when Judas showed up. "When they heard it, they were glad, and promised to give him money" (v. 11).

Sixth Bracket: Peter's Turn for Infamy

In 14:53–72, Peter also betrays Jesus—denying three times that he was a follower of the arrested Jesus. The Gospel of Mark often depicts characters as doing things in threes, such as Jesus telling his disciples three times in mid-Gospel of his looming death and resurrection. Though the disciples "all forsook him and fled" (v. 50) at Jesus' arrest, just as Jesus had predicted (v. 27), Peter followed at a distance and entered the courtyard of the high priest. "He was sitting with the guards, and warming himself at the fire," according to Mark 14:53–54, the opening scene.

The narrative then switches to Jesus standing before the chief priests and their council, which condemned him to death for blasphemy. Some council members spat on Jesus and struck him. As the middle scene ends, "the guards received him with blows" (v. 65)—perhaps some of the same guards with whom Peter sat warming himself earlier.

Back to the courtyard scene (vv. 66–72): a maid of the high priest spied Peter. "You also were with the Nazarene, Jesus," she declared. "I neither know nor understand what you mean," answered Peter, moving to the gateway. The maid again saw him and said, "This man is one of them." Again he denied being a Jesus follower. Bystanders said they were certain he was one of them. Cursing himself, Peter swore, "I do not know this man of whom you speak." Suddenly a rooster was heard crowing a second time, and Peter remembered that Jesus predicted he would deny him three times before the cock crows twice. And then Peter "broke down and wept."

Peter's betrayal in Mark may be worse than that of Judas, for when Jesus had foretold that all his disciples would forsake him, Peter protested. Peter "vehemently" pledged, "If I must die with you, I will not deny you" (14:31). The rest of the disciples echoed that vow. As

John Dominic Crossan put it, "Mark is severely and relentlessly critical of the Twelve in general, of Peter, James and John in particular, and of Peter above all the others."[10]

A Seventh Bracket?

James and John did suffer special embarrassment once. It was not part of a bracketed story, or was it? In Mark 10:35–45, the sons of Zebedee approached Jesus, demanding: "Teacher, we want you to do for us whatever we ask of you." Jesus replied, "What do you want me to do for you?" Envisioning in their afterlife a thronelike setting in heaven, the brothers asked, "Grant us to sit, one at your right hand and one at your left, in your glory." Jesus balked. Questioning whether they were able to meet the trials of discipleship, Jesus said that in any case it was not in his power to say who would sit next to him in heaven. Meanwhile, the ten other disciples became indignant at James and John, prompting Jesus to advise them all that one who aspires to greatness must serve others. "Whoever would be first among you must be slave to all," Jesus said.

In the text that Clement of Alexandria called the Secret Gospel of Mark, the James and John episode is immediately preceded by the story of the young man whom Jesus raised from the dead (after the youth's sister implored Jesus) and, after six days, taught him the secret of the kingdom in a nighttime initiation. The Secret Mark story seems to finish before Mark 10:35, but just after Mark 10:45, at 10:46a, a short resumption appears: "And they came to Jericho." Clement said that right after those words is the following in Secret Mark: "And the sister of the young man that Jesus loved and his mother and Salome were there, and Jesus did not receive them."[11]

Biblical Mark has Jesus first arriving in Jericho, then leaving without anything happening. Missing is this short postscript to the story of the resuscitated young man. It serves to bracket the episode of the misguided James and John with a story about the unnamed young man who loved Jesus and whom Jesus loved in return. Jesus treats this beloved disciple and the covetous brothers very differently.

The rebuff of the women by Jesus, without direct explanation, is not unprecedented in Mark. Earlier, Mark has Jesus express disdain for his mother and siblings at 3:31–35 and at 6:4, apparently for believing Jesus was "mad" and a prophet-pretender, respectively. Mother is ignored again in Secret Mark's 10:46. As for Salome, she doesn't appear in biblical Mark until 15:41, where she is described as having followed and ministered to Jesus while he was in Galilee. But, as Mark's readers know, Salome is in the trio of women—along with Jesus' mother and Mary Magdalene—who witness the crucifixion, go to the tomb to anoint Jesus' body, run away when told that Jesus had risen, and say nothing to anyone because of their great fear (16:1–8). The sister of the young man was blameless but happened to be in the wrong company when seeking Jesus' audience again.

The six bracketed stories described above in biblical Mark and this possible seventh example all invite comparison within each paired episodes. But a number of questions arise for anyone thinking this young man story was in Original Mark. Is the postscriptlike conclusion too short to be considered an end frame? I don't think so. Another example in Mark is at 6:30–32, where the travel-weary disciples reported back to Jesus. But what was needed was more evidence for this Secret Mark anecdote! Scholars today know of the two-part episode only from photographs of a copy of a letter by Clement of Alexandria. Biblical Mark has two appearances of a nameless young man, but nothing of the sort is in chapter 10. Luke and Matthew do not have the Secret Mark episode about the young man; that lightly dressed character shows up nowhere in their Gospels. I was alone in my suspicions. Smith and most of his supporters never proposed that this newly found story was part of the original gospel.

Nevertheless, I was gaining confidence that the Secret Mark episode was integral to the text from research on another important Markan writing technique—one that was not as easily seen as the bracketing format. The author's prolific use of this literary device promised to give startling evidence for recovering the original form of the oldest New Testament gospel.

Notes

1. David Rhoads et al., *Mark as Story: An Introduction to the Narrative of a Gospel* (2d ed.; Minneapolis: Fortress, 1999), 51–52.

2. "Six classic cases" were treated in detail by Tom Shepherd, *Markan Sandwich Stories: Narration, Definition, and Function* (Berrien Springs, Mich.: Andrews University Press, 1993).

3. Three pairings cited as brackets or sandwiches, which I do not treat in this chapter, are 4:1–9/10–12/13–20; 14:17–21/22–26/27–31; and 15:40–41/42–46/47–16:8. See W. R. Telford, *Mark* (NTG; Sheffield: Sheffield Academic Press, 1995), 103.

4. By referring to Jesus' real family, I follow studies that say the New Testament describes the siblings of Jesus as immediate family, not cousins or half-brothers as some church doctrines contend. Mark treats them as Jesus' mother, brothers, and sisters in a natural sense. The apostle Paul identified James of Jerusalem as "brother of the Lord" and spoke of the privileges accorded "the brothers of the Lord." The Letter of Jude identifies the author as "brother of James," a person assumed to be James of Jerusalem.

5. Rhoads, *Mark as Story*, 14.

6. Werner H. Kelber, *Mark's Story of Jesus* (Philadelphia: Fortress, 1979), 27.

7. Bas M. F. van Iersel, *Mark: A Reader-Response Commentary* (JSNTSup 164; (Sheffield: Sheffield Academic Press, 1998), 358–59.

8. Ibid., 359.

9. Rhoads, *Mark as Story*, 52.

10. John Dominic Crossan, *The Birth of Christianity: Discovering What Happened in the Years Immediately after the Execution of Jesus* (San Francisco: HarperSanFrancisco, 1998), 557.

11. Morton Smith, *The Secret Gospel: The Discovery and Interpretation of the Secret Gospel according to Mark* (New York: Harper & Row, 1973), 17.

CHAPTER 6

Deciphering the Code

IT'S A CATCHY SPEAKING TECHNIQUE, yet seldom heard today. President John F. Kennedy used it for a memorable line in his inauguration speech: "Ask not what your country can do for you—ask what you can do for your country." In prodding citizens toward public service, President Kennedy's key words in the first half of his sentence appear in reverse order to form a turnaround challenge.

A Mother Goose ditty remembered for its rhyme also uses this principle of reversing key words: "Hickory, dickory, dock, The mouse ran up the clock, The clock struck one, Down the mouse run, Hickory, dickory, dock."

Meet the long-neglected art of the *chiasmus,* a technique in writing and speaking used by the Greeks, Hebrews, and others in ancient times to help them remember stories and speeches that would be recited from memory. Audiences of old and a relatively small reading elite surely delighted in a nicely constructed chiasm with its clever connections. Instead of "chiasmus," I adopt the Anglicized spellings "chiasm" (pronounced ky-AZM) and "chiasms." The word derives from the Greek letter chi (X) representing lines one could draw to diagram a short, two-line chiasm.

The Hebrew Bible, the Old Testament to churchgoers, is peppered with chiastic constructions. Scholars have long known and cited their instances in the Hebrew Scriptures—just as they would take note of poetic writing, puns with words of the same roots, or even an "acrostic" to make the sequence of certain passages easier to recall. An acrostic uses words at the start of sentences that begin with successive letters of the (Hebrew) alphabet. Chiasms are so common that *The HarperCollins Study Bible,* in its introduction to the book of Genesis, outlines the actions and themes in the garden of Eden story (2:4–4:1) with the usual concave diagram for identifying chiasms.[1] From the top, each indented step to the right is labeled with a letter. The start at 2:4 is A. As the garden story unfolds, each step gets the next letter of the alphabet until the story's turning point—Eve's and Adam's eating the forbidden fruit at 3:6, a step labeled in this case with the letter I. As the themes and words occur in reverse order, the segments step to the left with the assigned letters H', G', and so on, until the finish at 4:1, which is labeled A'.

Some chiastic schemas stretch over many chapters. Whole books of the Bible, in some instances, are said to be written in chiastic patterns. Many are small and tightly wound—like the tower of Babel story (Gen 11:1–9). Here is how David A. Dorsey blueprinted it in *The Literary Structure of the Old Testament,* a masterful assemblage of chiasms as well as parallel patterns:

A introduction: **all the earth** had one language (11:1)
   B people settle together in Shinar (11:2)
      C resolution of the people: **come,** let us (11:3–4)
         D Yahweh discovers the plot (11:5)
      C' resolution of Yahweh: **come,** let us (11:6–7)
   B' people disperse from Shinar (11:8)
A' conclusion: **all the earth** now has many languages (11:9)[2]

Parallel patterns also appear in Jewish and Christian religious literature. The Gospel of Mark has about a dozen. For instance, consider Mark 4:22:

A For there is nothing hid,
   B except to be made manifest;
A' nor is anything secret.
   B' except to come to light.

These parallel constructions, at least in Mark, appear mostly in certain sayings of Jesus, such as "Render to Caesar the things . . ." (12:17), "Whoever divorces his wife . . ." (10:11), and a teaching about sewing an unshrunk patch on an old garment and putting new wine into old wineskins (2:21–22). Longer patterns (e.g., ABCDEA'B'C'D'E') occur, but it seems that the reversible, middle-pivot designs of chiasms were favored for long stretches of prose.

Chiasms in Mark are relatively recent discoveries in terms of any significance being attributed to them. For generations of scholarship, those who studied Mark regarded the Gospel as a patchwork of anecdotes and teachings strung together by someone who was more compiler than writer. When scholars found and duly noted chiasms, the concentric writing patterns tended to be attributed to Mark's sources, not to the author. But opinions shifted in the last third of the twentieth century to the point at which many extol that gospel's storytelling power. Many now bestow admiration on the drama of a miracle-working man who taught "with authority" about godly things, attracting followers and opponents alike, in a well-plotted sequence leading to climactic events in Jerusalem.

In the New Testament as a whole, scholars have cited here-and-there chiastic examples in the Gospels and in the Pauline Letters, but an appreciation of chiasms was especially slow in coming. For years, *Chiasmus in the New Testament* (1942), by Nils W. Lund, was the standard book on the subject.[3] Yet, disbelief often greeted Lund's own proposed chiastic patterns and those of later scholars in the pursuit. This wariness was described by David Noel Freedman in a preface to *The Chiasmus in Antiquity* (1981). Difficulties arise when chiastic steps "are defined in terms of thought and theme, rather than the more visible words and patterns," Freedman said. On those subjective terms, the existence of a given chiasm "can become almost a voter's choice." However, whenever well-written, self-evident chiasms appear, "these structures may add novel perspectives and unexpected dimension to the texts in which they appear," wrote Freedman.[4] Ian Thomson, in his book *Chiasmus in the Pauline Letters* (1995), elucidated five excellent examples in writings attributed to Paul. But Thomson acknowledged that the acceptance of chiastic claims in New Testament writings was controversial for most of the twentieth century because "the debate about chiasmus has been polarized between the incautious enthusiasm of its exponents and the legitimate skepticism of their critics."[5]

Model Chiasm in Mark

I wasn't aware of the debate when biblical chiasms first caught my interest. My introduction to them was through an article by Joanna Dewey
that appeared in 1985 in an anthology of essays on Mark. Dewey had
first published her article in the *Journal of Biblical Literature* twelve years
before, while she was studying at the Graduate Theological Union
(GTU) in Berkeley. She was the same Joanna Dewey who witnessed the
fierce debate at GTU two years later over Morton Smith's controversial
find and interpretation of the Secret Gospel of Mark.

What Dewey published was a classic exposition of the chiasm from
Mark 2:1 through Mark 3:6. That section has five so-called controversy
stories about Jesus, who was depicted moving about with his disciples
in Galilee and encountering antagonistic questioning from Judean religious figures. Dewey said she was startled when that chiastic pattern
first formed in her mind. She was poring over books published decades
earlier. "I was making my way through [Johannes] Sundwall's excellent
1934 study on Mark [in German], and what he was saying about Mark
2:1–3:6, and I thought, 'My God, This is an incredibly balanced section!'" said Dewey. She recalled in a conversation the experience for me
years later when she was a faculty member at the Episcopal Divinity
School in Massachusetts.[6]

Sundwall had paid particular attention to word repetitions and
observed the frequency of catchwords from one episode to another as
well as the use of similar words at the start and end of an episode,
according to Dewey. She said that Sundwall believed that these word
repetitions were common in the oral tradition available to Mark and
that the gospel author simply them took over. Sundwall did not look for
larger structural patterns in Mark, she said. But at the multiseminary
GTU, Jesuit John L. Boyle introduced Dewey to Catholic scholarship
on literary structures, including concentric structures in Mark, she
wrote. He was the coordinator of her dissertation project.

In her article on Mark 2:1–3:6, Dewey concluded that the five
episodes "form a tightly-constructed literary unit, predominantly chiastic in principle."[7] The themes of sin, sabbath lawbreaking, healings,
eating, and fasting were centered around an allusion to Jesus' fate—
when "the bridegroom" will be taken away from those who follow him.
As Dewey noted, within 2:1 to 3:6 there is "a linear development of
hostility in the opponents from silent criticism to the questioning of

Jesus' disciples, to the questioning of Jesus himself, to watching him, finally to plotting to destroy him."[8] In other words, Mark's Jesus has only started to perform mighty works and attract followers in Galilee when the gospel plot thickens. The story foreshadows Jesus' violent punishment and points the listener forward, anticipating the progression of events.

As other scholars examined the circular nature of 2:1–3:6, some differed slightly on the number of steps. Dewey depicted an ABCB'A' format, whereas some argued for an extra step on each side of the chiasm (ABCDC'B'A'). The important thing, however, is that the existence of a chiasm there has been confirmed repeatedly.

Here are the basic features of Dewey's chiasm as first published in 1973 and reprinted in 1985 (I present it here in a style used hereafter in this book—boldface for words and catchphrases with identical roots; underlining used for similar or opposite meanings, or other corresponding elements such as numbers, names, and Scripture allusions. Greek words are italicized and put inside parentheses after boldfaced words to show that though the English translation may differ, the Greek is the same or has the same root):

A (2:1–12) **And when he returned to** *(eiserchomai palin)* Capernaum; paralytic carried in; he **said to the** paralytic; scribes questioning in their hearts; in your **hearts;** (Jesus challenges opponents with alternatives, using word **or**); **rise** *(egeiro)*; he **said to the** paralytic; **rise;** he **rose;** (onlookers) amazed, glorified God.

  B (2:13–17) Levi, tax office, followed Jesus; in his **house;** scribes of Pharisees saw (Jesus, disciples) **eating** with sinners and tax collectors; why **eat;** have no **need** of a physician; (Jesus utters proverb, then a christological allusion).

    C (2:18–22) Fasting and not fasting; incompatibility of old and new.

  B' (2:23–28) One sabbath; Jesus, disciples; pluck heads of grain; what David did, when he was in **need** and hungry; **house** of God; **ate** the bread; to **eat;** (Jesus utters proverb, then a christological allusion).

A' (3:1–6) **Again he entered** *(eiserchomai palin)* the synagogue; man with a withered hand; he **said to the** man; Jesus: **come** *(egeiro)* here; (alternatives to opponents: good **or** harm, save life **or** kill); hardness of **heart;** he **said to the** man; Pharisees, held counsel with the Herodians against him, how to destroy him.

Dewey was certainly justified in claiming that the parallels between A and A' and between B and B' were purposely formed. "Such a structure as found in Mark 2:1–3:6 does not occur by accident," she wrote.[9] The gospel author, though often faulted for less-than-elegant Greek, possessed "considerable literary skill," Dewey asserted.[10] She could have added that Mark shows "determination" in building multiple tie-ins between the corresponding chiastic stages. She noted the unusual effort by the gospel writer to get one more link for A' with A. In A, the paralytic episode, the word "rise" *(egeiro)* is used three times, which is understandable in a story about enabling a disabled man to stand and walk. But A' is about the healing of a man with a withered hand, who presumably had no trouble standing. In most translations, Jesus summons the man to "come" to him or "stand up." But the literal meaning is a "rather odd expression," she said, to "get up *(egeiro)* to the middle." Using the word "rise" here "serves to bring the verb into the story," said Dewey.[11]

Chiastic parallels were achieved not only by catchwords and matching themes but also by grammatical constructions. A group of numbers or place-names in one part of the chiasm might be matched with numbers or place-names at the opposite spot in the chiasm. Opposite meanings also count as possible links—for instance, contrasting actions or reactions. Witnesses in Dewey's episode A and episode A' reacted quite differently to the healings by Jesus. In the first, the crowd witnessing the paralytic's standing and walking was "amazed and glorified God, saying, 'We never saw anything like this!'" (v. 12). In the last episode, upon seeing the man's withered hand restored, the Pharisees "went out, and immediately held counsel with the Herodians against him, how to destroy him." This reaction in 3:6 "is hostile, not admiring," wrote Dewey, indicating that antithetical actions or responses may serve as links in a chiasm, not just identical or similar elements.[12]

In coming years, Dewey and other scholars would spot and describe additional chiastic segments in Mark. Yet, many colleagues showed only modest interest at first. Chiastic patterns fall into the field of literary criticism and so-called reader-response studies, two of the many research specialties of biblical scholars. Also, my sense was that many found it hard to imagine Mark using chiasms extensively. Why would an author complicate the task of writing a religious work with the self-imposition of word linkups along each step of the way? Would Mark have gone to that much trouble? But the biggest question posed was, "Were most proposed chiasms unconvincing?"[13]

A Catholic scholar-monk, Augustine Stock of Conception Abbey in Missouri, observed that many might doubt that Mark's author "would indulge in such literary sophistication." In his 1984 article, Stock added: "And isn't it true that people read Mark's gospel for centuries without even considering the possibility?"[14] How could that escape notice for nearly 2,000 years? Yet, Stock declared that a case could be made that the author of Mark did indeed use chiasms and that learned people of that era would have recognized their presence. The chiasm— also described as "inverted parallelism" or "ring composition"—was pervasive in education systems of Greek and Roman antiquity. "If moderns have lost their appreciation for chiasmus, it is because they have been educated in a vastly different way," he wrote.[15] "Chiasmus afforded a seriously needed element of internal organization in ancient writings, which did not make use of paragraphs, punctuation, capitalization and other such synthetic devices to communicate the conclusion of one idea and the commencement of the next," he said.[16]

Ancient writings had no spaces between words, no subheads, and no chapter headings. Biblical writings had no chapters and numbered verses, an invention of many centuries later. Reading these tightly packed texts was one problem. But in an essentially oral culture, the learned were expected to memorize and recite texts as much as possible. Those exercises were standard school training for children in antiquity, Stock said.[17] Quick learners spread beloved stories widely among nonliterate folks. Stock's article cited Mark 2:1–3:6 as a particularly excellent example of a chiasm.[18]

Widening the Pattern

One thing troubled me about Mark 2:1–3:6 in spite of its seemingly self-contained structure. Wasn't it really longer than that?

I looked at the episodes immediately before and after. They, too, seemed to have chiastic matches. Just ahead of Mark 2:1 (in 1:40–45), Jesus responds favorably to a leper who asks to be made "clean." At the other end (in 3:7–12), he heals many diseases and often encountered "unclean" spirits. The Greek word that gives English the word "catharsis" was used four times in the earlier episode for "clean" and "cleansing" and once in the later episode as the root word for "unclean." Moreover, in both stories Jesus urged secrecy. First, he "sternly charged" the leper to not tell anyone of his cure except the priest (1:43). Second, he "strictly ordered" the unclean spirits not to make him known (3:12). In another matching motif, Jesus did his healings before large groups of people: first those coming "from every quarter" (1:45) and second "a great multitude" from four regions (3:7–8).

Eager to see if the chiasm could be carried another step, I compared 1:35–39 and 3:13–19. In the early episode, "Simon and those who were with him" (the thus-far amorphous group of followers) sought out and found Jesus, who had slipped away to pray in an isolated spot. Reenergized for his task, Jesus resumes his "preaching" and "casting out demons." The later episode reverses the situation. Jesus appoints the Twelve "to be with him, and to be sent out to preach and have authority to cast out demons." The first disciple appointed is "Simon whom he surnamed Peter"(3:16). Thus, the two stories link via the catchwords "preach" and "cast out demons" plus Simon's being named as the most prominent follower in both. Contrasts connect the passages, too. The followers urge Jesus to get about his work in one episode, and Jesus calls twelve disciples to help him in the other.

Stretching the chiasm longer yet, I saw that 1:29–34 and 3:20–27 each had to do with family members and the word "house" was used in both—relatively minor links by themselves. But "demons" appeared three times in the first story, and "Satan" was mentioned thrice in the corresponding episode, which is surely more than coincidence despite the fact that Jesus was exorcising plenty of evil spirits in this part of the Gospel.

Through trial and error, I found that happenstance was very unlikely. When several catchwords and/or motifs link each story, and when a succession of adjacent episodes also fulfill such chiastic requirements, you are in the middle of "growing" a chiastic flower from the middle outward.

What bloomed was a huge sunflower. The next steps outward (1:23–28 and 3:28–35) were also related. In the first, a man with an "unclean spirit" calls Jesus "the Holy One of God"; in the second, Jesus warns against blaspheming the Holy Spirit, and the short episode contains an accusation that Jesus had "an unclean spirit." I took one more step to stretch the core 2:1–3:6 chiastic pattern described by Dewey and others into an extensive one that began at 1:14–22 and ended at 4:1–12—the equivalent of three chapters in Mark! (See appendix 2.)

Why stop there? The chiasm ended there because the passages before 1:14 and those after 4:12 did not supply words or themes to make connections. Moreover, most studies describe the section before 1:14–15 as Mark's prologue, the introduction before Jesus' ministry in Galilee. This was my first indication that the surface narrative, one that people read and recite, probably had some relationships to underlying chiasms . . . if indeed there were more hidden patterns to be discovered.

Symmetric Introduction

The prologue of Mark begins with a Scripture quotation about "a messenger" to be sent, one crying in the wilderness—a reference in Mark to John the Baptist—who will prepare the way. "Messenger" in Greek is *aggelos;* and it also can mean, depending on the context, "angel," a messenger from heaven. The prologue began and ended with the catchword *aggelos*—"messenger" (John Baptist) and "angels" who ministered to Jesus in the wilderness for forty days. The prologue itself is a chiasm with the midpoint turning on Jesus' baptism. Here is the chiastic pattern of Mark's introduction in 1:1–14. Again, words having the same Greek root appear in boldface; words with similar or contrasting meanings are underlined. As with Dewey's 2:1–3:6 chiasm, I have compressed the longer chiasms so the structure may be better viewed.

A (1:1–6) Messengers/message. Beginning, **gospel** of **Jesus** Christ, Son of **God**; Isaiah, I send my **messenger** *(aggelos)* before thy face, prepare thy way; voice crying in the wilderness; prepare the way of the Lord, make his paths straight—**John** baptizer in **the wilderness,** preaching baptism of repentance, forgiveness of sins; went all of Judea, all of Jerusalem; baptized in Jordan, confessing sins; **John** clothed camel's hair, ate locusts, wild honey.

  B (1:7–9a) Recognition. Preached, after me comes he who mightier than I; not worthy; I baptized with **water;** he will baptize with Holy **Spirit.** In those days came[19]

    C (1:9b) Jesus from Nazareth of Galilee

      D (1:9c) and (he) was baptized

    C' (1:9d) in the Jordan by John

  B' (1:10–11) Recognition. Came up out of **water,** saw heavens opened, **Spirit** upon him like dove; voice from heaven, Thou art my beloved Son; with thee I am well pleased.

A' (1:12–14) Messengers/message. Spirit drove him into **the wilderness;** he was in wilderness forty days, tempted by Satan; was with wild beasts; and the **angels** *(aggelos)* ministered to him; after **John** was arrested, **Jesus** came into Galilee, preaching the **gospel of God.**

Verse 14 does double duty—serving as the end of the prologue's chiasm as well as starting the next long chiasm. It wasn't until years later, resuming research on Mark's chiastic patterns after a hiatus, that I found that the author was doing this in many transitions. I had long resisted that conclusion, thinking that a clean break between consecutive chiasms was logical for someone creating these puzzlelike word codes. But the author often borrowed from an adjacent chiasm. Another lesson in such research is not forcing rules on the puzzle maker, but letting the puzzle makers set the rules.

At any rate, this prologue chiasm addresses an academic debate over whether the author of Mark wrote all of 1:1 ("The beginning of the gospel of Jesus Christ, the Son of God") since some manuscripts omit "the Son of God." The chiastic connections between the opening and 1:14 would favor the original author as responsible for the whole opening verse. Also, Markan studies have disagreed on exactly where amid verses 13, 14, and 15 the prologue ends and the main narrative opens. It would seem that the dividing line was blurred there for chiastic purposes.

Messenger/Message and "Recognition"

Early in my search for chiasms the theme of "messenger/message" arose as a clue to the formal structure of Mark. Messenger John the Baptist is succeeded in his preaching by Jesus, who preaches the gospel of God, indeed the kingdom of God, calling upon people to repent (1:14–15). At the other end of this long chiasm, which I had expanded beyond the 2:1–3:6 core, was 4:10–12, a difficult-to-interpret teaching by Jesus. He told "those who were about him with the twelve" that they have been "given the secret of the kingdom of God." But the parables told by Jesus will confound outsiders, who will not understand—unless they "should turn again, and be forgiven."

Later in my research, I would see that for large chiasms especially Mark has tight turning points—some as short as a sentence or a phrase—that resonate with the start and/or finish. The chiastic center of my expanded chiasm from 1:14 to 4:12, I found, is 2:20, a cryptic self-reference from Jesus: "The days will come, when the bridegroom is taken away from [the disciples], and then they will fast in that day." The double use of "day" harks back to Jesus' announcement that the time is fulfilled. The term "bridegroom" is not explained, perhaps in keeping with the "secret" of the kingdom, which is also left to the readers or listeners to discern. Insiders "about" Jesus were "given" the secret, and it is a good thing since Jesus warns them that someday he will be "taken away."

Moving on, in a random fashion too haphazard for me to recall, I came up with a formal structure to Original Mark containing five major chiastic spans framed by the prologue and conclusion. Each of the five "acts," for lack of a better word, began with the themes of messenger and/or recognition. The recognition motif is evident in Mark from an ordinary reading of the Gospel—remembered best perhaps when Jesus asks, "Who do [people] say that I am?" (8:27). The prologue, from the opening verse and John the Baptist's prediction to the heavenly voice declaring Jesus to be the beloved Son, made it clear who Jesus is. But the reader is left to marvel at how many people in the rest of the Gospel do not recognize his divine connections, or only partially so. The following outline emerged:

    Prologue 1:1–1:14
    Act 1. 1:14–4:12
    Act 2. 4:13–6:46
    Act 3. 8:27–10:52
    Act 4. 11:1–14:9
    Act 5. 14:10–15:33
    Conclusion 15:34–16:8

Missing from the above is the section of Mark (6:47–8:26) that the author of Luke apparently did not see and which this study proposes was added by an editor (see ch. 3–4). Act 2 seemed to begin and end with messenger/message metaphors. A series of parables taught by Jesus (4:13–34) talks about seeds (= the Word), harvesting grain, mustard seed, and so on in a catchword journey to a midpoint (5:43) wherein, after healing a little girl, Jesus urged secrecy and told others to "give her something to eat." That instruction from Jesus seems oddly appended, but not when one sees that the Act 2 chiasm begins with grain and ends in a feast—the multiplication of bread and fish for the multitude (6:33–44), another metaphor for spreading the message.

Other links tie together the ends of Act 2. Numbers are important, for example. In the first, those who hear and accept the word bring forth "grain" (new believers) thirty-, sixty-, and a hundredfold. Another parable promised that "to him who has will more be given" (5:25), and the series includes the parable of the mustard seed, the small seed that grows

into a large bush. At the other end, Jesus instructs the disciples to go and
buy two hundred denarii worth of bread. He has the people sit in
groups of fifty and one hundred. The five loaves and two fish were multiplied miraculously to feed five thousand people (6:44).

After Act 2, the next story in the New Testament version of Mark
describes Jesus walking on water (6:47–52). That episode could not be
joined with the mass feeding story for a joint ending to Act 2, for the
catchwords were not there. At the other end of the editor's insertion,
healing the blind man (8:22–26) has often been identified by Markan
experts as the start of "the middle" of Mark, a section that ends with
another such cure at 10:46–52, the healing of the blind beggar
Bartimaeus. My inclination was to disagree.

I felt that the author of Mark had clearly delineated the start and finish of this middle section (Act 3) with an expression translated "on the
way." Bartimaeus, with his sight received, followed Jesus "on the way,"
ending the tenth chapter. That harked back in good chiastic manner to
8:27, where "on the way" Jesus asked his disciples, "Who do men say
that I am?" Peter spoke up, calling him the "Christ," thus becoming the
first follower to recognize this title of Jesus. Bartimaeus, though blind
and reduced to begging, called to Jesus for mercy, addressing him twice
as "Son of David," a title with messianic import. The episodes at both
ends of 8:27–10:52 lacked an obvious messenger motif but were strong
on the recognition theme.

Finding the Hidden Messenger Motif

Act 4 opens and closes with stories of messengers and messages,
although the motif is not easy to spot. At 11:1–6a, near Bethany, Jesus
sent two disciples to bring him a colt and told them what to say if anyone asked why. Indeed, people did ask, and the disciples told them what
Jesus said. In other words, they were "messengers" as well as errand boys.
Jesus then rides the colt into Jerusalem, where he is hailed as "blessed."
That story has links to Act 4's close at 14:7–9, following the act of an
unidentified woman who uses expensive oil to anoint Jesus—ironic
recognition that, contrary to his initial welcome, Jesus will die in
Jerusalem. At the end, Jesus exults, "Wherever the gospel is preached in
the whole world, what she has done will be told in memory of her." As
with the prologue, Acts 1 and 2 the messenger motif and the theme of
recognition pack a chiastic one-two punch at start and finish. The very

center of the Act 4 chiasm (12:32a) has a lone Jewish scribe telling Jesus, "You are right *(kalos)*." A very similar Greek word appears in the anointing scene, where Jesus declared the woman did something "beautiful" for him.

Finally, Act 5 also begins with the hidden messenger theme. In effect, the writer was telling the audience that if you did not detect the messenger motif at the start of Act 4, don't miss it here, too. Act 5 begins briefly with Judas being promised money by the chief priests to betray Jesus. Then Jesus instructs two disciples to locate a room in the city for him to observe the Passover supper (14:10–18). Just as when Jesus told two disciples earlier to find him a colt in town, the disciples seeking accommodations for a supper are told exactly what to say when they encounter a man carrying water. They could not perform the errands successfully unless they delivered specified messages.

Act 5's second step (14:19–21) portrays a non-recognition motif by the disciples. After Jesus told the assembled twelve that "one of you" will betray him, they all ask one another, "Is it I?" A different question of self-identity is posed by the high priest at the very center of Act 5, where Jesus is asked if he is the Christ. Jesus begins his answer, "I am; and you will see the Son of man . . ." (14:62a). In the opening, Jesus had alluded to himself twice as the Son of Man. In the closing passages (15:25–33), his persecutors mocked him as the "King of the Jews" and "Christ, the King of Israel," also a case of nonrecognition. Was there no messenger motif at the end of Act 5? No first-person reference? I struggled repeatedly with apparent inconsistencies, sometimes resolving them, other times giving up.

Certainly, numbers and the idea of sacrifice amply link A and A' in this fifth act. In 14:10–18, on the first day, when the Passover lamb is sacrificed, two disciples are sent to secure the upper room for the meal. There, Jesus says one of the Twelve will betray him. At 15:25–33, Jesus himself is sacrificed (crucified) at the third hour with two robbers; he was taunted about his claim to rebuild the temple in three days. When the sixth hour comes, darkness covers the earth until the ninth hour.

Finale: Shameful and Shining Messengers

The Gospel's conclusion is a chiasm as well and begins and ends with a messenger theme somewhat more oblique than elsewhere, yet it is there for people familiar with Mark's story. The conclusion opens at 15:34

with the God-sent Jesus crying with a loud voice, "Why has thou forsaken me?" Near death, he even seems to call to Elijah, whose image was attached to John the Baptist, the messenger at the Gospel's opening. The conclusion chiasm pivots at the midpoint, where he is confirmed dead. By the end of the conclusion, a "young man," dressed in a white robe, appears in the empty tomb when a trio of women comes to anoint his body. Mary Magdalene, Mary the mother of Jesus, and Salome are the only identified followers on the scene who could learn that Jesus has arisen from the dead—inasmuch as Jesus' blood brothers never left Galilee and the twelve male disciples all deserted Jesus.

But the women turn out to be disgracefully *failed* messengers in Mark's conclusion. The young man tells the women: "Go, tell his disciples and Peter that he is going before you to Galilee; there you will see him, as he told you" (16:7). But in the last line of the Gospel (16:8), the author writes emphatically that they definitely did not fulfill that duty: "And they went out and fled from the tomb; for trembling and astonishment had come upon them; and they said nothing to anyone, for they were afraid."

Many interpreters of Mark prefer to assume that Jesus would indeed be reunited with his disciples or that the women would recover from their shock to inform Peter and the others (as it is told in other gospels). But Mark's ending says that all the big name followers of Jesus and his family utterly forsook him.

Does that mean the Gospel ends on the note of *failed* messengers? Not entirely. The anonymous young man knows what happened, and it is left to him to tell others the good news of Jesus' resurrection. Similarly, all those characters in the Gospel—some named like the brave Joseph of Arimathea, who asked for Jesus' body to give him a decent burial and some unnamed like the centurion at the cross who said, "Truly this man was the Son of God"—were the ones who could witness to the divine nature of Jesus that they had recognized quickly and dared to speak. Mark's Gospel says that there were people throughout his ministry who could give a true account of what Jesus was about.

By highlighting the messenger and recognition motifs, the Gospel of Mark put a punctuation mark on the author's intended emphasis on who did and didn't fully perceive Jesus' nature and act as messengers for the gospel. For instance, the conclusion began with Jesus worrying that maybe God had forsaken him. That proved to be wrong; Jesus was raised from the dead. The conclusion ends, not with the catchword "forsake," but with the stark description of the women forsaking the role of messengers. Fortunately, according to Mark, that disappointing news at the Gospel's end was not the whole story. The mysterious young man—commonly thought by church and Bible experts for almost two thousand years to be an incidental, decidedly minor character in Mark—now will shine brightest among gospel characters who saved the day.

Notes

1. Joel W. Rosenberg, "Genesis: Introduction," in *HarperCollins Study Bible: NRSV* (New York: HarperCollins, 1989), 4.

2. David A. Dorsey, *The Literary Structure of the Old Testament: A Commentary on Genesis–Malachi* (Grand Rapids: Baker, 1999), 53.

3. Nils W. Lund, *Chiasmus in the New Testament: A Study in the Form and Function of Chiastic Patterns* (Peabody, Mass.: Hendrickson, 1992). The original of this reprint was published in 1942 by the University of North Carolina Press.

4. David Noel Freedman, preface to *Chiasmus in Antiquity: Structures, Analysis, Exegesis,* edited by John W. Welch (Hildesheim, Germany: Gerstenberg Verlag, 1981).

5. Ian H. Thomson, *Chiasmus in the Pauline Letters* (JSNTSup 111; Sheffield: Sheffield Academic Press, 1995), 44–45.

6. Joanna Dewey, "The Literary Structure of the Controversy Stories in Mark 2:1–3:6," in *The Interpretation of Mark* (ed. William Telford; IRT 7; Philadelphia: Fortress, 1985), 109–18; repr. from *Journal of Biblical Literature* 91 (1973): 394–401. Her 1977 dissertation was published as *Markan Public Debate: Literary Technique, Concentric Structure, and Theology in Mark 2:1–3:6* (SBLDS 48; Chico, Calif.: Scholars Press, 1980), in which she cites Hobbs's and Boyle's guidance in the acknowledgments and describes (on p. 24) Sundwall's book: *Die Zusarumensetzung des Markusevangeliums* (Abo, Finland: Abo Akademi, 1934).

7. Dewey, "The Literary Structure of the Controversy Stories," 113.

8. Ibid.

9. Ibid., 114.

10. Ibid., 116.

11. Ibid., 110, on 2:9 and 3:4.

12. Ibid., 111.

13. One source for many books and articles for biblical chiasms is John W. Welch and Daniel B. McKinley, eds., *Chiasmus Bibliography* (Provo, Utah: Research Press, 1999). Essays in a broader survey are in John W. Welch, ed., *Chiasmus in Antiquity: Structures, Analysis, Exegesis* (Hildesheim, Germany: Gerstenberg Verlag, 1981).

14. Augustine Stock, "Chiastic Awareness and Education in Antiquity," *Biblical Theology Bulletin* 14 (January 1984): 23–27.

15. Ibid., 23.

16. Ibid.

17. Ibid., 25.

18. Ibid., 23, 26, 27.

19. In verse 9, I used the word order in Greek, which makes the symmetry more apparent.

CHAPTER 7

Bringing Back the Lost Disciple

WITH THEIR MARCHING, matching steps, the underlying chiastic codes are in tune particularly with the surface travel narrative as Jesus and his following walk "on the way" from Mark 8:27 to 10:52. In this gospel middle (Act 3), the entourage switches southward at 10:1 from a Galilean-based ministry to the road to Jerusalem. Chiasms, by their nature, tend to be roughly symmetrical. Yet Act 3 is a bit lopsided, about ten verses longer in the first half.

Since editors of any era, by inclination, tend to delete passages as well as insert new material, it was time to see if, by reinserting the Secret Mark episode, I could right the chiastic balance of Act 3. It worked, along with an unexpected surprise. The editor had not only removed the young man episode but had also deleted the original midpoint, substituting his own verse, 10:1. Fortunately, Mark's original center was alive and well preserved, residing in another gospel. This is what I discovered:

The two-part episode, found in 1958 by Morton Smith, belongs in Original Mark in the same places where Clement of Alexandria said his Secret Gospel of Mark had it. The resurrection-initiation account belongs between 10:34 and 10:35. The postscript passage about the three women not received by Jesus in Jericho belongs within 10:46.

Biblical Mark's 10:1 had hardly met expectations for a tightly written chiastic center. It lacked catchwords and motifs to signal a pivotal shift. But an episode in the Gospel of Luke, in which Jesus sets out determinedly for Jerusalem, provided the missing centerpiece for Mark's midsection puzzle. Luke 9:51–56 was an episode "lifted" from Original Mark.

The chiastic journey through Act 3 has the signposts phrase "on the way" at either end. To repeat from the last chapter, the motif of recognition is strong in the A-level episodes (8:27–33 and 10:46–52). In A, Jesus asks his disciples who people say he is and who the twelve say he is. "The Christ" was a good answer from spokesman Peter, but when Jesus also identified himself as the suffering, rejected Son of man, Peter rebuked Jesus and in turn was vehemently rebuked by Jesus. At the other end, A', a blind beggar by the road perceived not only that Jesus approached, but appealed twice, despite being rebuked, to the Nazarene as "Son of David." The catchwords linking A and A' include "on the way, by the road" and "rebuked." The "Son of" man (8:31) has a parallel in "Son of" David and "son of" Timaeus, an identification of Bartimaeus that some have termed unnecessary since Bartimaeus already means "son of Timaeus." But the redundancy bolsters the chiastic linkage. (See the full design, appendix 2.)

My first test had arrived for "replacing" the Secret Mark episode in Biblical Mark's chapter 10. The verse 10:46 begins, "And they came to Jericho." Clement of Alexandria said that in Secret Mark he found, "And the sister of the young man whom Jesus loved and his mother and Salome were there, and Jesus did not receive them." Biblical Mark resumes, "and as he was leaving Jericho with his disciples. . . ." The rebuff of the three women in Jericho is a mild version of the rebuke of Peter, but nonetheless a parallel. Those familiar with Mark's story know mother Mary and Salome will be among the three women who failed to spread the news from the empty tomb. The snub at 10:46 certainly seems undeserved for the unnamed sister of the young man raised from the dead. She never again appears in the Gospel. Her mention appears to serve as a way to reveal that Jesus returned the young man's love.

At B and B' (8:34–38 and 10:42–45), the chief motif may be self-denying discipleship, though "messenger" may be intended. Teachings begin after Jesus "called to him" the disciples. Twice in each step, the word "whoever" precedes his advice. At 8:37 Jesus asks, "For what can a [person] give in return for [one's] life." He says at the other end, "The Son of man also came . . . to give his life as a ransom for many" (10:45).

The C sections contain embarrassing scenes for the lead disciples. At the forward side (9:1–16), Peter, James, and John see Jesus garbed in shining white garments while he is talking with (gulp) Moses and Elijah—a preview vision of a glorified Jesus in heaven with two biblical luminaries. But the disciples are confused and afraid; Peter volunteers to make a booth for each personage. And when the three disciples walk down the mountain with Jesus, they cannot understand what Jesus is talking about. In part of what C' offers (10:35–41), we see James and John make fools of themselves by demanding from Jesus that the two of them might sit "one at your right hand and one at your left, in your glory." This private request led Jesus to quiz the brothers on whether they were really up to the baptism that he was baptized with. The "young man" episode preceded 10:35, at least in Clement's Secret Mark. By including the initiation scene of this long-missing account in the C' step, Secret Mark's "and after six days" repeats the identical phrase that opens the transfiguration scene (9:2).

In the alternate "pairs format" below, C and C' can be easily compared for catchwords and corresponding ideas. Again, the abbreviated renditions put words with the same Greek root in boldface, the similar or otherwise corresponding words are underlined, and thematic signals and Greek words are italicized.

C (9:1–16) *Initiation images.* Some not <u>taste</u> death before **kingdom of God** has come. **And after six days** Jesus took Peter, **James and John** up mountain; <u>garment</u> became glistening, white; appeared Elijah, Moses; Peter: **make** *(poieo)* three booths, **one** for you, **one** for Moses, **one** for Elijah; he **did not know what** to say; voice came out of cloud: my **beloved** *(agapetos)* **Son, listen** *(akouo);* until **Son of** man **risen** from dead; what **rising** meant; first Elijah (John the <u>Baptist</u>) must come; **Son of** man suffer; Elijah, **did** to him what **pleased** *(thelo).* They came to <u>discples; scribes arguing with them.</u>

    C' (Secret Mark+10:35–41) *Initiation images.* Young man, **loved** *(agapao)* him; came to house; **and after six days** Jesus told him what to do; young man comes, <u>linen cloth</u> over naked; taught secret of **kingdom of God; arising,** across Jordan. **James and John, sons of** Zebedee: We **want** *(thelo)* you to **do** what we ask; what want me to **do?** Grant us sit **one** on right, **one** on left, <u>in your</u> <u>glory</u>; you **do not know what** asking; able to <u>drink</u> cup I <u>drink</u>, <u>baptized</u> with <u>baptism</u> I <u>baptized</u>? When <u>ten</u> **heard** *(akouo)* it, indignant at **James and John.**

The many matching phrases and catchwords above can hardly be coincidental or unintended. My labeling of C and C' with "initiation images" I explain in chapter 10, but it is obvious that Jesus is depicted in both C steps as revealing to followers certain secrets. The remark about "Elijah comes first" refers to John the Baptist, as Matthew 17:13 attests.

D and D' provide new life to Secret Mark's young man raised from the dead. That scene has parallels to biblical Mark's unnamed father who asked Jesus to heal his son. The boy had an unclean spirit that sometimes made him appear rigid, prompting onlookers to cry out, "He is dead" (9:26). The boy became like a corpse, Mark's Gospel emphasizes. But Jesus **took** *(krateo)* his **hand** and **lifted him up** *(egeiro)*. In the opening part of the Secret Mark episode, an unnamed sister asks Jesus to have mercy since her brother lies dead in a tomb. Entering that cavelike tomb, Jesus stretched forth his **hand** and **raised** *(egeiro)* him and **seized** *(krateo)* his **hand**. The disciples in the first story (D) had tried their hand, so to speak, but couldn't cast out the unclean spirit, which made Jesus lament the ineptitude of his disciples. In the D' story, the disciples erred by rebuking the woman's kneeling plea for mercy, making Jesus angry.

The story from Secret Mark, it appeared, was part of the original Gospel. Until I could see the rest of the chiastic pattern in this midsection of Mark, however, I needed to reserve judgment.

Zeroing In on the Center

The next steps inward (E and E') were easy enough to identify; they basically comprise the second and third predictions by Jesus of his suffering, death, and resurrection with some extra verses attached to each (9:28–35 and 10:28–34). Both stages also have versions of the "first shall be last" saying of Jesus. The F-stops have Jesus taking a child or children **into his arms.** He twice admonishes the disciples—**not to forbid** any outsiders exorcizing demons his name in one episode and **not to hinder** the children coming to him—making 9:36–41 and 10:13–27 solid tie-ins.

The G and G' word comparison is almost comical. Jesus advises in the first story that it would be better to chop off one body part than to sin; in the second that marriage should be forever because what God has joined together humans should not put asunder. He cites Genesis to say, twice, that in marriage the **two** become **one** flesh—key words in 9:42–47a as well. But we are not moving to a very exciting center. Look at the remaining verses:

> (9:47b–50) To be thrown into hell, where the worm does not die, and the fire is not quenched. For everyone will be salted with fire. Salt is good; but if the salt has lost its saltness, how will you season it? Have salt in yourselves, and be at peace with one another.
>
> (10:1) And he left there and went to the region of Judea and beyond the Jordan, and crowds gathered to him again; and again, as his custom was, he taught them.

The travel summary at 10:1 and the words about salt and seasoning are bland in the extreme, considering the cutting images on either side of this supposed midpoint in Act 3's chiasm. It was suspiciously ordinary for marking a major shift in Jesus' journey.

I turned to Luke to see how closely that gospel was replicating Mark's narrative. Starting at Mark 8:27 and Luke 9:18, where Jesus asks who people say he is, the two gospels present the same sequence of sayings and actions: the transfiguration account, the healing of a convulsive boy (greatly condensed in Luke), the second prediction by Jesus of his fate, a discussion about greatness as Jesus takes a child in his arms, and telling disciples not to forbid an exorcist healing in Jesus' name. At that point, the reader has come to Mark 9:41 and Luke 9:50. Luke uses, or has his own versions of, the consequences of sin seen in Mark 9:42–50, but Luke saves them for later in that gospel (17:1–4 and 14:34–35). The next passage in Mark is 10:1, which was seen and rewritten by Matthew—but was nowhere to be found in Luke.

Instead of Mark 10:1, Luke 9:51–56 has at that point a story of Jesus set to start his journey to Jerusalem. Upon approaching a Samaritan village, he learns through emissaries that the people would not receive him. Disciples James and John suggested bringing down fire from heaven upon the villagers, but Jesus rebuked the brothers, and the party moved on. The episode contains a small chiasm. The immediate tip-off that Luke 9:51–56 came from Original Mark was the word "messengers" in the very center of this chiasm! That motif appears at the very start and end of Mark's Gospel but was missing at the opening and finish of Act 3, where only the recognition theme was clearly present. Just as extraordinary, the "fiery" closing verses of Luke 9:51–56 link with Mark 9:47b–50 to complete the chiasm.

The recovered midpoint chiasm in Original Mark follows. Replacing the RSV rendition of Luke 9:52, I adopted literal wording here from Robert Tannehill.

> H (Mark 9:47b–50) To be <u>thrown into hell</u>, where their worm does not die, and the **fire** is <u>not quenched</u>. For everyone will be salted with **fire**. Salt is good; but if the salt has lost its saltness, how will you season it? Have salt in yourselves, and <u>be at peace with one another</u>.
>> I (Luke 9:51) When the days drew near for him to be <u>received up</u>, he <u>set</u> **his face** <u>to go</u> **to Jerusaelm.**
>>> J (Luke 9:52) And he sent messengers before his face, who went and entered a village of the Samaritans, to make ready for him;
>> I' (Luke 9:53) but the people would not <u>receive</u> him, because **his face** <u>was set</u> **toward Jerusalem.**
> H' (Luke 9:54–56) And when his disciples James and John saw it, they said, Lord, do you want us to bid **fire** <u>come down from heaven</u> and <u>consume them</u>? But he turned and rebuked them. And they went on to another village.[1]

After 9:56, Luke stops following Mark's sequence for a while. The next story in Mark (10:2–12), the question about divorce, is represented only briefly in Luke 17, and parts of Mark's account from 10:13 to 10:52 are used by Luke only in chapter 18. Not only that, beginning with chapter 10, Luke uses so many parables, sayings, and episodes from other sources that at least one expert on Luke has noted the odd placement of the story about Jesus' striking out for Jerusalem. In Luke, Jesus only arrives in Jersusalem at the end of chapter 19, while in Mark Jesus arrives in less than a chapter's time. To put it another way, Jesus' setting his face to Jerusalem fits well in Mark's narrative but seems unnaturally early in Luke's.

My reconstruction of Mark 10 posed some questions. Why did the editor delete both the story with "messengers" sent to the village of

Samaria and the story of the "young man"? As for the messenger story, the editor no doubt objected to the claims of James and John. They acted as if they possessed the miracle-working power of Elijah: "Lord, do you want us to bid fire come down from heaven and consume them?" Some manuscripts of Luke add "as Elijah did," but the allusion to the Hebrew prophet was clear without that scribal addition. Elijah had twice summoned fire to "come down from heaven and consume" a fifty-soldier contingent and its captain. The editor, I believe, wanted to reinforce Mark's depiction of John the Baptist as an Elijah-like figure. Allowing James and John to claim the power of Elijah confused the picture.

But why would the editor remove the two-part episode about the raising of the young man whom Jesus loved? Was it distasteful for a nearly naked young man spending the night with Jesus and for the declarations of mutual love? The editor did not remove the young man in two other appearances in the Gospel, including the scene after the arrest of Jesus when a young man, scantily dressed, escaped naked as the soldiers grabbed only his linen cloth. Also, why did Luke omit the young man story found today only in Secret Mark? I had some initial ideas to explain the omission. First, Luke already told a story at 7:11–17 of Jesus raising the son of a widow in the city of Nain. To that dead son, Jesus commands, "Young man, I say to you, arise." (The Greek word for "young man," *neaniskos,* is the same as that used in Secret Mark and biblical Mark.) Second, Luke left out *all* references to Mark's young man, including those after Jesus' arrest and at the empty tomb. Thirdly, Luke dislikes Mark's denigration of the disciples and family of Jesus and downplays Mark's favorable depiction of minor characters. I would have to mull over the possible motives for change by the editor and Luke.

Another Missing Piece Recovered

If it were not for the Gospel of Luke, yet another piece of Original Mark would have been lost. Luke has an admirable account of forgiveness by Jesus as he suffered with two criminals on their crosses. The editor deleted the story and substituted this short sentence: "Those who were crucified with him also reviled him" (Mark 15:32b).

What Luke drew from Mark was the last exchange Jesus had with another human. In Luke 23:39–43, one criminal shouts, "Save yourself and us!" But the other criminal rebukes him, saying that the two of them were justly sentenced: "We are receiving the due reward of our deeds; but this man has done nothing wrong." The repentant criminal then asks Jesus to "remember me when you come into your kingdom." Jesus promises, "Truly, I say to you, today you will be with me in Paradise."

My reasons for thinking that Luke borrowed Original Mark's scene were several. (1) Luke was following Mark's crucifixion before and after this point. (2) Mark introduces all kinds of people to recognize Jesus' divinity—from a tax collector to a blind beggar and, it would seem now, a convicted robber. The robber (Luke calls him a criminal) not only declares that Jesus has committed no crime but sees in Jesus a savior to open the doors of heaven for him. (3) This conversation on the crosses supplies a missing chiastic link to Act 5's Mark 14:10–18. The "messenger" motif is present in Mark at the start of Act 5, where two disciples were sent with messages to repeat in finding an upper room for the Passover meal. Luke 23:39–43 provides the missing messenger for A' at the end of Act 5. Jesus will speak on behalf of the second criminal, who asked Jesus to remember him in heaven. Jesus assures him he shortly will be in paradise. Another striking linkup occurs when the good robber tells the other criminal that they were justly punished, getting the "due reward of our deeds." At the start of Act 5, Judas was to get money for betraying Jesus, thereby also getting a "reward" for a criminal deed. The chief priests "promised" Judas money, and Jesus, in effect, promised heaven for the repentant robber. Lastly in A', the first-person reference appears in the verses Luke saved, "Truly, I say to you." At the Act's precise midpoint, Jesus admits, "I am (the Christ)."

There it was. I felt I had the original, preedited version of the Gospel of Mark—five large sections, or acts, plus a prologue and a conclusion. They were all authenticated by chiasms presenting evidence for additions and deletions. The Gospel of Luke saved two stories originally integral to Mark. Due to Smith's discovery of the writing quoting from a Secret Gospel of Mark, a key episode was returned to Original Mark.

Hoping to publish, I sought opinions from academic friends. I sent a sixty-page summary of the findings to several people prominent in New Testament studies and got mixed responses. All passed along some comments. I had no such luck with a shorter paper titled "Why Secret Mark Was Part of the Original Gospel of Mark" for the 1987 Pacific Coast regional conference of the Society of Biblical Literature (SBL). I had obtained some feedback when I read papers at four previous regional SBL meetings. This was a disaster, however. The moderator never showed up. As a result, the session started late. My mouth was dry as a bone with no water nearby, and I nervously tried to cover too much ground in the shortened time.

My training was in journalism, and I lacked an advanced degree, but that was not necessarily a drawback. An updated version of my 1976 book describing the significance of the Nag Hammadi Gnostic Library came out in 1988. But this new book proposal on Mark held no interest for two publishers that I approached in the winter of 1988–89. One editorial director said he'd look at a completed manuscript, but I was too busy. About that time, I had agreed to contribute a chapter each to three books on contemporary religion. I was still a full-time religion writer at the *Los Angeles Times*. My volunteer work increased in 1990–92 when I served as president of the Religion Newswriters Association (RNA).

The very day after I finished my RNA term, the director of the then-new First Amendment Center at Vanderbilt University offered me a fellowship for the 1992–93 school year to research and write a report with a clergy partner on the tensions between the news media and organized religion. *Bridging the Gap: Religion and the News Media,* published in the fall of 1993, helped to spark an awareness in print and broadcast journalism that religion deserved better news coverage. For the next few years, my non-*Times* activities focused on this field, including writing a primer on the God beat, *Deities and Deadlines.*

I didn't look again at Original Mark and my chiasms until the possibility loomed of early retirement from the *Times.* I had agonized over previous "golden handshakes" offered by the newspaper but always decided it was too soon. One buyout opportunity in late 1998 was irresistible, and I ended my thirty-one years with the newspaper that December. By then, I was finding chiastic patterns of all sizes in Mark, ones I never noticed before. I was exceedingly glad I did not rush into print a decade earlier.

Notes

1. On the midpoint of Act 3 in Original Mark, recovered with the help of Luke 9:51–56, I borrow a translation from Robert Tannehill, *Luke* (Nashville: Abingdon, 1996), 168. Instead of "he sent messengers ahead of him," Tannehill says it is literally, "he sent messengers before his face," wording that harks back to the same expression at Luke 7:27 and Mark 1:2, in turn an adaptation of Mal 3:1. The allusions to expressions in the Hebrew Bible are replete in both Luke and Mark. The

calling down of fire from heaven, of course, is Elijah-like (2 Kgs 1:9–12), which is written in a ABCD, A'B'C'D' parallelism. The expression "to set his face" may also remind some of Isa 50:7, but I think that its occurrence in Ezek 15:6–8 (NRSV) is most pertinent because it also speaks of Jerusalem and consumption by fire and was written chiastically.

> A (6a) Therefore thus says the Lord GOD:
> > B (6b) Like the wood of the vine among the trees of the forest, which I have given to the fire for fuel, so I will give up the inhabitants of Jerusalem.
> > > C (7a) I will set my face against them; although they escape from the fire,
> > > > D (7b) the fire shall still consume them;
> > > C' (7c) and you shall know that I am the LORD, when I set my face against them.
> > B' (8a) And I will make the land desolate, because they have acted faithlessly,
> A' (8b) says the Lord GOD.

The footnote in the *HarperCollins Study Bible* says the Jerusalem residents are destined for destruction, whether by literal fire or not.

CHAPTER 8

The Fabulous Word Mosaic of Mark

UPON REVISITING MY RESEARCH on Mark in the late 1990s, I began to notice that many individual episodes were chiastic patterns in their own right. Perhaps I saw some in the 1980s, but I was concentrating on the large coded word designs. Now, it was apparent that these smaller structures were so common that it meant that an episode had to satisfy not only the larger chiasm it was a part of, but also provide catchwords for internal use. Connections stood out once I knew what to expect; e.g. Jesus on a brief visit to his hometown (6:1–6):

A (1–2a) Came to own country; on Sabbath began to **teach** in synagogue; many <u>astonished</u>: <u>Where this man get all this? What is wisdom given to him?</u>

B (2b) What **mighty works** *(dynamis)* wrought by his **hands!**

C (3a) **Is not** this <u>carpenter</u>, son of <u>Mary</u>, <u>brother of James, Joses, Judas and Simon</u>, **are not** <u>his sisters</u> here with us?

D (3b) They took offense at him.

C' (4) Jesus said, A <u>prophet</u> **is not** without honor, except in own country, among <u>own kin</u>, and in <u>own house</u>.

B' (5) He could do no **mighty work** there, except laid **hands** upon a few sick, healed them.

A' (6) Marveled because of their unbelief; went about villages teaching.

As before, the words in boldface have the same root in Greek and the underlined words have similar (or contrasting) meanings, or correspond in some other way to the matching step. The Greek words for "astonished" and "marveled" are different, but the meaning is similar. I underlined "their unbelief" in verse 6 because it corresponds nicely to the skeptical questions of the hometown folk in verse 2.

Another story shouts for attention with its chiastic symmetry. On Pilate's reluctant orders, Jesus is taken away by soldiers to be crucified. But a Roman contingent assembles to mock and treat him with contempt. In Mark 15:15b–20, the chiastic steps could be put into a basic ABCB'A' arrangement. But the first four catchwords appear in the reverse order at the end, so why not make each phrase a separate step? Verses of 17c–18a and 19 lack catch words but they match because both are written in a parallel structure (A, B, C, A', B', C').

A (15b) delivered him to be **crucified**.
    B (16) soldiers **led him away** *(apago)* inside palace; praetorium; called together whole battalion;
        C (17a) they **clothed** *(endidysko)* him
            D (17b) in a **purple cloak,**
                E (17c–18a) (a) plaiting crown of thorns, (b) put it on him, (c) salute him,
                    F (18b) Hail, King of the Jews!
                E' (19) (a') struck his head with reed, (b') spat upon him, (c') knelt in homage.
            D' (20a) when had mocked him, stripped him of **purple cloak,**
        C' (20b) **put** *(endyo)* his own clothes on him.
    B' (20c) they **led him out** *(exago)*
A' (20d) to **crucify** him.

This was amazing. More individual chiasms emerged. I was filling folders with worksheets for each episode. Many months later, I was satisfied that Mark had back-to-back episodic chiasms throughout. I counted more than sixty-five. Clearly, the gospel author once mocked for an inelegant literary style now deserved homage for writing a marvelous story plaited with a network of word patterns mighty and small.

The Overlooked Clues

While congratulating myself for deciphering these word codes, I also kicked myself for another belated discovery. I had erected directional signals at either end of the gospel text back in the 1980s, but I did not recognize them as such. Students of Mark have observed in the past that the Gospel's opening and closing have parallel settings and words. The bleak wilderness in the prologue corresponds to the dreary tomb in the conclusion. The spirit went into Jesus at baptism; his breath left him at death. I had written down a number of verbal parallels, which were obviously intentional. But, so what? Writers through the ages have ended tales with images that echo their beginning. I had even arranged them this way on a sheet of paper:

Prologue
Messenger: John the Baptist: **Behold** *(idou),* send messenger **before** thy face.
John the Baptist, appeared, preaching.
    Setting: wilderness
        John the Baptist baptizes Jesus
            Saw heavens **open** *(schizo),* Spirit enters Jesus; Godly voice *(phone)* calls Jesus beloved **Son**.
                Jesus, sorely tested in wilderness, aided by angels

––––––––––––

Conclusion
                Jesus, nearing death, feared that God forsook him.
            Jesus breathes last, utters **cry** *(phone);* temple curtain **torn** *(schizo);* centurion: this man **Son** of God.
        Joseph of Arimathea buries Jesus
    Setting: the tomb
Messenger: Young man: Risen, **see** *(ide)* place they laid him; tell disciples and Peter he going **before** you to Galilee; but (women) said nothing to anyone (failed messengers).

It finally dawned on me. Both patterns are pointing toward the rest of the narrative. Why didn't I, long ago, take it further to see whether tie-ins showed up after the prologue and before the conclusion? I began the trial run one afternoon.

Just after the prologue, as Jesus enters Galilee preaching, he announces, "The time is fulfilled . . . believe in the gospel" (1:14). Immediately before the conclusion, at Mark 15:32–33, the chief priests are mocking Jesus, nailed to the cross, to come down "that we may see and believe." And verse 33 refers to the sixth hour and the ninth hour.

Now nervousness set in. Time references and the catchword "believe" in both spots were good. Immediately, my theory was tested on whether the repentant robber on the cross—now seen in Luke 23:39–43—was originally at Mark 15:32b, where the editor substituted, "Those who were crucified with him also reviled him." Would passages from Luke bolster the matchup with the start of Jesus' preaching mission in Galilee?

Yes, they did, to my great relief. For potentially long chiastic patterns, I wrote out pairs of matching episodes in the manner below.

> (1:14–15) After John arrested, Jesus **came** into Galilee, preaching gospel of **God:** The time is fulfilled; **kingdom** of **God** is at hand; repent, **believe** in the gospel.
>> (15:32+Luke 23:39–43+15:33]) Let Christ, King of Israel, come down now from cross, see, **believe.** One of criminals railed, You not Christ? Save yourself and us! Other rebuked, Do not fear **God;** under same condemnation, we justly; receiving due reward of deeds; this man done nothing wrong; Jesus, remember me when you **come** into **kingdom;** truly, today you be with me in Paradise. When sixth hour had come, darkness over whole land until ninth hour.

Additional catchwords provided in the episode used by Luke include "kingdom," "God," and the verb "to come." Another element of time saved by Luke was the word "today," which might seem to be an unnecessary word in that sentence, except that it is a word that helps cement the chiastic bridge to the opening of Jesus' ministry. And when Jesus started preaching salvation, he urged hearers to "repent." That is indeed what the God-fearing robber did. This pairing of distant episodes was a promising launch to what I hoped would be a lengthy chiasm. It looked to be so as I worked inward from front and back.

(1:16–20) **Passing along** *(parago)* Sea of Galilee, **Simon,** Andrew, **casting** *(amphiballo)* net; make you <u>fishers of [people]</u>; they followed; little farther, <u>James</u>, son of Zebedee, <u>John</u>, <u>brother</u>, mending nets; left **father** in boat.

(15:21–31) **Passerby** *(parago)* **Simon** of Cyrene; **father** (of two <u>brothers</u>), carry cross; brought to Golgotha; garments, **casting** *(ballo)* lots; crucified two robbers, <u>one on his right, one on his left</u>; mocked, <u>saved others</u>.

The big three disciples are treated sarcastically here. Simon Peter, James, and John (Andrew plays a minor role hereafter) are called by Jesus to be followers, but at the point of 15:21–31 they have deserted Jesus. It is another Simon who is compelled to carry Jesus' cross. James and John, who demanded of Jesus that they be allowed to sit on Jesus' right and left in his glory (10:37), have been replaced by two robbers, one of whom was granted a place in heaven.

The next paired steps rely minimally on catchwords to connect with each other. Rather, at the far end (15:1–20) Jesus is mocked as the "King of the Jews" four times even as he keeps his silence for the most part. The religious authorities bound Jesus and delivered him to the Roman authority, Pilate, who in turn let the angry crowd outside decide that he should be crucified. He is scourged, then led away by soldiers for more punishment and taunts. But early on (1:21–28), he was in full control and exercising so much authority that "he commanded even the unclean spirits, and they obeyed him." An unclean spirit possessing a man there was fearful; he recognized him right away. "I know who you are, the Holy One of God," it said. Jesus commanded the spirit to be silent and come out, which it did.

The following pairing includes Peter seemingly at his best (1:29–39) when the disciple went looking for and finds Jesus, who had risen early and gone off to pray. "Everyone is searching for you," Peter said. Jesus concedes that he should go on to the next town and preach there also, "for that is why I came out." And he went out through all of Galilee. But the matching episode depicts the disciple at his worst (14:66–72) as Peter, identified as a Galilean, denied knowing Jesus three times, as predicted.

Stepping further inward, I found that the pair below contains the first and last time in Mark that Jesus refers to himself as the Son of man (fourteen occasions altogether). Aside from the common matters of proof, testimony, false witness, and questioning in both segments, there was another clincher. The only two instances in which Jesus is accused of blasphemy are rendered grammatically alike. The scribes (2:7–8) think to themselves (somehow known to the author) in the same manner that the high priest (14:63–64) demonstrably speaks—first asking "why," then declaring Jesus' words to be blasphemy, followed by a second question.

> (1:40–2:12) Leper, make me clean; **I** will, be clean; **see** that you say nothing, but show to **priest,** as **proof** *(martyrion);* **reported** *(akouo)* he was home; to paralytic, your sins forgiven; scribes, **sitting,** questioning in hearts: **Why** does this man speak thus? It is **blasphemy! Who** can forgive sins but God alone? Jesus: that you may know **Son of man** has authority on earth to forgive sins; **I** say to you, rise.
>
> (14:55–65) **Testimony** (twice) *(martyria),* **false witness** (twice) *(pseudomartyreo),* **testify against** *(katamartyreo);* **heard** *(akouo)* to say, **I** will destroy; **I** will build another; high **priest:** You **Son of** the Blessed? **I am,** will **see Son of man seated** at right hand of Power, clouds heaven; high **priest: Why** we still need **witnesses** *(martys)?* You have **heard** *(akouo)* his **blasphemy! What** is your decision?

The next pair has to do with followers and who should be regarded as sinners. Jesus was criticized for sitting at the table (eating) with tax collectors and sinners. Should Peter be criticized for following the arrested Jesus at a distance (in contrast to the young man who followed so close that he was nearly captured), then sitting with the guards warming his hands in the high priest's courtyard?

> (2:13–17) **All** crowd **gathered** *(erchomai),* he taught; saw Levi, **sitting** at tax office; **follow** me, **followed** him; many tax collectors and sinners sitting with Jesus, many **followed; scribes:** Why? Jesus: I came not to call righteous, but sinners.
>
> (14:51–54) Young man **followed** him; ran away naked; **all** the chief priests, elders, scribes **assembled** *(synerchomai);* Peter had **followed** him at distance, **sitting** with guards, warming himself.

Why did Judas betray Jesus with a kiss? Mark has a suggestive chiastic link. The arrest of Jesus (14:43–50) goes back in this long chiasm to the time when Jesus was asked why his disciples do not fast like the disciples of John the Baptist and the Pharisees (2:18–22). Jesus responded: "Can the wedding guests (literally, sons of the bridal chamber) fast while the bridegroom is with them?" Not as long as the bridegroom is with them, he said. "The **days** will come, when the bridegroom is taken away from them, and then they will fast in that **day**" (2:20). At his arrest, Jesus lamented, "**Day** after **day** I was with you in the temple teaching, and you did not seize me" (14:49).

The full list of pairings (see appendix 5) contains other ingenious connections. One of the cleverest ties together the story of Jesus stilling the storm (4:35–41) and Jesus' description of tumultuous days ahead when the stars will fall and the heavens shake (13:24–27). Besides "day" the only catchword here is "wind." In the stormy boat scene, the author used "wind" four times. And in the other section, Jesus says the angels will come and "gather his elect from the four winds." Are people ready for a gospel laced with humorous word puzzles?

Seven more pairings appeared as I moved forward into chapter 6 and backward into chapter 12. It was well past midnight of the same day I had started work on this "macrocode," as I was calling it. I wouldn't be able to sleep without knowing whether the 6:47–8:26 addition to Mark was imaginary or real.

Two relatively long episodes paired up well—the feeding of five thousand people with only five loaves and two fishes (6:31–46) and the answer of Jesus to a scribe that the two greatest commandments were to love the one God totally and to love one's neighbor as oneself (12:28–34). The kindness of Jesus in feeding the multitude, despite the disciples' desire to send them away, resonates with the "greatest commandment" in Scripture of loving neighbors. Moreover, the feeding story has two clear allusions to Scripture—when Jesus compared the crowd to "sheep without a shepherd" and when he commanded (as Elisha did centuries ago) that the people be fed.

A Moment of Truth

An editor inserted the next episode in biblical Mark, that is, 6:47–52, when Jesus walks on water. If that story connected with elements of the next story at the other end, my theory had a problem. The other episode

(12:18–27) was one in which Jesus replies to a question about a much-widowed woman: Whose wife would she be in heaven? But I saw no links there to the story of Jesus walking on water; nor did the following "editor-inserted" episode of Jesus healing sick people provide a link. The verbal hitching posts that Mark typically provided readers were not there.

By skipping over the rest of the editor's material to the resumption of Original Mark—the story in which Jesus asks his disciples who people say he is (8:27–33)—I was back on track. Jesus' prediction in chapter 8 that he will be killed and "rise" again would find a chiastic partner in the chapter 12 story of Jesus' answer to the Sadducees that when people "rise" from the dead, they don't marry in heaven but are like angels. The concept of resurrection is vital to both episodes. Also, "God" and scriptural authority figures (Elijah in one; Moses, Abraham, Isaac, and Jacob in the other) are important in both episodes.

Would it work for the next step? Yes. At the front end, the memorable theme was the saying, "For what does it profit a man to gain the whole world and forfeit his life?" (8:36). At the back end, the comparable story was Jesus answering whether to pay taxes to Caesar. Next up were Mark's version of the transfiguration story (9:2–13), in which a heavenly voice says, "This is my beloved Son . . . ," and the parable of the wicked tenant farmers who killed the "beloved son" of the landowner (12:1–12).

A few more steps helped to confirm my restoring of Original Mark, including the Jesus-turns-his-face-toward-Jerusalem story now seen only in the Gospel of Luke. That story, in which messengers learned that Samaritan villagers would not receive (*dechomai*) Jesus, is paralleled in the postscript passage in Secret Mark when Jesus did not receive (*apodechomai*) his mother, Salome, and the sister of the young man Jesus loved. The chase on paper was narrowing down to a few last episodes as the bulk of the Secret Mark account came into play:

(10:20–27) **Teacher,** all these I observed from my youth *(neotes)*. Jesus, **looking upon him, loved him;** sell, give to poor, come, follow me; at that saying, went away sorrowful; Jesus **looked** around, hard for those with **riches** to **enter** *(eiserchomai)* **kingdom of God; enter kingdom of God;** amazed at words; for rich man to enter **kingdom of God;** who

can be saved? Jesus **looked at** them, with men impossible, not with
God, all possible with **God**.

(Secret Mark) Coming, she prostrated before Jesus: Son of David,
have mercy; disciples rebuked her. Jesus, angered, went with her to
garden, tomb was; cry heard; Jesus rolled stone from tomb, **going
in** *(eiserchomai)* where <u>young man</u> *(neaniskos);* raised him, seizing
his hand; <u>young man</u>, **looking on him, loved him,** beseeched to be
with him; going out of tomb, came to **house** <u>young man</u>; he was
rich; after six days, what to do; <u>young man</u> wearing linen cloth over
naked body; remained night; Jesus **taught** secret **kingdom of God**.
Arising, returned to other side of Jordan.

The center of the macrocode loomed ahead. I determined on that
first night and the next day that the third prediction by Jesus of his execution and resurrection (namely, 10:34) was the probable midpoint of
this gospel-length chiasm. I wrote 2/20/2000 on the notebook paper
because I considered it a breakthrough date. To be honest, I repeatedly
refined my macrocode by reexamining poor matchups. Indeed, I was
finally forced to see that the Jesus saying at 10:31 was the tightly wound
midpoint—in spite of fears that skeptics would say I "wanted" this dou-
ble-meaning verse to be the center. Knowing now how much this gospel
author loved chiastic patterns and storytelling ironies, it seemed only
logical that a prolific puzzle creator would offer this clue at the center!

(10:28–31a) Peter **began to say** *(archo lego):* **lo** *(idou),* left everything,
followed you; no one who left house, **brothers,** <u>sisters</u>, mother, father,
<u>children</u> or lands, for <u>my sake and for the gospel</u>, who will not **receive**
(lambano) <u>hundredfold</u> in this time houses, **brothers,** <u>sisters</u>, mothers,
children, lands <u>with persecutions</u>, and in age to **come** <u>eternal life</u>. <u>Many
that are will be</u>[1]

(10:31b–f) first
last
and
last
first.[2]

(10:32–34+Secret Mark) <u>They were</u> on road, going to
Jerusalem, Jesus ahead; amazed, those **followed** afraid; **taking**
(paralambano) <u>twelve</u>, he **began to tell** *(archo lego)* what going

to happen to him, **Behold** *(idou),* going up to Jerusalem; **Son of** man <u>delivered</u> to chief priest, scribes; will <u>condemn</u> him to <u>death</u>, <u>mock, spit upon him, scourge, kill</u> him; three days <u>he will rise</u>; **come** into Bethany, <u>woman</u> whose **brother** had died there.

Why Did the Macro-chiasm Remain Hidden?

It may not be surprising that this long chiasm was not recognized and published before. Anyone finding those early match-ups would have been totally frustrated upon hitting the section after 6:46, where the editor's insertion provided no sure links to other parts of Mark.

Biblical scholars, the likeliest ones to spend long hours of critical study on the Gospels, usually have so many duties in teaching or administration that they usually cannot afford time to pursue unconventional avenues of research. In other professions, scientists with a technological bent and medical sleuths often secure generous support from corporations, federal agencies, or foundations—and time—to answer nagging questions. Most biblical scholars don't have such support.

Other professors resist large-scope theories because, in fact, many a grand theory has bitten the dust in the past. Then there is the fear factor of presenting evidence that might receive damning adjectives such as "conjectural" and "unconvincing." A few weak spots in the evidence can lead critics to label a thesis "circular" or "arguing from silence." Certainly, not all research is good research. But in that atmosphere, where gaining faculty tenure is usually a career must, it is often safer for younger scholars to content themselves with smaller triumphs.

My professional refuge is journalism, which is somewhat insulated from academic jabs. But professionals in my field of endeavor abhor "sitting on a great story." And this one was getting better all the time. Newswriters relish the role of messenger, the chance to be first in disclosing significant discoveries and unexpected developments. I hope to be fully accurate the first time I tell the story, but even very close to right is good enough. If new findings are important and verifiable, they should be made public without undue delay.

With that credo off my chest, I confess further that many of these chiasms will be improved and fine-tuned by researchers adept in New Testament Greek. Many will offer corrections and better variations. My alphabetic "steps" are often tentative constructs. One has to decide somewhat arbitrarily on how many words, verses, or parts of verses to include in each step. If A and B have few obvious links to A' and B', then that problem might be solved by combining them into a larger A and larger A'. But I've tried to make each step as short as possible since I think Mark usually works that way.

Going Halfway with Mark

Mark has been grossly underestimated for centuries. This composition by the anonymous writer was a major achievement: a gospel with five major chiastic frameworks, plus a prologue and conclusion in that style. In addition, each episode forms its own self-contained chiasm, and the Gospel as a whole is one large chiasm, which means that each story along the way has to have words, phrases, names, Scripture citations, or whatever to serve its own internal chiasm as well as to touch base with an episode from afar or from a section only a chapter away. The writer's challenge in the first-century was to include so many "extra" words, actions, and grammatical constructions in each episode to make numerous other tie-ins.

Here, I thought, is the primary reason why this gospel's Greek has been deprecated for having a wordy and awkward flow at times. Yet, Mark's plain-view drama leading to the climax in Jerusalem nevertheless has won latter-day plaudits. The Gospel was sufficiently admired by Matthew and Luke for them to use Mark as a basic outline for their stories of Jesus' ministry and persecution.

Upon discovering the macrocode, I vowed not to underestimate Original Mark again. If the author was talented enough to weave these patterns, why not even more? This inquiry began when I noticed that within the prologue chiasm (1:1–14) were two different chiasms in the first and second half. I tried dividing the macrocode in half to see if two more chiasms would unfold.

The second-half code began strongly, starting just after the macrocode center at 10:31.

(10:32–34) Going up to Jerusalem, Jesus **walked ahead** *(proago)*; they **amazed,** those followed **afraid;** taking <u>the twelve</u>, [Jesus]: **behold** *(idou)*; will be delivered to Gentiles; they will <u>kill</u> him, after three days will <u>rise</u>.

(16:6–8) [Young man]: do not be **amazed;** you seek Jesus, was crucified, has risen; **see** *(ide)* place where they laid him. Tell his disciples and Peter he is **going before** *(proago)* you to Galilee; fled from tomb, said nothing to anyone; were **afraid**.

(Secret Mark+10:35–39) Woman whose brother died: mercy; Jesus went to **tomb; rolled away** *(apokylio)* **stone from door of tomb;** going where **young man** was, raised him; after six days, **young man, wearing** *(periballo)* **linen cloth** *(sindon)*. James, John: grant us to **sit at right hand** *(dexios)* and left in your glory.

(15:46b–16:5) [Joseph of Arimathea] wrapped him in **linen shroud** *(sindon)*, laid him in **tomb; rolled stone against** *(proskylio)* **door of tomb;** Mary Magdalene, Mary [his] mother, Salome, first day of week went to **tomb:** who will **roll away** *(apokylio)* stone from door of tomb? Saw **stone rolled back; young man sitting on right side** *(dexios),* **dressed** *(periballo)* in white robe.

A reader could conclude from this last pairing that the young man known from Secret Mark was the same person who would "roll away the stone," a big question on the minds of the three women as they approached the tomb of Jesus. The young man inside the tomb wears a white robe symbolic of his rather recent initiation in Bethany near the Jordan River. For chiasms that tell more or confirm suspicions about this young man, see appendix 3.

In the next step (10:40–45 and 15:42–46a), Jesus lectured the disciples about "those who are supposed to rule over the Gentiles lord it over them" but added that his followers should be servants, just as he came to serve and give his life. This is a reasonable counterpart to the episode following Jesus' crucifixion. Pilate, the Roman authority, inquiring whether Jesus was indeed dead, then granted to Joseph of Arimathea the body of Jesus to be wrapped and buried in a tomb.

The next short stops concern the women around Jesus. The editor-deleted sentence in Mark 10:46 about three women whom Jesus did not receive (the sister of the young man, Jesus' mother, and Salome) strikes a chord with the three women who watched the crucifixion from afar (and would later forsake him). The trio in both cases includes Salome and Jesus' mother, but the unnamed sister appears in the earlier group and Mary Magdalene in the second one. They probably are not the same woman; the sister lived in Bethany.

I was on my way toward another chiastic center: at 13:21–23, where Jesus warns some disciples against believing imposters—false Christs and false prophets—in troubled times ahead.

A Camel Ride to the First-Half Chiasm

If chopping the macrocode in two revealed a new chiasm in the last half, then another surely was waiting in the first half. The gospel opening, which cites prophetic words, matches up with Jesus' predictions of (1) who will meet his requirements for following him and receiving a full life, and (2) what will happen to him. The word for "way," or road, occurs twice in each, among other catchwords. Two verses from the macrocode's second half (10:32–33) contribute to this pairing, a borrowing practice common in Mark's chiasms.

> (1:1–5) **Beginning** *(arche)* of **gospel** Jesus Christ, **Son** of God. Written in Isaiah the <u>prophet</u>, **behold,** I send messenger <u>before</u> thy face, who shall prepare **way** *(hodos),* **way** of Lord. John baptizer; went to him <u>all</u> of <u>country</u> of Judea, <u>all</u> people of **Jerusalem;** they baptized by him in Jordan, confessing sins.
>
> (10:29–33) Jesus: [<u>prophecy</u>] Truly, I say, no one who left house, brother, sister, mother, father, children or lands, for my sake or for the **gospel,** who will not receive <u>hundredfold</u> now houses, brothers, sisters, mothers, children and <u>lands</u>, with persecution, eternal life. Many <u>first</u> will be last, last first. On road *(hodos)* going to **Jerusalem;** Jesus walking <u>ahead</u>. He **began** *(archo)* tell them, **behold,** going to **Jerusalem; Son** of man delivered to chief priests, scribes.

A camel aids the word "journey" between the second steps of the macrocode's first-half chiasm. The identical word *kamelos* at 1:6 and 10:25 occurs nowhere else in Mark. "Gospel" is used twice in the early segment and *logos* (word, or saying) twice in the later segment. That is hardly an accident. "The good news" and "the word" were synonyms in Mark and in churches to this day. Though Simon Peter and others readily left their families and jobs to follow Jesus at the start, they later appear amazed and "exceedingly astonished" (10:26) that followers must give up so much to be saved.

> (1:5–21) John clothed **camel's** hair; Jesus came, baptized; out of water, saw **heavens** opened; voice from **heaven:** my **beloved** *(agapetos)* **Son,** pleased. Jesus came into Galilee, <u>gospel</u> *(euaggelion)* of God; **kingdom of God** at hand, believe in <u>gospel</u> *(euaggelion);* saw Simon, Andrew, **brother,** casting net in sea; make you fishers of men; they **left** nets, **followed;** saw James, John, **brother,** in boat; they **left** their **father** with hired servants, **followed** *(aperchomai);* he **entered** *(eiserchomai)* synagogue and **taught** *(didasko).*
>> (10:19b–28) Do not defraud. Honor **father,** mother. **Teacher,** *(didaskolos)* All these observed from youth. Jesus looking upon him **loved** *(agapao)* him; sell, give, treasure in **heaven;** come, **follow** me. At that <u>saying</u> *(logos),* he **went away** *(aperchomai)* sorrowful. Jesus: Hard for those with riches to **enter** *(eiserchomai)* **kingdom of God;** disciples amazed at <u>words</u> *(logos);* **enter kingdom of God;** easier for **camel** go through eye of needle than rich man **enter kingdom of God;** disciples: who **can be** saved? with **God;** all things possible with **God.** Peter: we **left** everything, **followed** you.

Readers who want to try their hand at completing this first half chiasm in the asymmetrical macrocode to its center should be advised that the editor-added section of 6:47–8:26 took no part in this chiasm. Nor does it figure in another half-length chiasm covering roughly the same ground. Space does not permit the display here of either the chiasm I worked out from 1:1 to 10:34 (first half, macrocode) or another one built between 1:1 and the middle of Act 3 (the Luke episode which the editor deleted, substituting 10:1). It is mind-boggling to think that a gospel author would spend so much time constructing these word puzzles below the narrative. But why resist in the face of repeated examples? Immediately, one can see the possibilities that the symmetrical, seven-section structure of the Gospel has words at the very beginning and very middle (send messenger before thy face, make ready, Jerusalem, heaven) suggesting that this first-half chiasm is likely. Indeed, a second-half pattern can be found.

But contemplating too many chiasms in a short stretch can be dizzying. "Now, let's see this side is going frontwards and this side is going backwards, or is the other way around?" The principle of cutting lengthy chiastic patterns in half to produce two more, then four more, and so on, has worked in all the cases I've tried—an enormous testimony to the time spent and creativity exerted by the Gospel author. Sometimes they showed up unexpectedly.

I had proposed a paper of modest scope to read at the Spring 2000 meeting of the Society of Biblical Literature's Pacific Coast Region. In it, I planned to show how the well-attested 2:1–3:6 chiasm was really part of a larger one (1:14–4:12) and that each of the five episodes in this starting point were individual chiasms. But with my new slice-and-dice perspective, I noticed while preparing the paper that one could even cut 2:1–3:6 in half to have two new chiasms—2:1–2:20 and 2:21–3:6. In the first one, the B step has "sins forgiven" four times and B' step has "sinners" four times. Here is its center:

C (2:12a) [Healed paralytic] rose, took up pallet; **went out** before them **all;**
    D (2:12b) so that they were <u>all amazed</u> and
        E (2:12c) <u>glorified</u>
            F (2:12d) God
        E' (2:12e) <u>saying,</u>
    D' (2:12f) We <u>never saw anything like this</u>!
C' (2:13a) He **went out** again by sea; **all** the crowd gathered about him.

The other half has an equally admirable balance, tight center, and touch of humor. It opens with the proverb that "no one sews a piece of unshrunk cloth on an old garment" for if one does, the patch tears away and a worse tear results (2:21). At the other end, A' Jesus asked a man with a withered hand to "stretch out your hand." He "stretched it out" and his hand was restored—in contrast to stretching old and new cloth! The B and C steps have some matching catchwords, and then we arrive at another tightly wound center:

D (2:27b) **The sabbath for**
    E (2:27c) **[humankind]**
        F (2:27c) was made,
    E' (2:27d) not **[humankind]**
D' (2:27e) **for the sabbath**[3]

The samples displayed in these last three chapters do not exhaust the numbers of mind-stretching chiastic weavings. But we need a rest. I will turn to some of the "so what" questions raised by the restoring of Original Mark and recovery of the author's hero figures.

Notes

1. The word order in Greek.
2. The word order in Greek.
3. The word order in Greek. Also, the NRSV's humankind is used instead of RSV's man.

CHAPTER 9

Overlooked Heroes

WHEN POLITICAL PARTISANS today attack opponents viciously, accusing them of all sorts of evil, we say the tactic is "demonizing." It may be an effective way to besmirch rivals and enemies, but it's also unfair. An especially literal example in biblical history sits in Mark's Gospel. The author has Jesus demonizing his chief disciple, Peter, as "Satan" and opposing God. Those are devastating accusations, considering that Judas Iscariot was called nothing more than "betrayer" in the Gospel of Mark. In their adaptations of Mark's account, Luke omits the satanic accusation while Matthew uses the epithet only after Jesus promises Peter that he is the "rock" upon whom the church will be built.

The sharp rebuke of Peter came only moments after he identified his teacher as the Christ. Jesus had confirmed that answer by saying that no one should reveal it. Then, Jesus told his disciples plainly that he soon would suffer rejection and execution yet would rise again. The prediction angered Peter, who apparently thought a "messiah" should not expect to be killed. Peter grabbed Jesus, rebuking him. But looking to see if other disciples were watching, Jesus exclaimed, "Get behind me, Satan! For you are not on the side of God, but of men" (Mark 8:33). Then, calling crowds of people to him, along with the disciples, Jesus declared that following him would require forgoing worldly interests. "For what does it profit a man, to gain the whole world and forfeit his life?" he asked (v. 36).

Jesus next issued a warning: "Whoever is ashamed of me and of my words in this adulterous and sinful generation, of him will the Son of man also be ashamed, when he comes in the glory of his Father with the holy angels" (Mark 8:38). That is, when the resurrected Jesus was to appear in the near future as a heavenly being—the Son of Man—he would be ashamed of those who found his teachings objectionable and disgraceful. Today's Western culture may not regard a warning about feeling shame as troublesome. But in ancient Eastern Mediterranean lands, to have people ashamed of you could be devastating. Shame was to be avoided. Achieving and preserving honor, on the other hand, was a high goal. People desired very much to be held in esteem by others, of both higher and lower standing.

Mark heaps shame upon the big-name followers and family of Jesus in this oldest gospel of the New Testament. To acknowledge this, I think, is to see the Gospel of Mark leading a major shift in first-century Christian thinking. The Gospel's attack on these personalities is recognizable not only in the straightforward narrative but also in the sharp ironies of the bracketed episodes (discussed in ch. 5). Now, we see additional barbs woven into the many chiasms under the surface of Mark. To their credit, quite a few scholars had already dared to call Mark's treatment of the twelve disciples intentionally harsh. Relatively alone in braving criticism, Werner Kelber has said Mark also defamed the family of Jesus, and perhaps the Galilean women, as representatives of the Jerusalem church.[1] Of the women who flee from the tomb, Winsome Munro called Mark's ending a polemical treatment, but her reading has not won over many others.[2]

For an unflinching appraisal of Mark, however, I think scholarship must concede that the author excoriates all three groups of people honored in other circles: (1) the twelve disciples; (2) Jesus' mother and brothers; and (3) the followers Mary Magdalene and Salome. The polemic also includes the Judean religious authorities, but the Pharisees, scribes, high priest, and others do not get rehabilitated in other New Testament writings as do nearly all the disciples-turned-apostles, the family, and the named followers of Jesus. Paul, writing before Mark appeared, cited the Twelve and Jesus' brother James as among the many witnesses to the risen Christ. And the three gospels completed after Mark generally accord honor to every follower of Jesus except Judas Iscariot. Jesus' mother is the Spirit-impregnated virgin Mary gloriously portrayed in Matthew and Luke. Letters attributed to Peter, John, and Jesus' brothers James and Jude entered the New Testament canon.

Mark differs starkly from the other gospels in how the three women at the tomb are depicted. Mary Magdalene is sympathetically portrayed in Matthew, Luke, and John. She alone (in John) or with another Mary (in Matthew) or with several other women (in Luke) informs Peter and the disciples about the empty tomb. But in Mark, Mary Magdalene, mother Mary, and Salome are plainly described as so afraid that they fled in fear and told no one that Jesus had risen. Some scholars accept that seemingly disappointing end to the Gospel, then explain it as a temporary failure or as reasonable initial behavior for the women greeted by a strange young man in a tomb. Some others suggest that 16:8 was not the original ending to the Gospel, that the rest was lost.

Ending the Gospel on such a note of betrayal, for example, is illogical to Ben Witherington III. "Between 15:40 and 16:8 Mark has carefully built the case for the women to be the valid witnesses to the death, burial, empty tomb, and Easter message," he wrote.[3] Witherington contended that Mark "cannot have wished to undermine the case" by finishing the Gospel with the fearful women telling no one.[4] "Thus we have an authentic verse in 16:8 which is likely not Mark's true ending," which Witherington believes was lost.[5] Likewise, Markan specialist Larry W. Hurtado of the University of Edinburgh, in a paper presented at the 2001 meeting of the Society of Biblical Literature (SBL), said that discrediting these women would also fundamentally discredit the gospel author's own narrative. "Such a *kamikaze* move would ordinarily demand either a seriously demented author or one working with a strange sense of purpose!" Hurtado wrote in a footnote.[6] I suggested at that SBL workshop that the ending of Mark makes sense if it was the decisive conclusion to a full-scale polemic against the twelve disciples. Hurtado replied, "If the twelve are discredited, then Jesus is discredited."

Yet, my own investigation convinced me that the author of Mark believed that (1) these prominent followers and family members needed to be discredited and that (2) the perceptive, courageous witnesses—people who divined the God-sent nature of Jesus rather quickly, had faith in his miraculous powers, and brought honor to his name—needed to be recognized, and so he scattered them throughout the gospel story.

Honor and Heroism

A number of scholars in recent times have lifted up the importance of "honor and shame" for comprehending the New Testament world of social relations. Wealth, power, and status could help bring honor to leaders but only if they acted honorably as a patron to those of lower status and paid proper respect to their own superiors. People in Jesus' day valued wealth for its ability "for creating, preserving, displaying or recovering public reputation ('honor'), and for protecting the economic integrity of family and household," wrote scholars K. C. Hanson and Douglas E. Oakman. They also pointed to the high-level shame in family matters that John the Baptist made public in Mark's story of Herod and Herodias, who divorced to marry each other. "Beyond that, Herod virtually 'stole' this new wife from his half-brother, Philip, who was still alive," they wrote.[7] Of course, the jailed John the Baptist paid with his head for moral finger-wagging.

Another line of research illuminating gospel studies points to Greco-Roman literature for the "tragic hero," who was an admired figure in ancient epics and tales. In all four gospels, Jesus is predestined to live and die according to God's plan. One New Testament scholar, Gregory J. Riley, has suggested that the Jesus story resembles those of Greek heroes in which their personal character—"telling the truth" in Jesus' case—propels them to their fate. "He knows, as did Achilles, that if he continues on the course set for him, he will be killed," Riley wrote. "The Gospel of Mark turns on this very point." As both his fame and the forces opposing him increase, the anguished teacher from Nazareth prays at Gethsemane that his impending arrest not take place. "He is at last forced, or directed by the will of God, into a situation intriguingly like that of Achilles, choosing death with honor over life," said Riley.[8]

Describing the death of Jesus as honorable and heroic to many would-be believers in the first century was daunting, however. Crucifixion was a tortuous execution used by Romans to humiliate both the victims and, by extension, their surviving family and friends. The apostle Paul wrote that "Christ crucified [is] a stumbling block to Jews and folly to Gentiles" (1 Cor 1:23). "Crucified Lord" was an oxymoron of enormous proportion. Whereas some early sayings collections focused on wise maxims and parables of Jesus and were silent on his ignominious death, the author of Mark composed an action-oriented narrative that led to the persecution, crucifixion, and resurrection of Jesus as a glorious climax. In Mark—better yet, Original Mark—Jesus' cool actions amid adversity taught as much as his words. Except for that one outburst against Peter and creating a disturbance at the Jerusalem temple, Jesus showed great forbearance—with his slow-witted and fearful disciples, and with those who condemned and mocked him in Jerusalem.

One example of Jesus' patience toward the disciples occurs at the Gospel's ending in the sixteenth chapter. The young man in the empty tomb tells the stunned women to inform Peter and the disciples that the resurrected Jesus will go before them to Galilee, as previously planned (14:28; 16:7). For Jesus to keep alive this suggested rendezvous was gracious in the extreme, considering that the Twelve had forsaken Jesus before his trials. Yet, according to Mark, the frightened trio of women fled and informed no one that Jesus had risen. The "messenger" motif in the opening and closing scenes of Mark (and a key to the formal, seven-part chiastic structure) leaves the reader with the only witness available to spread the resurrection news—the "young man."

Polemic against the Family

A glaring exception to the kindly demeanor Jesus usually displays in Mark is his relations with his mother and his siblings. First appearing in Mark's third chapter, his family wanted to drag Jesus out of a crowded house because they evidently believed rumors that he was "beside himself"—crazy, and possibly possessed by demons. The mother and brothers of Jesus were persistent. Someone later tells Jesus they are standing outside calling for him, but he responds that "those who sat about him" were his mother and brothers, as was anyone who did the will of God.[9]

The next time the family appears in Mark, the location is Nazareth, and the occasion is Jesus' return home when he preaches in the synagogue. He startles the locals with his wisdom and reputation for wonderworking. "Is not this the carpenter, the son of Mary and brother of James and Joses and Judas and Simon, and are not his sisters here with us?" (6:3). Faced with skepticism in Nazareth, Jesus says resignedly, "A prophet is not without honor, except in his own country, and among his own kin, and in his own house" (v. 4). The basic form of this Jesus saying is attested in Matthew, Luke, John, and a couple of apocryphal gospels, but only Mark adds "and among his own kin." Mark makes sure that the family members are implicated in disbelief. Indeed, by calling Jesus "son of Mary" and never mentioning Joseph or any earthly father, the oldest gospel leaves the family background uncertain.

Mark's Jesus, who knows the future, may be seen as justified in his distaste for his natural family. When Jesus was killed, he should have been buried by either his closest disciples or the male members of his family. The other New Testament gospels describe Joseph as the man who functioned as, or was thought to be, the father of Jesus. He is not mentioned directly in Mark, but indirectly. Joseph of Arimathea asked for Jesus' body, bought a linen shroud, and placed him in a tomb. Dennis MacDonald of Claremont School of Theology suggested to me that father Joseph was the object of this dig, just as Simon Peter was obliquely slapped when Simon of Cyrene was compelled by soldiers to "carry" *(airo)* Jesus' cross at 15:21. If anyone would follow him, Jesus said earlier (8:34), they should deny themselves (not Jesus) and "take up" *(airo)* their cross. That's not all. The first two named brothers of Jesus in Nazareth (6:3) are James and Joses; they both are mentioned twice when Mark identifies Jesus' mother as a witness to his crucifixion and entombment. She is called "the mother of James the younger and of Joses" (15:40), "the mother of Joses" (15:47), and "the mother of James" (16:1).[10]

In Original Mark, Jesus' mother appears another time prior to the Gospel's ending—when Jesus' group arrived in Jericho. Biblical Mark (10:46) merely has the group arriving, then leaving. What actually happened in Jericho was in the second part of the Secret Mark episode excised by the editor. Jesus refused to receive three women in Jericho— the sister of the young man Jesus loved, his mother, and Salome. Salome here is fleetingly introduced with Jesus' mother—both are rebuffed in Jericho because, it would seem, those two will be joined by Mary Magdalene at the empty tomb, which they will flee as frightened, unwilling witnesses.

Unsung Heroes and Messengers

With no reference to Secret Mark, at least two scholars have drawn attention to the underrated role of secondary figures in Mark. Concluded Joel F. Williams, "Mark's narrative includes certain minor characters who live up to the demands and ideals of Jesus, and thus who serve to instruct the reader further in the proper response to Jesus."[11]

Defining minor characters as those who for the most part appear only once in Mark, Elizabeth Struthers Malbon said that they are "*most often* presented as exemplars," while "the disciples are *generally* presented as fallible followers"—fallible, but not irredeemable.[12]

Finding Original Mark has sharpened the juxtaposition of the shameful central characters in the Gospel and the alternative heroes unnoticed for so long. The unnamed young man found in Secret Mark—resuscitated, beloved, and initiated—now has a "best supporting actor" role in the Jesus drama when combined with the second and third appearances of such a figure in biblical Mark. Whether this is one, two, or three people in the story, this exemplary character also serves to elevate other "secondary" characters who appear fleetingly yet demonstrate significant recognition of Jesus and his mission. So viewed, the reconstructed gospel forces a new appraisal of "who's who in Mark" in terms of honor, shame, and heroics.

For this new vision, a debt is owed not only to Secret Mark but also to the Gospel of Luke. The Original Mark episodes found in Luke score one more against the bad guys and one more for the good guys. The gospel center, seen at Luke 9:51–56, portrays James and John wanting to summon fire from heaven to consume a Samaritan village. The brothers drew a quick rebuke from Jesus. From Luke 23:39–43, the list of perceptive Markan characters grows with the repentant robber on the cross, who declared that Jesus did no wrong and requested that Jesus save a place for him in heaven.

Even without the new episodes from Secret Mark and Luke, however, the biblical version of Mark is populated with seemingly incidental characters and followers who recognize Jesus' authority, sometimes braving censure by others for acting as they did. Here is a brief rundown of these messengers and witnesses for Jesus.

Women

Peter's mother-in-law, cured of a fever, "served" Jesus and his first four followers (1:31), though how long she served is not specified. Mark says there were women who "followed" and "ministered" to Jesus when he was in Galilee as well as "many other women who came up with him to Jerusalem" (15:40–41). Whether that included the healed woman who had suffered internal bleeding for a dozen years is not said, but she was praised by Jesus for her "faith" (5:25–34). The woman who earned lavish praise from Jesus, however, was the unnamed woman who poured costly ointment on Jesus' head, thereby anointing his body beforehand for burial (14:3–9). "She has done a beautiful thing to me," Jesus tells those who criticized her. He declared that "wherever the gospel is preached in the whole world, what she has done will be told in memory of her."

Men

The Gospel identifies at least two less-known followers of Jesus: Levi the tax collector and the roadside beggar Bartimaeus, who was healed of blindness. They both willingly "followed" Jesus. They were never cited again, but neither were they tainted by the shame of the Twelve. Three others did not become followers, but they had the right reactions to Jesus, even at his death. A daring scribe, hearing Jesus cite the two greatest commandments, declared, "You are right, Teacher"(Mark 12:32). That took courage because he was among Sadducees, Pharisees, and Herodians who were trying to trap Jesus in debate. Seeing that the scribe had understood, Jesus told him, "You are not far from the kingdom of God" (v. 34). A centurion, in contrast to other Roman soldiers who mistreated and mocked the prisoner Jesus, was able to see what his comrades did not. As Jesus drew his last breath on the cross, the centurion uttered, "Truly this man was the Son of God" (15:39). Joseph of Arimathea, who was "looking for the kingdom of God, took courage" and obtained permission from Pilate to bury Jesus' corpse properly in a tomb (15:43).

Anonymous Insiders

Some of the people in Jesus' circle were not part of the Twelve, yet clearly Jesus had given them the secret of the kingdom. These were the men and women sitting "about him" whom Jesus declared were his true family members by virtue of doing the will of God (3:34). A bit later (4:10–12), "those who were about him with the twelve asked him concerning the parables." Jesus told them, "To you has been given the secret of the kingdom of God, but for those outside everything is in parables; so that they may indeed see but not perceive, and may indeed hear but not understand; lest they should turn again, and be forgiven." Eventually, the gospel narrative demonstrates that the twelve male disciples—that is,

those whom Jesus appointed "to be with him" (3:14)—became outsiders who heard and saw without understanding. They were like the
examples of poor soil in the sower parable.

Now, in Original Mark, the young man is brought back to life and
taught "the secret of the kingdom of God," the gift received by those
about Jesus in 4:11. Receipt of the mystery by the young man culmi-
nated the nighttime teaching. He is either a devoted believer to the end
who risks arrest himself, then dares to roll back the stone from Jesus'
tomb, or he is the "type" of follower who shows up when one needs such
loyalty. At least two scholars have seen the young man as the model disciple. Hans-Martin Schenke described the young man as "prototype
and symbol of those who are to be initiated into the higher discipleship
of Jesus."[13] Marvin Meyer of Chapman University regards the young
man as coming close to being "a paradigm for discipleship in canonical
and *Secret Mark*."[14] But in his excellent study of the youth in Secret
Mark, in a 1990 article reprinted in a 2003 collection of essays, Meyer
saw the young man who escaped naked from soldiers (14:51–52) as forsaking his baptismal loyalties.[15] I think that is possible, but it is also true
that the young man showed a boldness not displayed by the Twelve, of
whom the gospel author plainly says, "They all forsook him" (14:50).

If there is a female equivalent to the beloved young man in Markan
heroics, it was the unnamed woman who poured costly ointment over
the head of Jesus to anoint "my body beforehand for burying" (14:8).
She braved the displeasure of others in the house of Simon the leper by
"wasting" the oil, when it could have been sold for donations to the
poor. For doing "a beautiful thing to me," Jesus commends her extrav-
agantly. How she could have known about his impending death is unex-
plained, though on the first and second occasion of Jesus' announcing
his coming fate, he said it to the "disciples," who in Mark at times can
be more than the Twelve.

This unnamed woman believed the prophecies of Jesus, wrote John
Dominic Crossan, a scholar convinced that Mark engaged in polemic.
"[I]f she does not anoint him for burial now, she will never be able to
do it later. That is why she gets that astonishing statement of praise,"
said Crossan. The woman's deed is "the first complete and unequivocal
act of faith in Jesus' suffering and rising destiny." Also, "Mark says that
a woman was first to *believe* in the resurrection," according to Crossan.[16]

Contrary to Witherington's assessment that Mark begins a positive
picture of Mary Magdalene, Jesus' mother, and Salome, starting with

15:40, Crossan observed that the Gospel has the three viewing the crucifixion from a "distance" which is the same Greek word Mark used to
describe how Peter followed the arresting soldiers "at a distance" (14:54)
to a spot where Peter would deny knowing Jesus three times. That was
"not a complimentary description," wrote Crossan, who pointed out
that the Gospel of John (19:25) has a group of women witnesses stand
right by the cross.[17]

Mark's story assignment for the final messenger goes to, not the three
women, but the young man, "a messenger entrusted with a heavenly
mission, as the reader understands from the color of his clothes," wrote
Bas van Iersel, the retired rector of Catholic University, Nijmegen, the
Netherlands. A scholar attuned to chiastic patterns in Mark, Iersel said
the Gospel starts in the wilderness and finishes at the tomb. The two
desolate places are distinctly parallel, he said: "They are the only places
where, besides Jesus, a messenger appears: John in 1:4–9, and a young
man in 16:5–7. Their dress is mentioned as well, which is exceptional
in Mark: the hairy mantle of the prophet and the white robe of the
bringer of good news. Both passages speak of the coming/going of Jesus,
of his coming after the baptist in 1:6, and of his going ahead of the disciples in 16:7." As for a young man's earlier flight from guards who
arrested Jesus, I agreed with Iersel in disputing claims that the scene
somehow symbolized the abandonment of Jesus by the disciples
moments earlier. Yes, the young man "fled," just as the disciples "fled."
But with the guards left holding his linen covering in their hands, "there
is something playful in the way he manages to give his pursuers the
slip," Iersel said. Indeed, in English we would quip that the young man
"barely escaped."[18]

Clues and Digs in Chiastic Links

The literary technique in Mark of bracketing one story with another,
described in chapter 5, frequently offered an ironical contrast between
two scenes. Jesus, under arrest, is questioned by the high priests and
pummeled by mockers urging him to "prophesy." Preceding that
episode and following it was the two-part story of the furtive Peter
warming himself at the fire outside the building in which Jesus was
being grilled; Peter then three times denies that he was an associate of
Jesus, as Jesus prophesized. Also, the two-part Secret Mark episode
about the young man who found great favor with Jesus brackets the

story of James and John demanding special seats beside Jesus in heaven. By juxtapositioning this action in a literary "sandwich," the puckish author is nudging the audience to evaluate the gospel figures.

Likewise, some chiastic patterns do the same beneath the story's surface. This is not to say that all chiastic links may be read for plot subtleties. The author had an astonishing, self-imposed burden just to supply every episode with enough parallel motifs, keywords, names or numbers, and grammatical constructs to connect chiastically with other episodes scattered about the text. Chiasms in Original Mark nonetheless do supply answers to some questions raised in Mark. Near the end of the Gospel, the three women asked themselves as they approach Jesus' burial place: "Who will roll away the stone for us from the door of the tomb?" (Mark 16:3). They arrive and see that the stone was already moved away. Biblical Mark does not explain by whom. Some commentators who label the young man as an "angel" may have felt it would have taken a creature with extraordinary strength to do it. But readers of the unedited version of Mark would have recalled that Jesus "rolled away the stone from the door of the tomb" of a young man midway in the Gospel. After Jesus' death and his entombment, a young man returns the favor. And a chiastic pattern confirms it. These two rock-rolling scenes provide links in the last-half chiasm within the asymmetrical macrocode described earlier (ch. 8).

Cutting that pattern in two, the last quarter length of the macrocode extends from 14:3–11 (A) to 16:1–8 (A'). The chiastic parallels drip with irony. It starts by contrasting the anointing woman with the frightened women who fled from the tomb. Whereas the unnamed heroine will be remembered "wherever the gospel is preached" (the message of Jesus' death and resurrection), the frightened women (A') kept their silence, just as Peter did in this chiasm's midpoint. Notice that the anointing of Jesus takes place in the house of "Simon" the leper and that Jesus, frustrated at Peter's inability to stay awake at Gethsemane, addresses him as "Simon" (14:37), his name before he was appointed as the leader of the twelve.

(14:3–11) House of <u>Simon</u> leper, woman with <u>alabaster</u> flask ointment, <u>very costly</u>, broke, poured over head. Some said **to themselves** *(pros heautou):* Why was ointment wasted? might have <u>sold</u>. Jesus: why trouble her? done beautiful thing; always poor with you; <u>you will not always have me</u>; did what she could; <u>anointed</u> body <u>beforehand</u> for <u>burying</u>.

Wherever gospel is preached what done told in memory. Judas, one of twelve, went to priests to betray him; promised money; he **sought** to betray him.

(16:1–8) Mary Magdalene, Mary mother James, Salome bought spices, anoint him; very early to tomb; they **said to one another** *(pros heautou):* Who roll away stone from door of tomb? Saw stone was rolled back—very large. Entering, saw young man: Do not be amazed; you **seek** Jesus of Nazareth, who was crucified. He has risen, he not here; see where laid him. Go, tell Peter, disciples he going before you to Galilee; went out, fled; said nothing to any one, for they were afraid.

(14:12–16) First day of Unleavened Bread, when sacrificed passover lamb, disciples: Where have us go, prepare for you eat passover? Sent two disciples, Man carrying water will meet you; follow him; to householder, my guest room, **where** I am to eat with my disciples? will show room, ready, prepare for us; disciples found it, prepared passover.

(15:42–47) Day of Preparation, day before sabbath, Joseph of Arimathea, looking for kingdom of God, went to Pilate, asked body of Jesus; Pilate, wondering if dead, summoned centurion; learned he was dead, granted body to Joseph. Bought linen, took him down, wrapped him, laid him in tomb hewn from rock; rolled stone against door. [Two Marys] saw **where** was laid.

(14:17–25) Eating with twelve, Jesus: Truly, one of you betray me, one of twelve. Is it I? said, one of twelve, dipping bread into the dish with me. **Son** of man goes as is written of him, but woe by whom **Son** of man betrayed [Psalm 41:9]. Better if that [person] not born; broke bread, take; this my body; took cup, they drank. Blood of covenant, poured out for many. Truly, I not drink again until day when drink it new in kingdom **of God.**

(15:34–41) At ninth hour, Jesus cried, My **God,** my **God,** why thou forsaken me? [Psalm 22:1] One ran, filling sponge full of vinegar, gave it to him to drink. See if Elijah take him down; breathed last; temple curtain torn in two. Centurion: Truly, this man was **Son of God.** Women looking on, Mary Magdalene, Mary mother of James and Joses, Salome, in Galilee followed him; other women came up to Jerusalem.

(14:26–31) Went to Mount of Olives. Jesus: all fall away *(skandalizo)*; is written, I will strike shepherd. After <u>I am raised up, I will go before you</u> to Galilee. Peter: Even though they all will fall away, I will **not. And Jesus said to him, Truly, I say to you, this very night** *(semeron),* before cock crows twice you will deny me three times. Peter: <u>If I must die with you,</u> I will **not** deny you, all said same.

(Luke 23:39–43) One criminal railed *(blasphemeo)* at Jesus: Are you not the Christ? Other rebuked him: Do you **not** fear God since you under condemnation? We justly, but has done nothing wrong. Said to Jesus: Remember me <u>when you come into your kingdom</u>. **And he said to him, Truly, I say to you, today** *(semeron),* <u>you will be with me</u> in Paradise.

(14:32–42) <u>They went to</u> **place called** <u>Gethsemane</u>. Jesus took with him Peter, James, John. Prayed; very sorrowful, even <u>to death</u>. Prayed **hour** might <u>pass</u> from him. Father, remove this <u>cup</u>; found them sleeping. **Simon,** could you not watch one **hour?** Spirit willing, <u>flesh is weak</u>; finds sleeping **third** time; **hour** has come, betrayed.

(15:21–32) Passerby **Simon** of Cyrene, to carry his cross. <u>They brought him to</u> **place called** <u>Golgotha</u>; offered <u>wine</u> mingled with myrrh, but not take it; divided garments; **third hour** when <u>crucified</u> him. <u>Crucified</u> with two robbers; those who <u>passed</u> by derided him: would destroy temple, build in <u>three</u> days. Chief priests: cannot save himself. Come down from cross, may see, believe.

(14:43–54) Judas came, with **crowd** with swords and clubs from **chief priests** and scribes; **betrayer** *(pardidomi)* given them a sign; one I shall kiss, seize him, **lead him away** under guard. <u>Master</u>! Kissed him; they seize him; one <u>struck</u> slave of high priest. Disciples forsake him; young man followed, nothing but <u>linen cloth</u> about his body; they seized him, but he left <u>linen cloth</u>, ran away <u>naked</u>. **Led** *(apago)* Jesus to high priest. Peter followed, to courtyard, sitting with guards.

(15:11–20) **Chief priests** stirred up **crowd** to release Barabbas instead. Pilate: What do with man you call King of the Jews? Crucify him, crucify him. Pilate, to satisfy **crowd,** released Barabbas, **delivered** *(pardidomi)* him to be crucified. Soldiers **led him away** in palace; battalion called together; <u>clothed</u> him in <u>purple cloak</u>, crown of thorns. Saluted him: Hail, <u>King of the Jews!</u> <u>Struck</u> his head with reed; <u>stripped off</u> purple cloak, put <u>clothes</u> back on. **Led** *(exago)* him out to crucify him.

(14:55–64) **Chief priests, whole council** sought testimony; false witness. High priest **asked** <u>Jesus</u>: **Have you no answer to make?** What these men testify against you? Silent and **made no answer.** Again, high priest: **Are you** <u>the Christ, Son of the Blessed</u>? I am. High priest to council: <u>What is your decision</u>? They all <u>condemned as deserving death</u>.

(15:1–10) **Chief priests, whole council** delivered Jesus. Pilate: **Are you** <u>King of the Jews</u>? You said so. Pilate **asked** <u>him</u>: **Have you no answer to make?** See how many charges bring against you. But Jesus **made no** further **answer.** Pilate to crowd: <u>Do you want me to release the King of the Jews</u>?

Arriving at the tightening chiastic pivot (14:66–72) of this last quarter-length of the macrocode, we switch to the indented form:

H (65–67) [Some] strike him, saying, <u>Prophesy</u>! Guards received him with blows. As **Peter** was <u>below</u> in courtyard, one of maids of high priest came; seeing **Peter** warming himself, looked at him, said, You also were with Nazarene, **Jesus.**

    I (68) But denied it, **I neither know** nor understand what **you mean** *(lego)*. And he went out into the gateway.

        J (69) The maid saw him, and began **again to say to the bystanders,** This man **is one of them.**

            K (70a) Again he denied it.

        J' (70b) After little while **again the bystanders said to** Peter, Certainly you **are one of them;** for you are a Galilean.

    I' (71) But he began to invoke curse on himself, to swear, **I do not know** this man of whom **you speak** *(lego)*.

H' (72) Immediately cock crowed second time. **Peter** remembered **Jesus** <u>said to him: Before cock crows twice, you will deny me three times.</u> He <u>broke down</u> and wept.

This stark ending for Peter is vivid. Yet, below Mark's surface narrative there are chiastic ties that embellish the story. In one of the pairings of the macrocode (appendix 5) that spans the Gospel, the humiliating scene above with Peter corresponds to the time when Peter was back in

Galilee with family (1:29–39). The catchwords are few, but the thematic links are a wicked blow at Peter, who was once called "Satan." Compare verses 71 and 72 above with the passages at 1:32 and 33: "And [Jesus] cast out many demons; and he would not permit the demons to speak, because they knew him. And early in the morning, a great while before day, he rose and went out to a lonely place, and there he prayed."

Jesus casts out demons and prays; Peter invokes a curse on himself. Jesus does not allow the demons to speak because they knew him; a fearful Peter does not permit himself to speak because he knows (oida) Jesus. And when most predictably does a rooster crow?

Notes

1. Werner H. Kelber, *Mark's Story of Jesus* (Philadelphia: Fortress, 1979), 90.

2. Winsome Munro, "Women Disciples in Mark?" *Catholic Biblical Quarterly* 44 (1982): 225–41. See also John Dominic Crossan, "The Relatives of Jesus in Mark," *Novum Testamentum* 15 (1973): 81–113.

3. Ben Witherington III, *The Gospel of Mark: A Socio-Rhetorical Commentary* (Grand Rapids: Eerdmans, 2001), 417–18.

4. Ibid.

5. Ibid., 46n.131.

6. Larry W. Hurtado, "Mission Accomplished: Apologetics, Witness, and Women in Mark's Passion-Resurrection Narrative" (paper presented at the SBL conference, Denver, November17, 2001). Hurtado said some other scholars suggested that the end of Mark once contained an account in which the women "overcame their fear and did speak to the disciples." But, he added, the suggestion that the original ending was lost through manuscript damage "remains only an interesting, but unproven, suggestion." See his *Mark, A Good News Commentary* (San Francisco: Harper & Row, 1983), 271.

7. K. C. Hanson and Douglas E. Oakman, *Palestine in the Time of Jesus: Social Structure and Social Conflicts* (Minneapolis: Fortress, 1998), 122, 86.

8. Gregory J. Riley, *One Jesus, Many Christs: How Jesus Inspired Not One True Christianity, but Many* (San Francisco: HarperSanFrancisco, 1997), 82–83.

9. For discussion of Jesus' family, see Hanson and Oakman, *Palestine in the Time of Jesus,* 57–58.

10. John Dart, "Who's Who in Jesus' Family," *The Christian Century,* May 3, 2003, 11, 12.

11. Joel F. Williams, *Other Followers of Jesus: Minor Characters as Major Figures in Mark's Gospel* (JSNTSup 102; Sheffield: Sheffield Academic Press, 1994), 205–6.

12. Elizabeth Struthers Malbon, *In the Company of Jesus: Characters in Mark's Gospel* (Louisville: Westminster John Knox, 2000), 192, 198.

13. Hans-Martin Schenke, "The Mystery of the Gospel of Mark," *Second Century* 4 (1984): 65–82, as quoted by Marvin Meyer, "The Youth in Secret Mark," *Semeia* 49 (1990): [The Apocryphal Jesus and Christian Origins] 137; idem, *Secret Gospels: Essays on Thomas and the Secret Gospel of Mark* (Harrisburg, Pa.: Trinity Press International, 2003).

14. Meyer, *Semeia,* 149; Meyer, *Secret Gospels,* 132.

15. Meyer, *Semeia,* 145; Meyer, *Secret Gospels,* 132. As noted by Meyer, Morton Smith felt the young man at 14:51–52 "deserted Christ and saved himself." Morton Smith, "Clement of Alexandria and Secret Mark: The Score at the End of the First Decade," *Harvard Theological Review* 75 (1982): 457. Harry Fledderman's oft-cited 1979 article, which did not take the Secret Mark story into account, pointed out that the young man who escaped naked from the guards "fled" (*phuego*, translated "ran away" in RSV), the same verb used to describe the flight of the Twelve at 14:50 and the women at the tomb at 16:8. Fledderman called it "a dramatization of the universal flight of the disciples." Harry Fledderman, "The Flight of a Naked Young Man (Mark 14:51–52)," *Catholica Biblical Quarterly* 41 (1979): 415.

16. John Dominic Crossan, *The Birth of Christianity: Discovering What Happened in the Years Immediately after the Execution of Jesus* (San Francisco: HarperSanFrancisco, 1998), 558–59.

17. Ibid., 571–72.

18. Bas M. F. van Iersel, *Mark: A Reader-Response Commentary* (JSNTSup 164; (Sheffield: Sheffield Academic Press, 1998), 82, 441, 496.

CHAPTER 10

Unashamed Naked Return to Oneness

SOME PEOPLE MIGHT BE UNEASY with the story of the young man if it were restored to the Gospel of Mark even on an unofficial basis. The whiff of sexual intimacy between Jesus and the young man twitches demure noses. Original Mark does not seem to imply that it was an erotic rendezvous, but perhaps some readers would draw that conclusion.

Folks unfriendly to anything outside the biblical canon would probably point out that Morton Smith, who discovered the long-lost episode, suggested that the Jesus of history engaged in physical, possibly homosexual, rituals with followers. If so, Smith said, that would account for erotic, anything-goes Christian sects in the church's early centuries. But that theory by Smith was not something he defended energetically, nor has the thesis gained notable backing in academia.

While the young man "loved" Jesus and in turn Jesus "loved" him, the word *agapao* "as used in the New Testament and therefore probably as used by Christians of the first century is the least sexual of the Greek words that we translate as 'love,'" said one scholar.[1] A couple of episodes earlier, Mark's Gospel said Jesus "loved" a rich man who asked about how to be saved. But the man walked away, unwilling to take up a life of poverty. In both Mark (12:30–33) and Matthew (19:19; 22:37, 39), that same Greek verb for love was used when Jesus quotes Hebrew Scripture that one is to "love" one's neighbor and "love the Lord your God." Then there is the Gospel of John in which an unidentified disciple

102

"whom Jesus loved" appears on the scene (19:26; 21:7). But this so-called beloved disciple is not discussed in hushed voices at churches for fear of extolling an intimate relationship between the two. More significant is the fact that an unnamed favorite of Jesus appears now in both Original Mark and John.

What about the scanty apparel of Mark's young man, only a linen cloth over his naked body, and the overnight stay with Jesus? The evidence is strong here for ritual, not romance. The story's elements suggest an archaic Christian rite of baptism, rather than a sexual liaison. Uncovering this inviting glimpse into initiation in the oldest New Testament gospel has implications for the history of early Christianity. Mark's young-man episodes, combined with other Christian literature alluding to baptisms, afford an opportunity to see features of a rite practiced by the mid-first century, if not earlier by Jesus himself.

Here again is the initiation half of the story:

But the young man, looking upon him, loved him and began to beseech him that he might be with him. And going out of the tomb, they came into the house of the young man, for he was rich. And after six days, Jesus told him what to do and in the evening the young man comes to him, wearing a linen cloth over [his] naked [body]. And he remained with him that night, for Jesus taught him the secret of the kingdom of God. And thence, arising, he returned to the other side of the Jordan.[2]

The next passages in Clement's copy of Secret Mark, a sequence confirmed by chiastic patterns, describe the demand by James and John that Jesus do whatever they wanted—specifically to grant them seats on either side of Jesus in heaven. When the story resumes ever so briefly at Mark 10:46, Clement said it is after "And he comes into Jericho" when the secret version adds, "and the sister of the young man whom Jesus loved and his mother and Salome were there, and Jesus did not receive them."

Garments of Shame

About a dozen years before the Secret Mark discovery, a spectacular new cache of writings relating to formative Christianity was found in 1945 near Nag Hammadi, Egypt. Buried by monks at a time when "heretical" writings were being destroyed, the bound codices included a full copy, in Coptic translation, of the noncanonical *Gospel of Thomas.* This collection of 114 sayings of Jesus, known previously only from church references and some Greek papyrus fragments, has eventually won (outside conservative circles) fairly wide acceptance as an independent source for Jesus' words aside from the New Testament gospels. The *Gospel of Thomas* is dated anywhere from the mid-first century to the mid-second century. Stephen Patterson suggests a date "in the vicinity of 70–80 C.E."[3] Some scholars believe the earliest stage of *Thomas* appeared before the Gospel of Mark. Historical-critical studies on *Thomas* and the Nag Hammadi Library proliferated in the last half of the twentieth century. My book *The Laughing Savior* (Harper & Row, 1976) was the first popularly written U.S. book on the collection's discovery and its importance for Christian origins and the churches' theological battle with gnostic theology and sects.

Though in the end it was called the "Gospel according to Thomas," this sayings collection was probably first known by its opening sentence. Missing some words but helped by comparing it to the complete version in Coptic, that first line in a Greek fragment reads: "These are the [secret] sayings [that] the living Jesus spoke, [and Judas, who is] also (called) Thomas, [recorded]." Judas, or Jude, a brother of Jesus, bears the second name Thomas in apocryphal texts from Nag Hammadi and elsewhere.[4]

One important avenue that *Thomas* opened was a research path to early baptismal imagery and practices of Jesus' followers. A good place to start is with Jonathan Z. Smith of the University of Chicago, a wide-ranging thinker respected by gospel scholars. In 1966, Smith published an impressive journal article, "The Garments of Shame," on primitive Christian baptismal rites.[5] He began with saying 37 in *Thomas:*

> His disciples asked, "When will you become revealed to us and when shall we see you?" Jesus said, "When you disrobe without being ashamed and take up your garments and place them under your feet like little children and tread on them, then [will you see] the son of the living one, and you will not be afraid."

Smith identified "four closely related elements" in the reply of Jesus: (1) the undressing of the disciples, (2) their being naked and unashamed, (3) their treading on the garments, and (4) their acting like little children. Smith went on to demonstrate that the origin of saying 37 "is to be found within archaic Christian baptismal practices" that suggest a return to the state of Adam and Eve before the fall.[6] "The nudity of the initiant [sic]—a feature shared by early Christianity with the initiation rites of the Hellenistic Mysteries and Jewish proselyte 'baptism'"—was found by Smith "to be consistently related to the symbolism of new life and birth."[7]

Jews and the early church shared a horror over nakedness, Smith wrote, "but held that in baptism it was necessary."[8] At first, Adam and Eve were "both naked, and were not ashamed" (Gen 2:25). Smith cited a fourth-century church figure who described an initiate as taking off all his garments, being anointed, then immersing naked in water, and being clothed in white garments upon completion of his baptism. In fact, his white garment is "wholly radiant" to remind him that his baptism is a sign of his new life. When Adam and Eve sinned, they fashioned body coverings to hide their shame. Smith and other scholars see the New Testament's Letter to the Colossians (3:9–10, NRSV) as referring to this custom: "Do not lie to one another, seeing that you have stripped off the old self with its practices and have clothed yourselves with the new self, which is being renewed in knowledge according to the image of its creator."

Smith also points to *Gos. Thom.* 21, which begins with Mary asking Jesus, "Whom are your disciples like?" Jesus responds, "They are like children who have settled in a field which is not theirs. When the owners of the field come, they will say, 'Let us have back our field.' They (will) undress in their presence in order to let them have back their field and to give it back to them." Both the "field" and the disciples' clothes here are metaphors for "the world," said Smith, commenting on *Gos. Thom.* 21. Smith noted that Tatian, a church apologist active around 160 C.E., also wrote of Christians stripping like little children. Both *Thomas* and the New Testament gospels have Jesus addressing followers as children or saying disciples must become like children. "The little child is a standard metaphor of innocence and sinlessness like that of Adam and Eve before the Fall," said Smith.[9]

The Chicago professor next cited a vital passage from Clement of Alexandria, who said he was quoting from the *Gospel of the Egyptians*, a text that has never been found:

When Salome asked when what she had inquired about would be known, the Lord said, "When you have trampled on the garment of shame and when the two become one and the male with the female [is] neither male nor female."[10]

Smith suggested that trampling on "the garment of shame" originally referred to baptism. But he felt "the two become one . . . neither male nor female" part reflected "an anti-sexual polemic" that became attached later to the baptismal language, a point with which I disagree.[11] Clement of Alexandria, of course, is the same churchman who saved the missing Markan episode of the young man.

The themes of an archaic Christian baptism occur all through the first four centuries, Jonathan Smith discovered. Jerome (b. 348–d. 420), the monk whose Latin translation of the Bible was a Roman Catholic standard for centuries, wrote that once an animal skin symbolizing one's mortality was discarded at baptism, the initiate puts on the linen "garment of Christ." That garment is "wholly white" so that "the entire shame of our past sins may be covered," according to Jerome, who lived into the fifth century.[12] Smith cited a New Testament passage going back to the first century conveying the idea that after shedding earthly material, then putting on the heavenly, "we will not be found naked" (2 Cor 5:1–4). Those passages speak of tent, house, and dwelling instead of clothes, garment, or skin, but Smith indicated the ideas behind the imagery are similar.

Smith did not refer to other, seemingly pertinent, Pauline passages— evidently in order not to stray far from common features of baptismal rebirth that he pulled together from Jewish, Hellenistic, apocryphal Christian, and church father writings. Smith's final point was that certain sayings in *Thomas,* then considered to be a pervasively "gnostic" text by some analysts, were not distinctly different from early church beliefs and practices.

Neither Male nor Female

Indeed, letters written by Paul some two decades after the death of Jesus invite comparisons with the "two become one . . . neither male nor female" imagery from *Thomas* and the *Gospel of the Egyptians.* In his Letter to the Galatians (3:26–28), Paul wrote: "For in Christ Jesus you are sons of God, through faith. For as many of you as were baptized into Christ have put on Christ. There is no Jew nor Greek, there is neither slave nor free, there is neither male nor female; for you are all one in Christ Jesus." And in 1 Cor 12:13: "For by the one Spirit we were all baptized into one body—Jews or Greeks, slaves or free—and all were made to drink of one Spirit."

One scholar concluded in his doctoral dissertation that the "garment of shame/two become one" formulas used in Gal 3:26–28 and in the *Gospel of the Egyptians* reflected the same earlier ideas known to Paul and were perhaps altered by the apostle. The *Gospel of the Egyptians* likely presented a version closer to the original than the formula in Galatians since Paul seemed to modify the formula to express the unity of Jews and Greeks, and to speak of the believers' unification into Christ, according to Dennis MacDonald.[13]

Put another way by Wayne A. Meeks in a 1974 journal article, Paul insists on outer preservation of the created, differentiated order.[14] "Women remain women and men remain men and dress accordingly, even though 'the end of the ages has come upon them,'" Meeks wrote. Yet the passages in Galatians and 1 Corinthians, and to some extent Col 3:9–11, represent "a 'baptismal reunification formula' familiar in congregations associated with Paul and his school," Meeks said. Paul himself may have introduced those ideas to churches in his circle, but that is unknown. "The point is, however, that it was not an idiosyncratic notion of his, but imbedded in the act of initiation into the Christian congregation," he said. As for the "no male and female" line in Gal 3:28, Meeks saw an unmistakable reference to Gen 2:21–22, in which God takes a rib from the sleeping Adam to form the first woman. The Christian baptism, at least at the start, restored the initiate into a Eden-like bisexual being, neither male nor female.[15]

"Myths of a bisexual progenitor of the human race were very common in antiquity," Meeks said. "Small wonder, then," he added, that some rabbis knew a version of the Septuagint, a Greek translation of the Hebrew Bible, "which translated Genesis 1:27 and 5:2, 'male and female he created *him*' (instead of *them*)." The mythic image of taking the initiate back to humankind's original state "received its most luxuriant development at the hands of the gnostics, who were particularly entranced by the androgynous character of the primal man," Meeks concluded.[16]

However, he said, the second generation of the Pauline school was unwilling to continue treating women and men as equals as they were in the earlier missions. "Perhaps Paul himself set in motion the conservative reaction," Meeks wrote. "The language of baptismal reunification persisted for a time, more and more enveloped in a myth of cosmic reconciliation, but ironically it was used to reinforce a conventional stratification of family and congregation and eventually rejected altogether in the misogyny of the [letters to Timothy and Titus]."[17]

Dying and Rising with Jesus

Besides nudity, an exchange of garments, and bisexual reunification, the baptism in early Christian teaching said the one being baptized dies and rises again to life as Jesus did. Writing to Rome (starting at Rom 6:3), Paul asked: "Do you not know that all of us who have been baptized into Christ Jesus were baptized into his death? We were buried therefore with him by baptism into death, so that as Christ was raised from the dead by the glory of the Father, we too might walk in newness of life."

Just before Morton Smith published his discovery, an article in the *Journal of Biblical Literature* looked at baptism in Mark, particularly the linen, or *sindon* (same word for the shroud that enveloped Jesus' corpse), worn by the young man at Jesus' arrest and the white robe worn by the young man in Jesus' tomb.[18] Authors Robin Scroggs and Kent Groff proposed, among other things, that the two biblical Mark appearances of a young man suggested that they were initiates at some stage of baptism. The Scroggs-Groff article was already being edited for the December 1973 issue when Smith's books on Secret Mark appeared. Permitted to write an addendum to the article, the pair found that Secret Mark and Smith's analysis generally supported their views on the baptismal significance of the young man's two appearances in biblical Mark. However, one problem was that Secret Mark said Jesus "taught" the young man the secret of the kingdom of God but didn't speak of baptizing him. "Why could not, however, the teaching be the pre-baptismal catechesis, necessarily preceding the actual baptism . . . ?" they asked.[19] Why not, indeed.

Echoes of a prebaptismal ritual have been detected in Mark's tenth chapter. First, discipleship is a principal theme from 8:27 to 10:52, the middle section of Mark forming one of seven chiasms in the formal literary structure of Original Mark. Second, what Jesus says to his disciples in the tenth chapter looks as if they were utterances lifted from rituals for early church baptism services. Though "disguised" in a sense as Jesus' teachings to his followers on their journey to Jerusalem, believers in the last third of the first century may have recognized instructions and questions they heard at the time of their initiations.

Morton Smith himself proposed that behind Mark 10:13–45 (including the Secret Mark episode) was a baptismal catechesis. Verses 13–16 insist that the kingdom of God belongs to "children," a word in Mark synonymous with new initiates. Already, Jonathan Smith and others have associated the "little children" image to archaic Christian baptism. Those passages close with Jesus taking children into his arms, "blessing them, laying hands on them." Then verses 17–31 begin with an outsider's question, "Good Teacher, what must I do to inherit eternal life?" Morton Smith points out the specific requirements in Jesus' answer: "Monotheism, obedience to the commandments, renunciation of property."[20] At verses 32–34, which in the narrative is Jesus' third prediction of his death and resurrection, is the "creedal prophecy" in the ritual, which assures the initiate that death will be followed by life. The principal Secret Mark segment, which comes before verse 35, describes the six-day interval, the nighttime ceremony for the linen-draped inductee, and the imparting of the kingdom's mystery.

Verses 35–45 in the narrative serve first to embarrass James and John, who will forsake Jesus in the end, unlike the ideal initiate who was just given special teaching. At verse 38 comes a question that could have been posed to initiates (but probably earlier in the ritual): "Are you able to drink the cup that I drink, or to be baptized with the baptism with which I am baptized?" The answer of James and John was perhaps the expected response of baptism candidates: "We are able." When Jesus then says that the two brothers also will drink from the cup and be baptized the same as Jesus was, the words sound like metaphors for a baptism of fire or martyrdom. But in Mark's Gospel James and John abandoned Jesus. In 10:38, Jesus referred to a baptism he has already had. His dip in the Jordan River water was characteristic of the baptism administered by John the Baptist, but Jesus was also "baptized" by the Holy Spirit at that time. The Baptist said Jesus would in turn baptize with the Holy Spirit (1:8). Now that reconstructed Original Mark has Jesus inducting an ideal disciple into the kingdom, it does not seem far-fetched to say that receiving the Holy Spirit was also a feature of this secret baptism. The recovered young-man story does not call it a baptism, but a chiastic pattern strongly suggests Jesus' baptism references to the ritual in the Secret Mark episode (see pp. 175–76, for last-quarter chiasm of Act 3).

Two Shall Become One

Expanding on Morton Smith's schema, I hear echoes of initiation/ baptismal rites in passages before Mark 10:13 where the Gospel has Pharisees testing Jesus on his stance on divorce (10:2–12). The response of Jesus recalls Gen 1:27 and 2:24: "But from the beginning of creation,

'God made them male and female,'" and "'For this reason a man shall leave his father and mother *and be joined to his wife* and the two shall become one flesh.' So they are no longer two but one flesh."

The phrase that I italicized above does not appear in the oldest and most reliable manuscripts of Mark. Codex Sinaiticus and Codex Vaticanus (fourth-century texts) plus an early Syrian text omit the words "and be joined to his wife." (Sinaiticus and Vaticanus also are the leading textual witnesses for Mark's Gospel ending at 16:8, where the women flee from the tomb.) "A man" (*anthropos*) could be translated "a person" here. True, Mark's Jesus is ostensibly talking about marriage, but the first-century baptized readers could see something different in the original wording: "A person shall leave father and mother and the two shall become one flesh." The requirement by Jesus for would-be followers to leave their natural parents is well attested in Luke 14:26; *Gos. Thom.* 55, 101; and in Mark 10:29–30.

If anyone has previously described the baptismal symbolism behind Mark's "divorce" episode, I am unaware of it. That particular piece of the puzzle was something I came upon years ago. Relating it to most of the above sources, starting with the "garments of shame" study, I summarized the evidence for archaic baptismal features in a light-hearted article in 1978 for the journal *Theology Today.*[21]

Things move slowly in biblical research. I read a paper entitled "'The Two Shall Become One' in the Gospel of Mark" at the Society of Biblical Literature's Pacific Coast regional meeting in 1982 at Stanford University. At the same conference, I gave another paper about "the child of seven days" in the *Gospel of Thomas* and how the Secret Mark episode sheds light on that saying. Both papers elicited a few helpful comments, but interest was minimal since the Secret Mark passages were generally regarded, at best, as short-lived additions to Mark omitted before that Gospel entered the biblical canon.

After Six Days . . .

But with evidence today that the young man's story is an integral part of Original Mark, I think the situation has changed. Saying 4 in the *Gospel of Thomas* now assumes added importance: "Jesus said, 'The man old in days will not hesitate to ask a small child seven days old about the place of life, and he will live. For many who are first will become last, and they will become one and the same.'"[22]

Taken literally, this makes no sense. Some would say it is apocryphal drivel, resembling nothing in the New Testament. Wrong. Picking up a prayer from the sayings collection known as Q, the gospels of Matthew (11:25) and Luke (10:21) both have Jesus say the following: "I thank thee, Father, Lord of heaven and earth, that thou hast hidden these things from the wise and understanding and revealed them to babes; yea, Father, for such was thy gracious will." If the small child or babe is not the new disciple or believer, who else is?

The number of days meshes *Gos. Thom.* 4 and the story from Secret Mark. The "child of seven days" is the equivalent to the young man in Secret Mark, for "after six days, Jesus told him what to do and in the evening the young man comes to him, wearing a linen cloth over [his] naked [body]. And he remained with him that night, for Jesus taught him the secret of the kingdom of God."[23] When that all-night session ended, the young man was a child seven days old who knew the mystery of the kingdom.

The *Gospel of Thomas*, subject to more than four decades of study, is known to have appeared in different versions, as determined simply by comparing sayings in Greek fragments with the Coptic manuscript. "We probably should be speaking of multiple versions of the *Gospel of Thomas*," Marvin Meyer once remarked to a seminar on the text.[24] Many New Testament scholars quite naturally take *Thomas* seriously to study comparisons of the parables, proverbs, and other sayings of Jesus that also appear in the canonical gospels.

But many also shy away from assigning authenticity to sayings peculiar to *Thomas*, such as 37 and 21 relating to baptism. Even *Gos. Thom.* 4, with its parallel motif in the wise "babes" praised by Jesus in Matthew and Luke, is often ignored. Much of *Thomas* shows traces of sectarian (though arguably not "gnostic") emendations. The end of *Gos. Thom.* 4, for instance, is also translated "become a single one," a term that appears often enough in that text to suggest wording introduced by celibate sectarians or monks. But *Gos. Thom.* 4's linking of the "child of seven days" with the idea that "many who are first will become last" would not be strange; that cryptic Jesus axiom appears twice (9:35 and 10:31) in Mark's section on requirements for discipleship.

The phrase "and after six days" shows up twice in Original Mark. It comes not only at the start of the young man's ceremony but also earlier when it begins Mark's story of the transfiguration (9:2). A common theory in the 1900s was that the transfiguration story originated as an appearance of the risen Christ, that is, a postresurrection vision of Jesus that Mark moved back into the life of Jesus. Mark portrays Peter, James, and John as experiencing a vision after accompanying Jesus to a mountaintop. Dressed in a radiant white garment, Jesus talked to Moses and Elijah, and a voice from heaven is heard. The scene recalls Moses' encounter with God on Mount Sinai (Exod 24), which had been clouded over for six days until the seventh day when God appeared as a bright fire and spoke to Moses.

But since "after six days" in the young man account appears to be a baptism, an initiation rite should be suspected here, especially since the two episodes are paralleled in Act 3's chiasm. Mark's point seems to be that the trio of disciples botched the vision experience. Spokesman Peter was dumbfounded at the sight and proposed making booths for the three figures. "For he did not know what to say, for they were exceedingly afraid," says Mark 9:6. Walking down the mountain, Jesus told them to say nothing about this until the Son of Man arose from the dead. That instruction also confounded the three disciples.

Luke Balks at Ritual Words

The Gospel of Matthew (17:1), like Mark, begins the transfiguration story with the phrase "And after six days." But Luke (9:28) says instead, "Now about eight days after these sayings . . ." Remember that Luke picks up nothing from Mark about the mysterious young man character. And Luke will have nothing to do, I suspect, with the barely disguised symbols of secret baptismal rituals—certainly not with the two-shall-become-one words attributed to Jesus in Mark 10:2–9. Luke's Jesus speaks only briefly (16:18) of divorce, saying that a man commits adultery when he divorces and marries another, or marries a divorced woman. In other words, Luke surely recognized the six-day reference in Mark as the introductory period before the overnight induction as a follower. He omits completely the young man account but still wants to use the transfiguration story, so he transforms the suggestive ritual phrase "after six days" into a vague reference for elapsed time. In that way, no implication can be made in the Gospel of Luke that Peter, James, and John flunked the visionary part of their initiation.

But, it might be asked, weren't Peter, James, and John already initiated? If not initiated when they were appointed to the Twelve (3:13–19), weren't they at some point soon thereafter? That is hardly certain. The only other time Mark says the "secret of the kingdom of God" was given was when Jesus answered a question about his parables asked by "those who were about him with the twelve" (4:10). When Jesus answers "them," it could mean only "those who were about him," not including the disciples. Just two episodes earlier, Mark described the crowd that "was sitting <u>about him</u>" (3:32) and "those who sat <u>about him</u>" (3:34) as his true family members, in contrast to his actual mother and brothers who were "outside" calling for Jesus because they thought him crazy. When Peter and the other eleven were named as disciples, Mark said, "He appointed twelve to be <u>with him</u>" and to preach and cast out demons (3:14–15).

First-Century Ascents to the Heavens

Morton Smith declared that claims of heavenly ascent by humans had circulated through the eastern Mediterranean lands from ancient times and were the keys to understanding the transfiguration account.[25] "The stories of Jesus' transfiguration seem distorted reflections of such an illusory ascent into the heavens, together with a few disciples," Smith wrote.[26] Some Jewish sages of that period engaged in mystical studies inspired by passages in the Hebrew Bible, such as the whirlwind on which Elijah ascended accompanied by chariots and horses of fire (2 Kgs 2:11). But Jewish sages and the earliest rabbis also warned of the dangers inherent in these visions. The apocryphal *Secret Book of James* from the Nag Hammadi Library describes James and Peter kneeling in prayer, hearing music, and beholding sights as their hearts reached the first and second heavens, but they were not permitted to view the Majesty in the third because other disciples came interrupting their reverie with questions.

The apostle Paul said he ascended skyward into the heavens, but he, too, was cautious describing how it happened and claimed he could not reveal what he heard at the third level. In 2 Cor 12:1–5, Paul apologetically boasts of his own heavenly ascent, albeit speaking indirectly of himself. A footnote in *The HarperCollins Study Bible* commented, "The *person* is Paul himself, who . . . is describing one ecstatic experience." And further: "Heavenly journeys were a popular means of claiming divine authentication and were apparently used by Paul's opponents for this purpose."[27]

Those first five verses in 2 Cor 12 (NRSV used here), by the way, were written as a chiasm:

A It is necessary to **boast;** nothing is to be gained by it, but I will go on
    B to visions and revelations of the Lord. I know a **person** *(anthro-*
    pos) in Christ who fourteen years ago
        C **was caught up** to the third heaven—
            D **whether in the body or out of the body I do not know;**
            God knows.
                E And I know that such a person
            D' **whether in the body or out of the body I do not know;**
            God knows—
        C' **was caught up** in Paradise
    B' and heard things that are not to be told, that no **mortal** *(anthro-*
    pos) is permitted to repeat.
A' On behalf of such a one I will **boast,** but on my own behalf I will
not **boast,** except of my weaknesses.

In the last half of the twentieth century, a number of leading-edge
scholars have found that Mark, Q, and the *Gospel of Thomas* are likely
to contain the oldest materials—along with Paul's letters—for research-
ing the beginnings of the Jesus movement. When new manuscripts or
fragments have surfaced, these scholars have reviewed long-known
apocryphal texts and reread New Testament writings in that light
despite the sometimes jarring or curious elements in the new finds. And
they do this knowing that many other scholars, by creed or personal
preference, do not deal with noncanonical works, regarding them as
imaginative, often heretical, writings.

More the pity, for the assembled evidence from biblical and extrabib-
lical sources strongly points to a seven-day initiation and baptism that
incorporated a ritual climax of dying and rising with Jesus, signified by
wearing a linen shroud, then trampling on this garment of shame to
reject the sins of the world, and stepping into baptismal water naked
and unashamed. The initiate was returning, at least in symbolic ways,
to the pre-fall whole human, neither simply male nor simply female.
The white garment stood for this new life that would continue in
heaven. The nighttime culmination after six days may have also
included heavenly visions. At the least, in the view of Original Mark, the
compilers of Q, and *Thomas,* these born-again babes in faith received
revelations and secrets that were outside the grasp of ordinary sages.

Notes

1. Sherman E. Johnson, "Response," in *Longer Mark: Forgery, Interpolation, or Old Tradition?* (ed. William Wuellner; Colloquy 18; Berkeley, Calif.: Center for Hermeneutical Studies, 1976), 26.

2. Morton Smith, *The Secret Gospel: The Discovery and Interpretation of the Secret Gospel According to Mark* (New York: Harper & Row, 1973), 17. I substituted "young man" and "secret" for "youth and "mystery" in Smith's translation.

3. Risto Uro, ed., *Thomas at the Crossroads: Essays on the Gospel of Thomas* (Edinburgh: T&T Clark, 1998), 1; Ron Cameron, ed., *The Other Gospels: Non-Canonical Gospel Texts* (Philadelphia: Westminster, 1982); Stephen J. Patterson, *The Gospel of Thomas and Jesus* (Sonoma, Calif.: Polebridge, 1993), 120; James M. Robinson, ed., *The Nag Hammadi Library in English* (rev. ed; San Francisco: Harper & Row, 1988).

4. Robert J. Miller, ed., "The Greek fragments of *The Gospel of Thomas*," in *The Complete Gospels* (Annotated scholars edition; San Francisco: HarperSanFranisco, 1994), 325.

5. Jonathan Z. Smith, "The Garments of Shame," *History of Religions* 5 (1966): 217–38.

6. Ibid., 218.

7. Ibid., 237.

8. Ibid., 220.

9. Ibid., 235, 233.

10. Ibid., 236

11. Ibid., 237.

12. Ibid., 232–33.

13. Dennis R. MacDonald, *There Is No Male and Female: The Fate of a Dominical Saying in Paul and Gnosticism* (Harvard Dissertations in Religion 20; Philadelphia: Fortress, 1987).

14. Wayne A. Meeks, "The Image of the Androgyne: Some Uses of a Symbol in Earliest Christianity," *History of Religions* 13 (February 1974): 165–208.

15. Ibid., 208, 181.

16. Ibid., 185, 188.

17. Ibid., 208.

18. Robin Scroggs and Kent I. Groff, "Baptism in Mark: Dying and Rising with Christ," *Journal of Biblical Literature* 92 (1973): 531–48.

19. Ibid., 548.

20. Morton Smith, *Clement of Alexandria and a Secret Gospel of Mark* (Cambridge: Harvard University Press, 1973), 187–88.

21. John Dart, "The Two Shall Become One," *Theology Today* 35 (October 1978): 321–25.

22. Robinson, *The Nag Hammadi Library in English,* 126.

23. Smith, *The Secret Gospel,* 16–17.

24. Also, Marvin Meyer, *Secret Gospels,* 98: "If, then, sayings in the Thomas tradition may have gone through significant change and modification, we may well speak of Gospels of Thomas rather than a *Gospel of Thomas.*"

25. Smith, *The Secret Gospel,* 108–11. Also, Smith, "The Origin and History of the Transfiguration Story," *Union Seminary Quarterly Review* 36 (fall 1980): 39–44.

26. Smith, *The Secret Gospel,* 110.

27. *The HarperCollins Study Bible,* NRSV (New York: Harper Collins, 1989), 2179, footnotes to 2 Cor 12:1–12.

CHAPTER 11

Editor's Motives, Luke's Preferences

HAVING SHELVED MY INITIAL FINDINGS about Original Mark for nearly a decade, I didn't follow New Testament studies as closely as I had in the 1970s and 1980s. Upon pulling my notes from storage in the late 1990s, I was consumed by uncovering one new chiastic puzzle after another, occasionally thinking I had exhausted Mark's ingenuity only to find new networks of words. When I did look up to scan the biblical studies landscape, I saw a growing pack of scholars doing their ABCB'A's on Bible texts.

"What are we to make of this current critical zeal for chiasm?" Robert M. Fowler had asked already in a 1991 book on Mark. He praised Joanna Dewey's "convincing case" in Mark 2:1–3:6, but suggested that typographical displays of passages arranged concentrically are not always convincing under close examination.[1] Good point, I thought. The successive indentation of verses, all neatly labeled with letters and then reversed after midpoint, may simply give the illusion of chiasms unless they meet requirements of consistency and clever connections. Some scholars proposed chiasms in a casual, "by-the-way" manner. Others gave repeated chiastic examples that they claimed clarified an author's intent, including patterns in Mark.

This added attention to concentric word designs was encouraging and, to be truthful, worrisome: encouraging because if chiasms were not being dismissed as fanciful or inconsequential, then my own efforts might not fall flat; worrisome because someone else may have already found the lengthy patterns in Mark! As far as I could tell, no one had. Some intriguing studies had appeared. The most challenging to me was published in 1994 by Father John Breck, a professor at St. Vladimir's Orthodox Theological Seminary.[2] He proposed that biblical Mark has—except for a few gaps—a succession of sixty-six chiasms from front to end. I agreed basically with more than half of his episodic chiasms, disagreed with others, and thanked him silently for several things I had missed.[3] However, his book did force me to admit that there were episodic chiasms in the section I assigned to an editor.

Breck also cited an article from 1985 in which Catholic scholar M. Philip Scott proposed a gospel-length chiasm.[4] It has problems. Scott's chiasm takes only ten steps to reach a midpoint at Mark 9:7 before reversing the pattern. Moreover, those steps were sometimes two verses apart or two *chapters* apart—a disparity that gives a researcher too much leeway to locate matching words and motifs. Still, the larger scholarly trend was heartening. More sleuths were joining the hunt.

Ignoring the Linchpin

During my research hiatus, however, no one seemed to see the promise in the published theory of Helmut Koester, namely, that Luke used an unedited version of Mark and that Matthew worked with the edited version, the one that became canonical Mark.[5] Here was a key reason why the large and overlapping chiasms in Mark went undiscovered for centuries. Would-be discoverers would have hit the wall every time they tried to tie chiastic steps to parts of the big chunk inserted by the editor in the first half of the Gospel. Of the three episodes removed by the editor, the mid-Gospel episode in which Jesus sets his face toward Jerusalem was damaging. It neatly divided the Gospel between the Galilee half and the on-to-Jerusalem half. That pivot point had catchwords and motifs that, had they been left in Mark, would have caused readers to recall the Gospel's opening words and make many other chiastic connections.

I can only speculate that Koester's idea made no progress partly because when he postulated this editor, he also pointed to the controversial Secret Mark episode as an example of the instability of religious texts in that era. Koester thought the episode was inserted by someone into the original gospel, then removed again before the Gospel of Mark assumed its final form.

One of the few scholars to assess Koester's theory at length was a former student of his, Philip Sellew. He contended that Luke saw but omitted the big section before 8:27 because Luke did not use duplicate stories. More than that, Sellew called 6:45–8:26 an integral part of "Original Mark" (a term chosen by Sellew over Koester's "proto-Mark") for plot reasons; that is, the denigration of the disciples there was "crucial in the portrayal of this central narrative theme."[6] My sense, however, was that the editor overdid the berating of the disciples and used other language untypical of the author. Sellew disagreed with Koester also by suggesting that the Secret Mark fragment was inserted into Mark, not in the first century, but in the late second century by Clement's Alexandria church. One piece of evidence, he said, was that when the young man at Jesus' arrest is introduced at 14:51–52, it says literally, "And a *certain youth (neaniskos tis)* was following." Mark and other gospel writers employ such wording "when introducing a *previously unmentioned character*" (Sellew's italics).[7] Sellew said it was "unsatisfying" to have this young man as a different person than the one in the Secret Mark fragment, or even different from the young man in the tomb.

On the contrary, I find it satisfying because the *neaniskos* is a character type, an exemplar, and Mark scattered throughout his gospel story alternate heroes and potential messengers who could bear witness to the various events in Jesus' ministry. Mark, puzzle-maker extraordinaire and one who delighted in hidden clues and in parables as riddles not comprehended by outsiders, does not disclose to the reader all that is happening in the gospel story. The appearance of another young man at Jesus' arrest—wearing only a linen cloth *(sindon)* like that used to wrap a corpse—is likely yet another initiate who was with Jesus at Gethsemane as Peter, James, and John were at a distance away, assigned to be on watch but repeatedly falling asleep. It was not satisfying to have the beloved young man initiated by Jesus and the young man at 14:51–52 as the same person because the question arises as to why the young man at Jesus' arrest was still wearing the linen cloth symbolic of dying and not a white garment symbolic of his rebirth. The young man in the empty tomb wears the white robe of "a child of seven days," one fully initiated into new, eternal life. Therefore, in terms of plot, it would be plausible to link the young man whom Jesus loved with the one who alone rolled back the stone, who sat "on the right," dressed in white, and announced the gospel: "You seek Jesus of Nazareth, who was crucified. He has risen, he is not here" (16:6).

To be fair, Koester's theories about Secret Mark grew more complicated after he presented his basic idea of an editor (chapter 3). By 1990,
Koester said that after Luke used the earliest version of Mark and
Matthew used a version "amplified" by the long trip to Bethsaida, a new
edition appeared (that could account for phrases that Luke and
Matthew supposedly copied faithfully from Mark but are now different
in Mark), then a Secret Mark edition, and finally what became canonical Mark.[8] John Dominic Crossan, on the other hand, said Secret Mark
was the original gospel, but that its young man story was dismembered
and scattered about the Gospel by whoever edited the canonical version.[9] Recently, Scott G. Brown disputed the theory that Secret Mark
was the first version. He told me by email on May 6, 2003, that in a
forthcoming book he will argue that Mark wrote the Gospel we see
today, then wrote an expanded, more spiritual *Secret Gospel of Mark* for
advanced believers, as stated by Clement of Alexandria. Brown and I
agree that the original author wrote the two-part young man story that
brackets Mark 10:35–45, a point he made in his 1999 doctoral dissertation.[10] Rather than critiquing these studies, I have put heaping por-
tions of finely layered chiasms on the dinner table with a menu that I
think distinguishes the chef-created entrees from the short-order cook's
superfluous "miracle" side dishes and deletions. One too many cooks
tainted this literary fete. But finding the original recipes allows us to
serve the meal anew.

Luke's "Little Omission"

The general neglect of the editor theory and Secret Mark left me with a
chance to show how the two were connected in a way previously unsus-
pected. Nothing in my renewed research was appearing to contradict
evidence that the oldest New Testament gospel had three major stages
of composition: (1) Original Mark, (2) Edited Mark, and (3) Mark with
"longer endings," passages added after Mark 16:8 by others.

Another matter remained. Despite the sheer number of chiastic
patterns covering every stitch of word-coded passages to insure a confident reconstruction of Mark, I had to offer reasonable motives for
Luke's ignoring and the editor's deleting the young-man story in
Mark's tenth chapter. I had reached some tentative ideas years earlier
on what could be called Luke's "little omission." Now I thought it could
be explained.

At least three reasons coalesce. First, as discussed in the last chapter, Luke evidently did not want to use allusions to the early church's baptism/initiation rites and perhaps did not wish to depict Jesus himself inducting a follower into the movement. In Luke, John the Baptist says before Jesus arrives on the scene that the one to come will baptize with the Holy Spirit and with fire. And Jesus later says, "I have a baptism to be baptized with" (Luke 12:50). But Luke and Matthew do not portray Jesus baptizing anyone. The Gospel of John is ambivalent: saying he did, then saying only his disciples performed baptisms (3:22–26; 4:1–2). At any rate, Luke changed the ritually important "after six days" phrase before the transfiguration story to "after about eight days," skips the "two-shall-become-one" discussion in Mark's tenth chapter, and ignores the appearances in biblical Mark of young men in the arrest scene and in the empty tomb—perhaps because they are wearing baptismal garb.

A second motive for Luke to bypass the Secret Mark story is that Luke frequently softens the harsh portrayal of the Twelve. As such, Luke apparently does not want Mark's nameless characters depicted as alternate heroes to the Twelve, Jesus' family, Salome, and Mary Magdalene. Luke seems to reject Mark's story line that has a beloved male follower, or the prototype of one, showing the very devotion, courage, and special knowledge that the Twelve and others lacked. From Luke's point of view, the beloved "young man" figure has to go. Also, Luke altered the story of the most admirable woman, who in Mark did "a beautiful thing" for Jesus by anointing him beforehand for burial. In Mark (14:3–9), Jesus predicted that what the unnamed woman did with the expensive ointment would be long remembered. In Luke's version (7:36–50), she is a sinner who serves as a better host than Peter by welcoming Jesus into the house with kisses and by wetting and anointing his feet. Luke ends the story with Jesus forgiving her sins—and with no implication that she is a memorable figure to be henceforth extolled. Even the centurion by the cross, who exclaims in Mark, "Truly this man was the Son of God" (15:39), is said by Luke to praise God but to say only of Jesus, "Certainly this man was innocent" (23:47).

Finally, prior to reaching Mark 10, Luke had already used in his narrative two accounts of Jesus raising young people from the dead. In an account found only in Luke, Jesus raises another "young man" from the dead (7:11–17). In the city of Nain, Jesus takes pity upon a widowed mother whose son has just died. Addressing the corpse, Jesus says,

"Young man, I say to you, arise." The young man does so. Onlookers glorify God and exclaim, "A great prophet has arisen among us!" This feat comes amid other healings in Luke and just before Jesus tells the inquiring disciples of John the Baptist that he has fulfilled many of the messianic expectations with these wonders, including that "the dead are raised up" (7:22). For Luke's purposes, then, this raising of a corpse in the seventh chapter establishes Jesus' messianic credentials early in his ministry.

Also, in his next chapter, Luke borrowed the episode from Mark in which the daughter of a man named Jairus (Mark 5:35–43 = Luke 8:49–56) was revived by Jesus. That means that at this point Luke's Jesus has raised two youths. Next, in Luke 9, he greatly condenses Mark's story of the boy convulsed by a spirit but eliminates any suggestion that the boy *died* as the demon left (Luke 9:37–42; cf. Mark 9:26–27). By the time Luke reaches the young man's resurrection in Original Mark, he is likewise disinterested in having Jesus perform another resuscitation miracle here. An intriguing possibility is that, for his story of raising the "young man" in Nain, Luke drew inspiration from both Jesus' raising of a woman's brother in Original Mark and Elijah's raising a widow's son in 1 Kings.

Editor's Miracle Motives

Like Luke, whoever altered Original Mark wanted to signal soon the significance of Jesus' accomplishments in the light of Israel's history. The editor did this by grafting six more miracles onto the Gospel after 6:46. With the fourth of these miracles, when Jesus cures a deaf mute, the editor says people exclaimed, "He has done everything well; he even makes the deaf to hear and the mute to speak" (7:37 NRSV). The restoring of hearing and speech to the afflicted recalls Isaiah 35:5, where the Hebrew prophet proclaims what will happen when Israel is redeemed.

Seminary professor Wolfgang Roth, as credited in chapter 4, enumerated Jesus' supernatural acts, comparing their number to the Jewish tradition that Elijah did eight and Elisha did sixteen. But I had difficulty with Roth's totals, and not simply because he ruled out the role of an editor. The crowd's observation, "He has done everything well," was meaningful to Roth because by his count the affirmation came after the sixteenth miracle occasion. But to do that, Roth left out one occasion when Jesus went about Galilee "casting out demons" (Mark 1:39). And

Roth also counted the bracketed stories of healing the bleeding woman and raising Jairus's daughter as only one miracle (Mark 5:21–43). Whether the crowd's exclamation was after sixteen or eighteen feats did not matter, I decided.

But it also seemed to me that *both* the editor and Mark's original author were keeping miracle counts. The original author was being purposeful about the number of specific feats. The editor was tallying both specific feats and the summary descriptions of healings/exorcisms.

Original Mark

If we ignore four short summary descriptions of healings and exorcisms, Jesus' total of individual healings, casting out demons, and other supernatural acts comes to exactly sixteen, including the raising of the young man. The last two in Original Mark would be shriveling the symbolic fig tree with a curse in chapter 11 and the resurrection. Mark has Jesus, calling himself the Son of Man, say "after three days he will rise" (9:31; 10:34), suggesting a shared feat with his Father—the crowning miracle of this man sent by God. Thus, Original Mark had sixteen specific mighty works of Jesus, matching the great Elisha.

Edited (Canonical) Mark

Someone in the late first century—our editor—evidently believed sixteen was not good enough. This self-appointed, or community-appointed, redactor felt that if Elijah had eight miracles to his credit and Elisha eight more, then why shouldn't Jesus have another eight? Elisha was granted "a double portion of the spirit" of Elijah, according to Hebrew Scriptures. Shouldn't Jesus receive a *triple* portion of the spirit?

The editor perhaps did not worry that the second feeding of the multitude hardly differed from the first one except for a lower number fed—four thousand. Walking on the sea is called by Koester a variant of the stilling of the sea storm. Aware that Original Mark has a blind man cured in the tenth chapter, the editor still adds another sight-restoring story. These doublets served a purpose: they allowed Jesus to equal or exceed Elisha's power in certain *types* of feats.

With two feedings of thousands, Jesus bested Elisha's feeding of one hundred people with twenty loaves (2 Kgs 4:42–44). With two displays of divine authority on the Sea of Galilee, Jesus equaled Elisha's parting

of the Jordan River and raising an ax head that had sunk. Whereas
Elisha called upon God first to blind and then to restore the sight of
attacking troops (2 Kgs 6:15–23), Jesus uses his God-given ability to cure
blind men on two separate occasions. As for raising the dead, Elisha
revived a mother's son (2 Kgs 4:18–27), a story that mimics the achievement by Elijah (1 Kgs 17:17–24). But early in Mark, Jesus had raised
two youths—the daughter of Jairus and the boy who was rigid as a
corpse—already having topped Elisha's one. To the editor, this could
have meant that Original Mark's raising of the young man is superfluous.

To bring the miracle total to twenty-four in the expanded gospel, the
editor counts both the specific feats *and* short summaries of healings.
Besides the four summaries in Original Mark, the editor adds a fifth in
6:54–56, where in villages beside the Sea of Galilee people brought to
him the sick on pallets. Those with diseases sought to touch him. This
summary appears to be written by borrowing elements from other miracles in Original Mark (1:32–34; 3:7–10). Once the young man story is
reached, the editor has twenty-one wonder-working instances. Then,
Jesus heals the blind beggar Bartimaeus (no. 22), curses the fig tree as he
approaches Jerusalem (no. 23), and cheats death (no. 24).

For both the original writer and the editor, the climactic crucifixion
carries a tension related to the godly spirit once possessed by Elijah. The
resurrection would complete a double portion of the spirit for Jesus in
Original Mark and a triple portion for Jesus in edited Mark. Though
Jesus thrice told his disciples with seeming confidence that after his
death he would rise again in three days, Jesus is depicted praying
moments before his arrest for an escape from this fate. Later, he pleads
on the cross for a rescue from God. He cried, "My God, my God, why
hast thou forsaken me?" (15:34). Bystanders thought he was calling
Elijah. Hinting that some truth or irony was at work, Mark likes to tease
the readers with onlookers' impressions. "Let us see whether Elijah will
come to take him down," they mocked in verse 36. Just then Jesus utters
a loud cry and breathes his last. In other words, Jesus succumbs before
what he hoped would be a last-minute rescue by God—or Elijah.

But if the editor was bent on boosting the miracle total, it might be
asked, why take out the dramatic resuscitation of an entombed corpse
and keep two episodes in which revived children were perhaps only
questionably dead? Could the editor have objected to the mutual love
between the young man and Jesus? Was the editor fearful that the nighttime rendezvous of Jesus with a seminude male sounded like a sexual

tryst? It would seem so. The editor did not object to the two young men appearing later in Mark; those segments were untouched. But the editor took care to excise both the long, initial story about this young man and the postscript at 10:46, since the latter verse said Jesus also loved the young man.

The editor had Jesus endorse strict behavior and pure thoughts, as indicated by Jesus' defining "defilement" and criticizing the purity rituals of the Pharisees at 7:1–23. At the close of this section (vv. 20–23), Jesus said,

> A What comes out of a **man** is what **defiles a man.**
>   B For **from within,** out of the heart of man, **come** <u>evil</u> thoughts:
>   C fornication, theft, murder, adultery, coveting, wickedness,
>   C' deceit, licentiousness, envy, slander, pride, foolishness.
>   B' All these <u>evil</u> things **come from within,**
> A' and they **defile a man.**

Yes, the editor knew how to do chiasms, too. But this one, which Breck did not list, breaks Original Mark's rule against double, or parallel, centers, that is, ABCC'B'A'. In Greek, as scholars have noted, the first six vices are plural nouns; the next six are singular nouns. Original Mark's author always used an ABCB'A' style of chiastic pattern.

The list, headed by fornication, is quite long, typical of the editor's emotional excesses and earthy language. The Gospel of Matthew, whose author followed the edited copy of Mark, cut these vices down to six. The editor fell short of Paul, who rattled off some twenty examples of wickedness in his Letter to the Romans and cited fifteen sins of the flesh in writing to the Galatians. Even if the editor himself had likened Jesus's "love" for the young man to "love your neighbor as yourself" (Mark 12:31), he must have worried about what readers could infer from the scene with the young man coming to Jesus wearing a linen cloth over his naked body, remaining with him overnight. The Hellenistic world knew of mystery religions in which licentious rites were cloaked under the guise of holiness.

The Editor's Geography

Question: Why did Jesus cross the sea? Answer: To get to the other side. Yet to Original Mark's lines about Jesus sending the disciples ahead of him to Bethsaida, the editor added a long, confusing travelogue from 6:47 through 8:26.[11] In Original Mark they no doubt arrived separately but directly in Bethsaida, then headed farther inland toward the villages of Caesarea Philippi. On the way, Jesus raises the "recognition" question to his disciples. His feats and fame had escalated to the point, or so the original narrative indicates, that now was the time to learn what people and his disciples thought of him.

Why did Jesus ask on the way to Caesarea Philippi? Eduard Schweizer, in his study of Mark, suggests that it was a very appropriate place. "According to rabbinical statements, it is on the boundary between the Holy Land and Gentile territory," he wrote. "This is the place where Jesus must decide whether he will abandon Israel or do the exact opposite—set out on the perilous journey to Jerusalem."[12] Original Mark had Jesus preaching to people who have come from Gentile lands as well as to Jewish crowds. Jesus' first venture outside Galilee was to sail with his disciples to the country of the Gerasenes in Gentile territory. Jesus cures a demoniac, expelling demons and sending them into a herd of two thousand swine—animals that would be raised in a non-Jewish land. The man freed of the demons began to proclaim what happened to him "in the Decapolis" (5:20), the large Gentile territory to the southeast of the Sea of Galilee.

The editor apparently wanted to take Jesus and his disciples much farther into Gentile territory. The entourage travels to Tyre (7:24) on the Mediterranean coast, where Jesus has an encounter with a Gentile woman whose daughter has an unclean spirit. Then the group leaves Tyre, goes through Sidon to the north "to the Sea of Galilee, through the region of the Decapolis" (7:31). Scholars have found that itinerary strange. "To travel from Tyre by way of Sidon in the direction of the lake is a detour, for which the reader would expect an explanation," observed scholar Bas van Iersel, who speculated that the writer "never knew the region from personal experience."[13] Scholars have disparaged Mark for faulty geography, but many of the errors occur in passages written by the editor. Consider this verse written by the editor in biblical Mark: "And he left there and went to the region of Judea and beyond the Jordan, and crowds gathered to him again; and again, as his custom was, he taught them" (10:1). Vocabulary unique to the editor occurs at 10:1. The word for "region" in Mark appears only in the editor's section at 7:24 and 7:31 in reference to Tyre and Sidon. Nowhere else does Mark write "crowds" (plural), observed scholar William L. Lane.[14] The

Greek word for "gathered to" occurs only at Mark 10:1; when people "gather" in Original Mark, other Greek words are used. The expression "as his custom was," or similar forms of "custom" or "accustomed," appears only here in Mark.[15]

By taking out the two-part young man episode rediscovered in 1958, the editor eliminated an episode that began, "And they come to Bethany." This Bethany, east of the Jordan River, is the traditional site of John the Baptist's activity (John 1:28).[16] This is another clue to the editor's bumbling. Knowing that Jesus earlier went to a Bethany on the other side of the Jordan, we can understand why Mark then took such pains at 11:1 to distinguish a second Bethany of the journey: "And when they drew near to Jerusalem, to Bethpage and Bethany, at the Mount of Olives, he sent two disciples. . . ." This done, Mark refers thereafter to this second Bethany without further description (11:11, 11:12, 14:3).

If future studies of Mark accept the presence of an editor, researchers will no doubt arrive at a clearer profile of the redactor. Certainly, the editor goes overboard in describing Jesus' emotions—having Jesus sigh heavily, actually groan, and viciously attack his disciples. The editor mimicked Original Mark by making the Twelve look bad, but he had Jesus rip into the dozen with a long series of accusing questions, which is uncharacteristic for the Gospel as a whole. Original Mark has Jesus showing only brief moments of impatience or anger with them. And in contrast to Original Mark's depiction of Jesus restoring a sufferer or a deceased person with a few words and a gesture, the editor twice has Jesus healing someone using his spittle and exaggerated efforts said to be characteristic of such tales in Greek-dominated culture. The editor's Jesus also uses coarse language—speaking of defecating in one case and, in another, describing Gentiles as "dogs," an ancient Jewish slur of non-Jews.

Though the editor composed some episodes chiastically within 6:47–8:26, that large section has stymied chiasm pursuers such as John Breck. He also begins a long chiasm (like my bridge code, which skips over that insertion; see pages 184–86) at Jesus' reviving a father's daughter and ends it with Jesus' reviving a father's epileptic son, but Breck includes nearly all of the editor's insertions along the way. Admitting he could not fit into his chiasm the blind man at Bethsaida (8:22–26), Breck conceded "unevenness in the quality of the various parallels."[17] In addition, his midpoint was ten verses long (7:14–23), a bulkiness at odds with the gospel author's practice of forming ever tighter centers.

Another big technical mistake made by some Markan scholars with chiastic proposals is the minimal interest they show in citing catchwords and matching phrases. Their tendency is to be satisfied with themes perceived to be similar or antithetical, but those judgments are often rightly seen as subjective. To signify the stepped parallels, Mark uses *both motifs and/or catchwords,* as does the Gospel of John, the Pauline Letters, and many Hebrew biblical books. Exceptions can occur. Sometimes the verbal hooks, grammatical parallels, Scripture references, numbers, and other gimmicks carry the burden. At other times, the motifs, actions, and ironies in the narrative are so striking that catchwords are less important, and may be absent.

Breck concluded that Mark "unquestionably relied on the principles of chiasmus to work out various sections of his gospel," but he was pessimistic about a grand overall scheme. "Perhaps there is a definitive pattern that will someday be recovered, to prove once and for all that the evangelist first created an elaborate plan and then followed it to the letter, although that seems unlikely," wrote Breck.[18]

Searching for the Center

Dutch scholar Iersel was encountering similar dead ends. In an extensive treatment published in 1998, the New Testament professor offered many good small chiasms, but what he published relied more on themes than catchwords. He faulted the larger chiastic attempts of Breck and others.[19] Mary Ann Tolbert and Hugh M. Humphrey separately suggested different thematic chiasms for Mark's middle section. Humphrey's structure identified the second resurrection prediction (9:30–32) as the midpoint, but Iersel declared that "a number of correspondences perceived by Humphrey are based on a selective if not arbitrary way of reading the text."[20]

Iersel limited his own chiastic steps in the middle section to five: two healings and the three resurrection predictions. "[I]t seems wiser, as long as no better proposals are put forward, to abandon a detailed concentric structuring," he wrote.[21] Iersel simplified his basic gospel-length chiasm to a mere outline in which "Galilee" (1:16–8:21) and "Jerusalem" (11:1–15:39) are the huge C sections and "the way" (8:27–10:45) is the middle (E). Claremont scholar Burton Mack, in a 1988 book primarily on mythic elements in Mark, presented his own candidate for a chiastic structure based solely on corresponding themes.[22] The transfiguration

(9:2–8) sits at Mack's center (G)—not an unusual choice. That scene "forms the central theme of the whole gospel," said Werner Kelber, who added, "Structurally, in terms of number of verses, it stands almost exactly at midpoint in the gospel story. . . . Outside of baptism this is the only time the life of Jesus is marked by divine intervention in visible and audible terms."[23]

As mentioned earlier, I had discovered belatedly that Original Mark includes two more verses (6:45–46) that Koester had labeled part of the editor's insertion. That find prompted me to seek again the likely center of Original Mark by tallying up the verses, as Kelber did above. My previous attempts were hasty and did not land very close to where Jesus declared it was time to head to Jerusalem (where I thought it should be). Nor did my tries take me close to what I was calling the "asymmetrical" midpoint for the gospel-length chiasm just before Jesus' third prediction (10:31). This time I took care to exclude four verses that were once assigned numbers (9:44, 46; 11:26; 15:28) but have been dropped from modern translations since the verses are missing from reliable manuscripts. That noted, I subtracted the editor's insertions and added the two deleted stories saved by Luke. I allowed one verse (now missing or truncated) for the separate arrivals of Jesus and the disciples in Bethsaida. Finally, by comparing the number of Greek words in the two-part Secret Mark story to episodes of similar length in Mark, I figured that would add 10 verses to the total for Original Mark.[24]

I came up with 305 verses on the front side and 305 on the back side. The last six verses on the front side were supplied by Luke 9:51–56, the episode removed by the editor and replaced by Mark 10:1. Mark 10:2 began the last 305 verses in Original Mark. Though counting verses can only give an approximation of the symmetrical center, this total brought us very close to the chiastic center below:

When the days drew near for him to be received up, he set his face to go to Jerusalem. And he sent messengers ahead of him [literally, "before his face"], who went and entered a village of the Samaritans, to make ready for him; but the people would not receive him because his face was set toward Jerusalem (Luke 9:51–53).[25]

Thanks, Luke.

Notes

1. Robert M. Fowler, *Let the Reader Understand: Reader-Response Criticism and the Gospel of Mark* (Minneapolis: Fortress, 1991), 151.

2. John Breck, *The Shape of Biblical Language: Chiasmus in the Scriptures and Beyond* (Crestwood, N.Y.: St. Vladimir's Seminary Press, 1994).

3. Ibid., 144–64.

4. M. Philip Scott, "Chiastic Structures: A Key to the Interpretation of Mark's Gospel," *Biblical Theology Bulletin* 15, no. 11 (January 1985): 17–26.

5. Helmut Koester, "History and Development of Mark's Gospel," in *Colloquy on New Testament Studies: A Time for Reappraisal and Fresh Approaches* (ed. Bruce C. Corley; Macon, Ga.: Mercer University Press, 1983), 35–85.

6. Philip Sellew, "Secret Mark and the History of Canonical Mark," in *The Future of Early Christianity: Essays in Honor of Helmut Koester* (ed. Birger A. Pearson; Minneapolis: Fortress, 1991), 242–57. Koester's theories on proto-Mark, but especially on Secret Mark, are discussed in Robert H. Gundry, *Mark: A Commentary on His Apology for the Cross* (Grand Rapids: Eerdmans, 1993), 603–23.

7. Sellew, "Secret Mark," 251–52.

8. Helmut Koester, *Ancient Christian Gospels: Their History and Development* (Harrisburg, Pa.: Trinity Press International, 1990), 285–86.

9. John Dominic Crossan, *Four Other Gospels: Shadows on the Contours of the Canon* (Minneapolis: Winston, 1985), 91–121; "Thoughts on Two Extracanonical Gospels," *Semeia* 49 (1990): 155–68; *The Historical Jesus: The Life of a Mediterranean Peasant* (San Francisco: Harper, 1991), 328–32, 411–16, 429–30.

10. Scott G. Brown, "The More Spiritual Gospel: Markan Literary Techniques in the Longer Gospel of Mark" (Ph.D. diss., University of Toronto, 1999); "On the Composition History of the Longer ('Secret') Gospel of Mark," *Journal of Biblical Literature* 122 (Spring 2003): 89–110.

11. Howard Clark Kee, *Miracle in the Early Christian World: A Study in Sociohistorical Method* (New Haven: Yale University Press, 1983), 206. In retrospect, it had been difficult to explain how Luke could place his version of the feeding story *at* Bethsaida (9:10) if, like Koester, I contended that Luke did not see the editor's reference to Bethsaida. Thus, Luke *did* see the place-name at Mark 6:45 but moved it, as explained by Kee. In reproducing the feeding story, Kee said, Luke changed some details: "[I]nstead of a desert area, as in Mark, the miracle takes place in the city of Bethsaida . . . which is consonant with Luke's emphasis throughout both volumes of his work [Luke-Acts] on the urban setting of the mission of Jesus and his Apostles" (p. 206). Having made Bethsaida the site of the mass feeding, Luke keeps Jesus and his disciples there for the identity question at Luke 9:18.

12. Eduard Schweizer, *The Good News according to Mark* (trans. Donald H. Madvig; Atlanta: John Knox, 1970), 171.

13. Bas M. F. van Iersel, *Mark: A Reader-Response Commentary* (JSNTSup 164; (Sheffield: Sheffield Academic Press, 1998), 252.

14. William L. Lane, *The Gospel of Mark* (Grand Rapids: Eerdmans, 1974), 351.

15. Another unique word for Mark also appears in the brief line inserted by the editor in place of the repentant robber story, "Those who were crucified with him also <u>reviled</u> him" (15:32b). The Greek *oneidizo* is also translated "reproach" or "upbraid" in the New Testament.

16. See Rainer Riesner, "Bethany Beyond the Jordan," in *The Anchor Bible Dictionary* (trans. Siegfried S. Schatzmann; New York: Doubleday, 1992), 1:703–5.

17. Breck, *The Shape of Biblical Language,* 169.

18. Ibid., 169–70.

19. Iersel, *Mark,* 84, 272–76. He cites Mary Ann Tolbert, *Sowing the Gospel: Mark's World in Literary-Historical Perspective* (Minneapolis: Fortress, 1991); and Hugh M. Humphrey, *He Is Risen! A New Reading of Mark's Gospel* (New York: Paulist, 1992).

20. Iersel, *Mark,* 272.

21. Ibid., 276.

22. Burton L. Mack, *A Myth of Innocence: Mark and Christian Origins* (Philadelphia: Fortress, 1988), 331.

23. Werner H. Kelber, *Mark's Story of Jesus* (Philadelphia: Fortress, 1979), 53. My tally of the verses in canonical Mark has the center around 9:32.

24. Studies that have numbered the verses in the Secret Mark episode (e.g., *The Complete Gospels,* op.cit., 411) have thirteen in the first part and two in the second. I think that's too high compared to the ratio of Greek words and verse numbers in the rest of Mark. I counted 159 Greek words in Secret Mark's first part. A sampling of comparable "action" episodes in canonical Mark shows that 9:2–10 has 155 words and 9 verses, 9:24–34 has 165 Greek words and 11 verses, 9:35–43 has 151 words and 9 verses, 11:12–20 has 160 words and 9 verses, and 14:1–9 has 158 words and 9 verses. Pending other analyses, I counted Secret Mark 1 as 9 verses and Secret Mark 2 as 1 verse; thus 10 more verses added to the total.

25. Remarkably, Luke must have kept most of the wording from Original Mark because nearly all the words have ties to many other chiasms. The RSV English can be deceiving. The word for "face" (*prosopon*) is in verses 51, 52, and 53; likewise the word *poreuomai* is the root of "go" (51), "went" (52), and "set toward" (53). The Greek word for "received up" (51) and "receive" (53) is not identical, although the meanings are related.

CHAPTER 12

In Praise of Secret Mark's Discoverer

"THIS WAS A PLEASANT SURPRISE," Morton Smith had written me from his Columbia University office on August 6, 1989. "Nothing so challenging and original has come in for a long time," he said. He was responding to a sixty-page summary I mailed to him on my initial research. That sentence of praise was typed over an earlier sentence that he had obliterated with a white "wipe-out" substance. His postscript indicated why: he gave me advance permission to quote any of his comments, and he wanted to choose his words carefully.

It might be expected that Smith would commend any plausible theory supporting his discovery, especially since my theory declared that the Secret Mark episode was pure Markan prose, part of the original gospel. Smith had rejected that possibility years before as too good to be true.

My request for his reactions did not come out of the blue. Smith had helped me with comments before. Our correspondence dated back to 1977, when he provided an encouraging critique of a conference paper I was giving on a Jesus saying in the *Gospel of Thomas* about the "small child seven days old." In addition, he periodically sent me journal offprints of his articles. In 1982, he wrote to me about a book manuscript on *Thomas* circulating among scholars that argued the sayings collection was written in the mid-first century, earlier than usually thought. "I hope it will find a publisher in spite of being intelligent and original (two major handicaps, as you know)," Smith wrote wryly.

We were both invited in 1985 as speakers at a University of Michigan symposium on "Jesus and the Gospels," which was cosponsored by a skeptics group linked to *Free Inquiry* magazine.[1] My paper on the brothers of Jesus depicted them as real, historical figures. Smith's talk would have surprised some seminary professors who have cringed at Smith's sarcastic treatment of certain Christian doctrines. Smith affirmed that Jesus was an actual person, responding in his customary acerbic manner to a speech by a British professor who cast doubt on the historical Jesus by arguing that since the Pauline Letters and other epistles in the New Testament said little about the earthly life of Jesus, their authors knew nothing about it, and thus there was no Jesus of history. Smith called the professor's argument "absurd." The paper also had "a great many trivial arguments," according to Smith, and "a piece of private mythology that I find incredible beyond anything I find in the gospels."

As for my basic ideas in 1989 on the original Gospel of Mark, Smith said he especially liked the roles Luke and the editor played. As he put it, the idea that biblical Mark may be an expansion of an earlier text that was used by Luke "has much more to be said for it than I realized, and certainly deserves to be published. That whoever made the expansion should also have [deleted material] is altogether likely, and some of your proposals to restore abbreviated material by reliance on Luke are persuasive."

However, on my chiastic patterns in the prologue, conclusion, and five major sections, Smith admitted he was "of two minds." He viewed Mark as a writer with few signs of literary craft or stylistic niceties. He admitted he was prejudiced on this, but his bias resulted from a long study of Mark, he said. "On the other hand, your evidence for your first chiasm—[Joanna] Dewey's for hers [2:1–3:6], and yours for taking it somewhat further [1:14–4:12]—is surprisingly good." Smith cautioned that scholars who find chiastic patterns in ancient texts tend to meet heavy resistance from peers. Smith cited a classics scholar who in the 1960s tried to show extensive chiasms in Homer, but he lost the battle against skeptical colleagues.

"Thinking this over," he said in another note to me, "I continue to be bothered by the weakness of many of the parallels/antitheses you have to rely on to work out the chiastic structures to such length." (In my own defense, most of the seven long patterns that I summarized showed only *some* of the catchwords and parallels because I wanted to squeeze each long concentric pattern on a single page. Also, I made improvements in later years.) He advised that I should blunt the attacks of doubters by featuring "only the clearest, strongest, central parts" of these long word patterns.

Arthur Dewey of Xaxier University also responded to my summary that summer of 1989. "First, this is very, very compelling," he wrote. "You have been able to suggest a number of solutions to problems that have been long outstanding. Your emphasis upon the anonymous followers is quite good." Dewey (no relation to Joanna Dewey) liked the arguments about Luke's supposed "great omission" and the editor's motive for adding more miracles. "The point about Jesus being 'bigger and better' than Elisha is capital," he said in his July 25, 1989 letter. Ominously, Dewey warned, "I think that your biggest opposition will come from those who would like the origins of Christianity to be plain and simple." He said my theories would place me among a group of New Testament scholars, including himself, who "are making things complicated, suggesting that our ancestors were complex and imaginative, too."

And like Smith, Dewey worried about the acceptance level for the lengthy chiastic designs. "You are making a major shift in the way scholars usually use chiasm in their arguments," he said. He indicated that his colleagues were comfortable with the appearance of short chiasms, seeing them as reflecting an oral culture in which brief concentric passages were easily remembered and recited. "You are assuming very much a written environment," he said.

A Gospel for Listeners *and* Readers

Indeed, several specialists view Mark as written expressly for an oral culture. "Mark's gospel was written to be heard, and hearing requires performance," wrote Donald H. Juel, a New Testament theology professor at Princeton Theological Seminary.[2] Indeed, David Rhoads, who teaches at Lutheran School of Theology at Chicago, has performed Mark's Gospel live in one-man shows and on video. In 2002, Elizabeth Struthers Malbon published *Hearing Mark: A Listener's Guide*.[3] And Whitney Shiner of George Mason University has given exuberant readings of Markan passages at seminars. "It 'works' orally," claimed Juel, saying whenever he had students watch a performance of Mark they reacted emotionally. One student was upset. She suspected the actor reciting Mark was an unbeliever because of "his portrayal of the disciples as buffoons," said Juel.[4]

Obviously, a writer needs readers. In Mark, Jesus asks three times, "Have you not read . . . ," to the Pharisees (2:25); to chief priests, scribes, and elders (12:10); and to the Saducees (12:26). The Scripture citations by Jesus are rejoinders to literate religious authorities, to be sure. But Mark's author also writes in an aside, "Let the reader understand" (13:14), when referring to a "desolating sacrilege" in the tumultuous end times. That seems aimed at a reader of Mark, but Joanna Dewey suggested the "reader" refers instead to a reader of the book of Daniel, where the cryptic phrase appears.[5]

I straddle the fence on the question of oral or written emphasis in Mark. The gospel author writes for the pleasure of ear and eye. An aspect of Mark previously unknown—the enormously prolific number of chiastic patterns—indicates to me that both listeners and readers are being served. For recitations, the speaker can find chiasms as small as a sentence or two, or a single episode. Orators of greater skill, however, might tackle the longer chiasms. "Find what section(s) you like, and you'll find a word pattern to help you," a teacher could tell students.

But when well-read people of that era found the gospel-length macrocode that ends up at an asymmetric midpoint (10:31), then happened to find half-gospel-length chiasms within either side, they probably said, "Aha," or "Lo, behold." When they discovered the same principle applied to the symmetrical midpoint for the formal chiastic structure, they might have murmured anachronistically, "Wow!" They probably saw that one can chop all long chiasms in half: "Zounds! They multiply faster than hares."

Readers must have had great fun doing a kind of early-centuries "word search" within the blocks of solidly packed Greek letters (no spaces, no punctuation, no indentations). Finding the start and end of various lengths of chiasms, the readers would chuckle at the double entendre in Jesus' words that "many that are first will be last, and the last first" (10:31). There was extra meaning in "For there is nothing hid, except to be made manifest; nor is anything secret, except to come to light" (4:22). Those who liked the narrative's subtle ironies surely enjoyed the below-surface chiastic links. Such steps wedded the phrase "when the bridegroom is taken away" to the arrest of Jesus after a kiss from Judas or the ironical contrast between Peter's protestations that he would die with Jesus before disavowing him and the crucified robber's declaration of Jesus' innocence while dying with him. To find most of the patterns would require reading and rereading the text, something I can vouch for.

A related issue, I think, is the challenge that New Testament scholar Richard Bauckham has raised to the common belief that the four author-evangelists wrote their gospels for the communities in which they lived. "Why should he go to the considerable trouble of writing a Gospel for a community to which he was regularly preaching?" he asked.[6] Most of the Christian leaders in that period "moved around" the eastern Mediterranean cities quite a bit, as did merchants, soldiers, health seekers, enthusiasts for the pan-Hellenic games, and government officials, said Bauckham, who teaches New Testament studies at St. Mary's College, University of St. Andrews, Scotland. The gospel authors' "implied readership is not a specific audience, large or small, but an indefinite readership: any or every church of the late first century to which his Gospel might circulate," Bauckham said.[7]

Timing, Timing, Timing

Studies like Bauckham's were either not yet published or had escaped my notice back in 1989–1990, when I had ended my own attempts to find a publisher. My reluctance was based on time constraints—my job at the *L.A. Times* and other journalistic work. Certainly, the mixed reactions from Morton Smith, Arthur Dewey, and a few other scholars also caused me to shy from opposing standard views on Mark. It was one thing for me to write journalistic-style books and articles on the discovery and scholarly analyses of Christian and gnostic manuscripts found in Nag Hammadi, Egypt; it was another to present my own research findings as a journalist. I would need clear, undeniable evidence of Mark's use of the underlying "coded" writing.

Timing surely helps in scholarship and journalism. News writers and editors know that you can be "too early" on some stories. Journalists typically have a plateful of potential news stories they want to report. They are loath to push aside these surefire stories-in-waiting to take on new, complicated claims on unfamiliar topics for fear that few would understand them or care—even if the claims turned out to be true. When obscure issues do rise to public awareness and stimulate curiosity, the moment may be right. My decade-later return to chiastic structures in Mark—uncovering larger, smaller and overlapping patterns—gave me the solid evidence I needed at a time, coincidentally, when New Testament studies were increasingly admiring Mark's narrative skill and the art of chiastic patterns.

The only obstacle was the lingering dismissal of Smith's controversial theories in academia. At his death in 1991, some New Testament specialists thought his ideas involved a forgery and many thought the Secret Mark fragment was a piece of apocrypha hardly worth bothering with.

Of course, Smith sowed the seeds of that disdain. What Smith meted out to academics he regarded as mediocre or mistaken returned on his head tenfold after the 1973 publication of his two books on Secret Mark. A scathing review by Jesuit scholar Joseph Fitzmyer compared Smith's enterprise to the religious freakiness of the early '70s, when "all you have to tell a publisher is that you have discovered a 'secret gospel,' and Faust sells his soul." Edwin Yarnuachi wrote: "It is not likely that Professor Smith will succeed in damaging the reputation of Jesus. However, he many well have irreparably damaged his own."[8]

One major objection to Smith's story was that he was the only person—or so it was thought—to see and photograph the handwritten copy of a portion of the letter from Clement of Alexandria that quoted an episode in Secret Mark. Yet, timing was propitious in this part of the story, too. By the year 2000, Charles Hedrick, a manuscript detective of sorts, would cast out some demons of doubt surrounding the discovery.

More Photos and the Missing Book

While he worked on the Nag Hammadi manuscripts, Hedrick helped me many times at Claremont to understand those texts, even after he joined the faculty at Southwest Missouri State University. Like others who studied the "secret books," "apocalypses," and "gospels" never seen before and found in 1945 in buried jars in the upper Nile region of Egypt, Hedrick valued apocryphal writings for illuminating the history of early Christianity. In 1995, for instance, he was working in the Berlin Egyptian Museum when he chanced upon some fragments of a parchment manuscript written in Coptic. He later learned that another American scholar, Paul Mirecki of the University of Kansas, had also come across the fragments four years earlier. Collaborating on a study of the thirty-four pieces from thirty pages, they dubbed this previously unknown text the *Gospel of the Savior*. Missing were the start and end of the Christian text, but the fragments had a dialogue between "the savior" (Jesus) and disciples such as Andrew, John, and Jude (or Judas), as they anticipated his crucifixion and resurrection.[9]

With his long interest in noncanonical writings, Hedrick was acquainted with Smith's work. In his personal dealings, Hedrick said that he found the Columbia professor "always courteous and polite" despite a reputation for being "somewhat idiosyncratic, irascible and downright obnoxious." Hedrick admitted that Smith "did not suffer those whom he considered fools gladly, and I have seen others on more than one occasion on the receiving end of his public ire."[10]

In 1990, Hedrick lectured in Israel on the Secret Gospel of Mark to students and staff participating in archaeological digs at the site of ancient Caesarea Philippi. After hearing the lecture, Old Testament professor Nikolaos Olympiou of the University of Athens volunteered to take Hedrick to the Mar Saba Greek Orthodox Monastery to see if together they could locate the book containing the copy of Clement's letter on the final blank pages. The book was an edition of the letters of Ignatius of Antioch, published by Isaac Voss in 1646. When they got to the monastery, however, the men were told that the book had been taken to the Greek patriarchate's library in Jerusalem.

What they didn't know then was that Smith had already reported that an Episcopal priest, Thomas Talley, was told ten years earlier that a Father Melito had taken it to Jerusalem to the patriarchate. Details of the book's transfer in the mid-1970s did not emerge until 2003 when Guy G. Stroumsa, director of the Center for the Study of Christianity at Hebrew University in Jerusalem, wrote up his first-hand experience of seeing the complete book at the monastery.[11]

By the 1990s, inquiries by Hedrick and Olympiou at the patriarchate yielded little at first. In 1992, the two men were told the book could not be located. Eventually, Olympiou found the priest who had served as librarian there from 1975 to 1990, one Kallistos Dourvas, a former student of Professor Olympiou at the University of Athens, who was serving a parish outside Athens, Hedrick said.[12] The librarian told Olympiou that shortly after he received the Voss book from the monastery (in 1977, he said), he removed the two end pages with the script and photographed them. Indeed, the priest gave black-and-white photographs of the manuscript to Olympiou, "who later gave copies to me," said Hedrick.

Hedrick had informed me in the late 1990s that a professor from Athens had located someone with photographs, but not the same ones taken by Smith. He said he was trying to learn whether the pages themselves were available. Since I was going to Jerusalem in March 2000, to take part in a conference on religion and the news media, I tried to look up the current librarian, Bishop Aristarchos. But the patriarchate's library—a small, stand-alone building in the Greek Orthodox quarters adjacent to the Church of the Holy Sepulchre—was closed. I was advised to fax Aristarchos with my inquiry. The bishop, who spoke English, telephoned me later at my hotel to say that neither the Voss book nor the pages had been found. Aristarchos complained that the previous librarian, one who had succeeded Kallistos, left the library in relative disarray.

I didn't know that Olympiou had had better luck. He had seen the Voss book (minus the Clement letter) in the library at the end of 1998. Then in June 2000, with Aristarchos's help at the library, he secured photographs of the Voss book. And that same month in Greece, he obtained color photographs from Kallistos. Olympiou permitted use of the photos for an article Hedrick wrote in the September–October 2000 issue of *The Fourth R,* a magazine of the Westar Institute. In an interview with Hedrick in August 2000, Kallistos said that as long as he was librarian (until 1990), the Clement letter was kept with the Voss book, though as separate items. "Kallistos does not know what has happened to the manuscript since," according to Hedrick. Asking Kallistos why he photographed the Clement letter, Hedrick said the priest replied that it was important, being the only copy of the manuscript in existence and also containing a great deal of "diversity." Hedrick took that to mean the text diverges from church tradition. "He further said (without a question from me) that the manuscript may provide the basis for a 'sexual Jesus' as has been portrayed in popular movies and books," Hedrick said. According to Hedrick, Olympiou has guessed that the missing leaves "were likely concealed by certain well-meaning persons at the patriarchate library for reasons of piety."[13]

What the Photos Show

The photographs taken in Jerusalem yielded unexpected evidence to support Smith's accounts. At the top right corner of the opening page of the book, "Smith 65" was written with blue ink, which Stroumsa saw in 1976 at Mar Saba. On the last printed page, well below the "FINIS" and at the bottom left corner, was a small, circular blotch—possibly a water stain. A discoloration of the same size is on the first page of the Clement letter at the corresponding right bottom. These were facing pages in the book, so the researchers could conclude the photographed pages were once in this book. The second page of the Clement letter, which was written on the back of the first, also had a spot where one would expect a stain to seep through. "The small circular mark is just visible at the bottom right hand side of the sheet of binder's paper, which is the last page of the Clement manuscript," Hedrick said.[14] That agrees with Smith's description of what he found. An intact copy of the same book—with two blank leaves at the end—sits in the library of Union Theological Seminary in New York City, the American scholar learned.

What Smith encountered in the desert monastery in 1958 was the handwriting of a monk in the last half of the eighteenth century who copied the fragment of Clement's letter. It was not so odd a place to preserve historically important information. "It was a common practice of monks," Hedrick said, "to hand copy manuscripts onto the unused pages of old books."[15]

Hedrick, with the aid of Olympiou, was still hoping to track down the pages. The letter definitely exists, Hedrick told a session of Mark scholars at the annual Society of Biblical Literature meeting in November 2001. Its whereabouts are unknown, "but probably it is in the Greek Orthodox Patriarchate library in Jerusalem, either misplaced, sequestered, or destroyed," he said, adding in an aside, "Personally I don't think it was destroyed."[16]

Notes

1. Papers given at the 1985 conference appear in *Jesus in History and Myth* (ed. R. Joseph Hoffman and Gerald A. Larue; Buffalo: Prometheus Books, 1986). Responding to G. A. Wells, "The Historicity of Jesus," 27–45, was Morton Smith, "The Historical Jesus," 47–54. My paper was "Jesus and His Brothers," 181–90.

2. Donald H. Juel, *The Gospel of Mark* (Nashville: Abingdon, 1999), 28.

3. Elizabeth Struthers Malbon, *Hearing Mark: A Listener's Guide* (Harrisburg, Pa.: Trinity Press International, 2002).

4. Juel, *The Gospel of Mark,* 17, 35.

5. Joanna Dewey, "Oral Methods of Structuring Narrative in Mark," *Interpretation* 43 (1989): 32–44.

6. Richard Bauckham, ed., *The Gospels for All Christians: Rethinking the Gospel Audiences* (Grand Rapids: Eerdmans, 1998), 29; see his chapter "For Whom Were the Gospels Written?" 9–48.

7. Ibid., 33, 45.

8. As quoted by Charles Hedrick, "The Secret Gospel of Mark: Manuscript and Interpretation," paper presented at SBL seminar, November 19, 2001, at Denver Colorado. Joseph A. Fitzmyer, "How to Exploit a Secret Gospel," *America* (June 23, 1973): 570–71; Edwin Yamauchi, "A Secret Gospel of Jesus as 'Magus'? A Review of the Recent Works of Morton Smith," *Christian Scholars Review* 4, no. 3 (1975): 238–51.

9. Hedrick, "The Secret Gospel of Mark," 3.

10. Charles Hedrick and Paul Mirecki, *The Gospel of the Savior: A New Ancient Gospel* (Santa Rosa, Calif.: Polebridge, 1999). For a popular description of the new gospel fragment and other noncanonical gospels, see Hedrick, "The 34 Gospels, Diversity and Division among the Earliest Christians," *Bible Review* 18, no. 3 (June 2002): 20–31, 46–47.

11. Guy G. Stroumsa emailed me on April 18, 2003, an article he wrote for a forthcoming issue of *The Journal of Early Christian Studies*. He said it was the spring of 1976 when, fascinated by Morton Smith's find at Mar Saba, he drove to the monastery with Father Meliton (Stroumsa's spelling) and two professors (since deceased) at Hebrew University, David Flusser and Shlomo Pines. Shown the Voss book with its three manuscript pages intact at Mar Saba, they were permitted to take it with them to the patriarchate's library in Jerusalem for safekeeping. Upon hearing of a still-simmering controversy over Secret Mark some 25 years later, Stroumsa said he had a duty to testify to the book's actual existence.

12. Charles Hedrick's story of his tracking down photographs comes from his November 2001 SBL seminar paper and his article "Secret Mark: New Photographs, New Witnesses," *The Fourth R,* 13 (September/October 2000): 3–11, 14–16.

13. Hedrick, "Secret Mark," 8–9.

14. Ibid., 9.

15. Ibid., 3.

16. Hedrick, "The Secret Gospel of Mark," 7.

CHAPTER 13

Solving Mysteries, Facing New Ones

WHILE ADMIRING THE IRONICAL TWISTS in the Gospel of Mark, Robert M. Fowler conceded that two intriguing scenes had long eluded solutions. "[N]o one has ever been able to solve satisfactorily . . . the mystery of the *neaniskos,* the 'young man' who runs from Gethsemane undressed in 14:52 and either reappears or is replaced" by another young man at 16:5, "this time gloriously dressed, inside a vacated tomb at the crack of dawn."[1] Frank Kermode, an eminent British literary critic expressed it succinctly, "The difficulty is to explain where the deuce he popped up from."[2]

That mystery is over, I dare say. The young man's long-lost introductory scene enables readers to recognize him as the kind of model follower beloved by Jesus, according to Mark. The *neaniskos* first appears in Original Mark as a contrast to the twelve disciples, whom Jesus urges to be humble servants instead of arguing among themselves who is the greatest (9:34; 10:43).

This shining character type (not to mention admirable others who pop up), together with the illuminating chiastic codes, forces out of the research shadows two troubling mysteries in Mark. They especially may disturb people of faith accustomed to reading gospel stories as historically reliable accounts of Jesus' followers and family. Trouble no. 1: Mark unmistakably attacked those saints-to-be, but just how much damage the Gospel tried to inflict—and why—has vexed gospel studies

142

for a long time. Church-based interpretations tend to harmonize the four gospels into one story of Jesus, glossing over the differences, a practice legitimate for a pastoral setting. But even in scholarly circles, the apologetic approach to Mark's bashing retains the upper hand. Yes, it is said, Mark was rough on the disciples and family of Jesus, but that was done to make readers/hearers face their own failings and doubts, as surely the disciples and the women did eventually.

Trouble no. 2: Mark undeniably makes things up, even if some core aspects of Jesus' adult life have a historical basis. Historical-literary criticism has acknowledged for at least a century that early Christian thinkers reread the biblical history of Israel to articulate what they saw as the saving significance of a crucified Lord. The Hebrew Bible inspired writers on what Jesus would have done and would have said beyond what was available in sayings collections. Recent studies that dare say more about Mark's fictionalizing suffer either from being too cautiously stated or from being ignored as off-base and unconvincing.

I think the return of Original Mark will push scholarship to face more openly the twinned question of polemics and fiction in that influential, groundbreaking gospel. It may seem, to some, a travesty to say that Mark not only attempted to defame Peter, Mary, and company but also shaped Jesus traditions in a fictional framework. But it may in fact be fortunate that invective and imagination in Mark are related issues because acknowledging the reality of one should soften the shock of the other. I have come to admire enormously Mark's author for the coded word puzzles and a surprising sense of humor. But if Mark engaged in polemics, then one must say the Gospel's depictions of certain people are a fiction, even falsehoods. That explains in part why the church kept all four gospels in a New Testament canon. But can believers live with the notion that there was a dark side to Mark? They might; more on that later. First, as a journalist, I want to summarize some of what scholarly proponents say of Mark's polemic and literary invention.

Mark's Novel Approach

The first gospel, Mark, viewed from different perspectives, wrote British scholar W. R. Telford, "is a historical document, a literary composition and a religious (or sacred) text." Though it gives information about Jesus, "as a historical source it must be approached cautiously and critically," Telford said. As a composition, it has all the possibilities and limitations of a written text. "Being also a religious text, it is a mixture of fact and fiction, a blend of history and theology, a product of literary artifice and faith-inspired imagination," he said.[3] That overview is general enough not to offend those outside of conservative, traditionalist circles. Burton L. Mack of Claremont Graduate University went much further in 1988, by indicating that Mark indulged in full-blown mythmaking.[4] A small but growing number of scholars contend that the *Odyssey,* the *Iliad,* and other epics inspired the storytelling of Mark and Luke. Others see the Greco-Roman novel or the Jewish novel as akin to Mark's literary style.[5] But regardless of what genre(s) the Gospel fits best, most acknowledge that Mark is a literary composition that involved countless storytelling decisions by its writer.

For her part, Mary Ann Tolbert, of the Pacific School of Religion in Berkeley, criticized fellow scholars who declined to acknowledge Mark as "a self-consciously crafted narrative, a fiction, resulting from literary imagination." She added, in *Sowing the Gospel,* "To say it is a fiction does not necessarily mean it has no connection with events in history; rather, describing Mark as a fiction serves to underscore the selection, construction, and choice behind the story it tells." Mark displays striking stylistic similarities to the Greek ancient novel with its episodic plot, minimal introduction, central turning point, final recognition scene, and fairly crude narrative style, she said. Yet, it is "obviously not an ancient novel of the erotic type," said Tolbert.[6]

One literary device that helps readers to suspend disbelief is placing the story in known places and among historical figures. Tolbert cited literary analyst Robert Alter's characterization of the Hebrew Bible as "historicized fiction."[7] Critics usually do not intend to demean the use of creative storytelling in ancient texts because, they say, the modern demand for factual accuracy was not present or very possible two thousand years ago. By giving seemingly factual details, the novelists render the story believable, Tolbert said. "Mark's descriptions of the Jewish hierarchy and its practices, the Roman rulers, the crowds, the villages of Galilee, and even Jerusalem and the temple may well be set pieces, more stereotypical than typical," wrote Tolbert.[8]

Jewish novels may be a better comparison to Mark owing to their "expectation of divine deliverance" amid threats against God's people, said Michael Vines in a recent book.[9] Vines nonetheless acknowledges that Mark resembles Greco-Roman novels in some ways. "As in Greek romance, the tension between recognition and non-recognition [in

Mark] produces irony."[10] Heroines like Esther may use their beauty to outwit enemies, but Vines says that the Jewish novel does not contain "the essentially bourgeois entertainment" typical of the Greek romance.[11] As for Jewish novels such as Esther, Tobit, and a Greek version of Daniel, Vines said that "historical accuracy is not a major concern," although the story frameworks are realistic and allude to historical events.[12] "The Jewish novels display a careless, almost playful attitude toward historical accuracy," he said.[13] Some of them, I would add, are written in chiastic and ironic style as well, such as Judith, one of the Jewish apocryphal books.[14]

The chiastic patterns that facilitated the recovery of Original Mark could reinforce the argument that the author was using imagination as much as information. To make so many lengthy chiasms work right, the author had to move the pieces of the word mosaic over and over again. Each time a new episode is inserted, it potentially throws off other stepped patterns—words or motifs must be moved to fix the adjusted sequences. Jesus' adversaries might be shifted to the next episode or back one scene. Even if a teaching or act of Jesus is not shifted in the narrative, it may mean the crowd or the disciples will say or do something else to provide the links.

The "young man" in all three appearances is certainly not a real person or persons. At Jesus' arrest he is not the author's autobiographical signature, an oft-cited idea most scholars reject. In the tomb he is not an angel, which unfortunately many accept. The *neaniskos* can be seen as a fictional type whose devotion and bravery shame the named disciples and the blood brothers of Jesus. One may say he furthers Mark's polemical and novelistic purposes.

The ancient Greek novels are called romances since they typically featured lovers who are separated and finally reunited at the end. In a milder way, Mark has "love" interests. In biblical Mark, a Jesus frustrated with the failings of his twelve disciples "loves" at first sight a man (10:21) who sought to "inherit eternal life" but was told he must give up his wealth. He went away sorrowful. Not long afterward, the restored Gospel says a young man "loves" the man who raised him from the dead, and although he too was rich, Jesus must feel this one is willing to give it all up. He is given the secret of the kingdom by Jesus, who Original Mark notes later, loved him in return. At the end of the Gospel, Jesus is reunited at the tomb with his beloved. In addition, the "recognition" scenes typical of the romances abound at story's end: the persecuting authorities unknowingly "recognize" Jesus as "King of the Jews" and "Christ, the King of Israel," though their intent was mockery. As Jesus hung helplessly from his cross, two individuals—a repentant robber and a centurion—perceived Jesus' divine power. And the young man in the tomb proclaimed the church's Easter message, "He has risen."

Advocates for Polemic

The most-cited proponent of a Markan polemic is Theodore Weeden, though his 1971 book credited two scholars for paving the way a decade earlier—Johannes Schreiber of Germany and American Joseph Tyson. Weeden said the two "have argued that Mark's portrayal of the disciples must be seen as a literary device in the service of a polemic against a conservative Jewish Christian group in Palestine which placed no positive meaning in Jesus' death, held to the long-established Jewish practices, and rejected the necessity of the gentile mission."[15] Differing with those scholars on the motives, Weeden theorized in essence that Mark used Peter and the disciples as foils, or stand-ins, for real opponents in the Markan community. These "divine-men" boasters in Mark's circles emphasized the wonder-working, supernatural image of Jesus and claimed to possess such powers themselves. Therefore when the Gospel of Mark depicts Peter and the disciples as unable to understand that Jesus is a suffering servant ready for execution, the author is really attacking his own adversaries. My difficulty with that theory is that the early Christian leaders took a heavy hit in reputation just so the author can lay waste to contemporary rivals.

Werner Kelber saw the polemical motive differently: "Mark's combined critique of the Twelve, the Three, Peter, Jesus' family and the Galilean women is directed against people who are identifiable as representative figures of the Jerusalem church." These followers, he wrote, failed to understand what was said in Galilee, abandoned Jesus, and "thus were stalled in Jerusalem, never reaching the goal of Galilee." Readers living after 70 C.E., when the Jerusalem temple was destroyed by Roman soldiers in quelling a Jewish revolt, also can understand "the demise of the Jerusalem church as a consequence of the abortive discipleship."[16]

Moreover, Kelber argued, the Gospel was making a break with oral traditions about Jesus. The biggest oral authorities were the Jerusalem leaders and the family of Jesus, kinfolk to whom "Mark's gospel registers consistent hostility," Kelber said. The author of Mark was a writer, that is, "no mere custodian, preserving and presiding over the collective memories of the past," said Kelber. "Truly creative stages in tradition involve alienation," Kelber wrote, "and genuine innovation is destructive to tradition."[17] Again, the recovered episodes of Original Mark bolster the polemic theories. The Gospel now has two new model images of faith (the beloved young man found in Secret Mark and the repentant robber found in Luke). Conversely, the recovered gospel adds another damaging story about James and John (rebuked by Jesus after they suggested raining fire on Samaritans) and another shunning of mother Mary by Jesus (when he refused to receive her and Salome in Jericho).

Mark presents alternate heroes and indicates that the true understanding of Jesus, Son of God and Son of Man, was derived from Jesus' followers such as the *neaniskos* and those "about him [Jesus]" who were likewise given the secret of the kingdom. Other knowing witnesses included the woman with the expensive ointment, the centurion, the scribe, and those healed of disease and freed from unclean spirits. Onlookers to Jesus' exorcisms and five thousand participants in the miracle feeding offset the instances that Jesus admonished some to keep his feats a secret.

But I will keep quiet for practical reasons about why I think Mark relentlessly attacked the early followers of Jesus. Some theories come close, but I believe there was a larger, theological crisis during which our storyteller decided it was imperative (1) to shatter the reputations of figures whose names lent authority to written and oral traditions regarded as inadequate and misleading by those who eventually defined orthodox Christianity and (2) to draw a word picture of Jesus that was more compelling and dramatic and seemingly better informed than other influential beliefs. It will take another book to make a case for why Mark took these risky steps, inflicting some permanent damage to history in the process. My present effort—with all its chiastic diagrams and complicated aspects—needs time for critique, corrections, and refinement.

Yet, my reportorial instincts warn against sitting too long on significant news, no matter how potentially upsetting. In all modesty and with concern for those who find great comfort in the present Christian story, I think that many believers would divide into (1) those who would thank Mark for a polemic that is much bolder than that of the apostle Paul's—that saved Christianity from a narrower understanding of Jesus and (2) those who would feel that the "who's who" ranks of early Jesus followers and their witness were betrayed by the Gospel of Mark.

One Last Mystery—Solved?

The final mystery concerns the last words in Mark. The sudden, seemingly unresolved ending leaves modern readers perplexed when they recall the happy final scenes in Luke, Matthew, and John. Besides that, scholars have puzzled over the peculiar grammatical ending in Mark. The last phrase is usually translated "for they were afraid" (16:8), but the word order leads to a literal rendering of "they were afraid, for." As Daryl D. Schmidt of Texas Christian University explained, the conjunction "for" (*gar*) "is usually the second word in its sentence, but usually with something following it." Schmidt rendered it aptly, "Talk about terrified . . ."[18]

Another rendition is, "They were scared, you see," according to Frank Kermode, the British literary analyst.[19] Knighted in 1991, he has had a long career, including a 2001 published collection of his essays for the *London Review of Books* in the 1990s. Other Kermode books include *The Sense of an Ending* (1967) and *The Genesis of Secrecy* (1979). The latter dealt with the nature of narratives, including the Gospel of Mark, and even mentioned Morton Smith's Secret Mark discovery and analysis in one chapter. While working to finish my own book's last chapter, I came across the photocopied pages of that chapter that he mailed to me in 1983 around the time he was a visiting scholar at Columbia University. Apparently I had requested a copy upon meeting him, though I don't recall it. At any rate, his words in that chapter and in the rest of *The Genesis of Secrecy* gave me grist for my own "sense of an ending" to solving some of the mysteries Kermode wrote about.[20]

Admitting that the Gospel of Mark tantalizes with its intimations of secrets to be discovered, Kermode wrote that perhaps "there is a secret at the heart of Mark which is not a theology and perhaps not even really a secret; but rather some habit of narrative paradox or conjunction that might, in the end, be best represented without the use of words, in a diagram or by algebra."[21] He suggested at that point that maybe it was a giant form of "intercalation," or what many call bracketing or sandwiching of one episode by another. (Sandwiching, of course, is a primitive chiasm with its ABA' pattern.) The Harvard University lectures that became his *The Genesis of Secrecy* book were written before the summer of 1978, when sandwiching was a frequently cited mechanistic literary device in Mark and one widely accepted by scholars. He did not cite chiasms, but in repeating his curiosity about Mark's organizing principle he mentioned "catchwords, topics, [and] the requirements of a lectionary" as possibilities.[22] Those three, I think, now can be seen respectively in chiasms, messenger/recognition themes outlining the formal structure, and baptism-initiation ritual words seen especially in Mark 10.

Let's return to Kermode's observations on "They were afraid, you see"—the supposed weak ending of the Gospel:

> The scandal is, of course, much more than merely philological. Omitting any post-Easter appearance of Jesus, Mark has only this empty tomb and the terrified women. The final mention of Peter (omitted by Matthew) can only remind us that our last view of him was not as a champion of the faith but as the image of denial. Mark's book began with a trumpet call: "This is the beginning of the gospel of Jesus Christ, the son of God." It ends with this faint whisper of timid women.[23]

The main obstacle for accepting 16:8 as the true ending "and going about our business of finding internal validation for it," Kermode continued, was that Mark has not been considered capable of such literary refinement. "The conclusion is either intolerably clumsy; or it is incredibly subtle," he wrote.[24]

Fowler, quoted at the beginning of this chapter, also wondered if Mark's author had some purpose behind the unusual ending. "Thus, the awkward *gar* at Mark 16:8, coupled with the ambiguous allusion to Galilee in 16:7, signals the reader to return to the beginning of the Gospel, to begin reading all over."[25]

Breaking the Boundaries

When people learn the solution to a magic trick, the answer to a riddle, or the missing clues to a mystery, a common reaction is, "Oh, yes, that's makes sense." It looks easy in retrospect, if one only had not been stuck on a faulty premise or thwarted by flaws or missing parts to the mystery. A rebuilt Original Mark perhaps provides the "Aha!"

The last chiasm I must show was also the last one I found while working on this chapter. "Fortuitous" is hardly strong enough to describe these late-arriving insights. What will it prove? At the least it will establish (along with other chiasms) that the original author did not write anything more after 16:8. No ending was lost in the mail. We have the true, intended *finis* to the Gospel . . . or not.

This became clear after I had noticed that Mark wrote "fulfilled" and "at hand" in two momentous sections. One was at the arrest, literally the "handing over" of John the Baptist before Jesus began his preaching. The other was at the betrayal, the "handing over" of Jesus. Maybe these were starting points for another new, asymmetrical chiastic center. But it really wasn't there, so I looked at passages before the arrest of John the Baptist and after the arrest of Jesus. That was going the wrong direction—outward not inward. But here is what resulted:

(1:14–28) After John was **arrested** *(paradidomi),* Jesus preached gospel, Time is **fulfilled.** Kingdom of God **at hand.** Saw Simon and Andrew, who left nets, **followed** him. Called James and John, who left father to follow him. Jesus entered synagogue and **taught** as one with authority, not as the **scribes.** Unclean spirit recognized Jesus of Nazareth. Have you **come** to destroy us? I know you. You are Holy One of God. Jesus commanded, **Come out** of him. Spirit **came out.**

(14:41b–54) Enough; hour has **come.** Son of Man is **betrayed** *(paradidomi).* My **betrayer** is **at hand.** Judas directed mob, **scribes** to Jesus; **betrayer** had given sign. When he **came,** he went up to kiss him. Seized him; bystander wielded sword. Have you **come out** as against a robber? I was in temple **teaching;** you did not seize me. But let the scriptures be **fulfilled.** They all forsook him. Young man **followed** him; they seized him, but he left linen cloth, ran away naked. As Jesus was led away, Peter followed at a distance.

(1:1–13) Beginning *(arche)* of gospel Jesus **Christ, Son** of God. Isaiah **prophet,** messenger before thy **face.** John Baptist preaching baptism forgiveness of sin; people baptized. After me **comes** he who is mightier than I. Jesus **came** from Nazareth. Baptized, Jesus saw **heavens** open; voice from **heaven** said, My beloved **Son.** In wilderness forty **days.**

(14:55–65) Council sought testimony to execute Jesus. He said he will destroy temple; in three **days** I will build another. High priest *(archiereus)* asked, Are you the **Christ, Son** of the Blessed? I am; you will see **Son** of man at right hand of Power, **coming** with clouds of

heaven. <u>High priest tore</u> garments; You heard his blasphemy. Condemned him, spit, covered his **face,** saying, **Prophesy!**

Continuing on this chiastic pathway would shatter literary convention. From 1:1 we move to the end of Mark. The matching steps below arguably tells what the women would have said whenever they were asked what they saw at Jesus' tomb, according to Mark.

(16:1–8) Mary Magdalene, Mary mother of James, and Salome (<u>three</u>) took spices to the tomb to anoint him; saw stone was rolled away. Saw the young man in white robe. <u>Amazed</u>. Do not be amazed, he said. You seek **Jesus of Nazareth.** He is risen. Tell his disciples and Peter he is going <u>before</u> you to **Galilee.** They fled from tomb, <u>trembling and astonishment</u>, <u>said nothing to anyone</u>, for they were <u>afraid</u>.

(14:66–72) To **Peter,** maid of high priest said, You were with the **Nazarene, Jesus.** He denied it, I neither know nor understand what you mean. Maid told bystanders, He is one of them, but he denied it again. Bystanders said to him, Certainly you are one of them, a **Galilean.** He <u>cursed himself and swore</u>, I do not know this man. Cock crowed second time; he recalled Jesus said, <u>Before</u> cock crows second time, <u>you will deny me three</u> times. He <u>broke down, wept</u>.

(15:42–47) Joseph of Arimathea, respected member of council, went to **Pilate,** asking for the body of Jesus. **Pilate wondered** if he were already dead. And when he **learned** *(ginosko)* that he was, he <u>granted the body</u> to Joseph. He <u>wrapped his body</u>, laid it in a tomb.

(15:1–15) Priests' council <u>bound Jesus</u>, delivered him to **Pilate,** who asked questions. Jesus made no further answer, so that **Pilate wondered.** Do you want me to release for you the King of the Jews? For he **perceived** *(ginosko)* it was envy that made the priests deliver up Jesus. Crowd cried, Crucify; Pilate <u>released Barabbas</u>, a criminal, instead.

(15:39–41) When <u>centurion</u> saw him breathe his last, he said, Truly <u>this man was the Son of God</u>! Women were looking from afar, among whom were Mary Magdalene, Mary <u>mother of James the lesser and Joses</u>, and Salome, who, when in <u>Galilee</u>, ministered to him; also many others <u>came</u> with him to Jerusalem.

(15:16–21) <u>Soldiers</u> led Jesus to front of assembled battalion, put purple cloak on him, mocking him and saluting him, <u>Hail, King of the Jews</u>! Struck him, led him out to crucify him. They compelled passer-by Simon of <u>Cyrene</u>, <u>coming</u> in from the country, the <u>father of Alexander and Rufus</u>, to carry his cross.

(15:34–38) Jesus cried, Eloi, Eloi, lama sabach-thani? **which means, <u>My God, my God, why hast thou forsaken me?</u>** (<u>Ps 22:1</u>). Bystanders thought he called Elijah. One <u>filled sponge full of vinegar, put it on a reed and gave it to him to drink</u> (<u>Ps 69:21</u>). Jesus uttered loud cry; curtain tore in two.

(15:22–24) They brought him to place called Golgotha, **which means** the place of a skull. They <u>offered him wine mingled with myrrh</u> (<u>Prov 31:6</u>); but he did not take it. They crucified him, <u>divided his garments, casting lots</u> on which each should take (<u>Ps 22:18</u>).

Now, when Mark's chiastic patterns move to a midpoint, the stitches are more tightly woven. Here are the final steps in the indented format. This chiasm shows again that Luke 23:39–43 came from the scene in Original Mark. Luke changed Mark's "robber" to "criminal" but little else because Luke's account attaches smoothly here and to other chiasms in Mark. (Mark 15:28 is omitted because it is not in older manuscripts; Mark 15:32b is left out because it was inserted by the editor of Original Mark.)

G (15:25) And it was the **third hour,** when <u>they crucified him</u>.

   H (15:26) And the inscription of the charge against him read, **The King** of the Jews.

      I (15:27) And with him they <u>crucified two robbers</u>, one on his right and one on his left.

         J (15:29–30) And those who passed by **derided** *(blasphemo)* **him,** wagging their heads, and saying, Aha! You who would destroy the temple and build it in three days, **save yourself,**

            K (15:31a) and **come down from the cross!** So also the chief priests <u>mocked</u> him to one another with the scribes, saying,

               L (15:31b) He saved others; he cannot save himself.

            K' (15:32a) Let Christ, the King of Israel, **come down now from the cross,** that we may see and <u>believe</u>.

J' (Luke 23:39) One of the criminals who were hanged **railed** *(blasphemo)* **at him,** saying, Are you not the Christ? **Save yourself** and us!

I' (Luke 23:40–41) But the <u>other rebuked him</u>, saying, Do you not fear God, since you are under the <u>same sentence of condemnation</u>? And we indeed justly; for <u>we</u> are receiving the due reward of our deeds; but this man has done nothing wrong.

H' (Luke 23:42–43) And he said, Jesus, remember me when you come into **your kingdom.** And he said to him, Truly, I say to you, today you will be with me in Paradise.

G' (Mark 15:33 = Luke 23:44) And when the **sixth hour** had come, there was <u>darkness over the whole land</u> until the **ninth hour.**

Mixed feelings may be in order when considering what conclusions to make. Morton Smith, for all his rough treatment of other scholars and provocative theories, deserves posthumous praise for his discovery of a missing piece of the oldest New Testament gospel. Long-hidden coded word patterns laced through the Gospel have exposed more than ever the polemic and novelistic strategies of the author. Despite Mark's harsh attack on Jesus' disciples, family, and named women followers, the writer should be admired for a wonderfully crafted story that won centuries of believers in the God-sent man who "saved others but could not save himself" from a tortuous death. Remarkably, the writing is so multi-leveled and multidirectional that you cannot be sure you've read it all, even when you reach the end.

Notes

1. Robert M. Fowler, *Let the Reader Understand: Reader-Response Criticism and the Gospel of Mark* (Minneapolis: Fortress, 1991), 216.

2. Frank Kermode, *The Genesis of Secrecy: On the Interpretation of Narrative* (Cambridge: Harvard University Press, 1979), 55.

3. W. R. Telford, *Mark* (NTG; Sheffield: Sheffield Academic Press, 1995), 34.

4. Burton L. Mack, *A Myth of Innocence: Mark and Christian Origins* (Philadelphia: Fortress, 1988).

5. On the use of epic literature, see Dennis R. MacDonald, *The Homeric Epics and the Gospel of Mark* (New Haven: Yale University Press, 2000). See also Ronald F. Hock et al., ed., *Ancient Fiction and Early Christian Narrative* (SBLSymS; Atlanta: Scholars Press, 1998).

6. Mary Ann Tolbert, *Sowing the Gospel: Mark's World in Literary-Historical Perspective* (Minneapolis: Fortress, 1989), 30, 65.

7. On p. 30 n. 16, Tolbert quotes Robert Alter from his *Art of Biblical Narrative* (New York: Basic Books, 1981).

8. Tolbert, *Sowing the Gospel,* 74.

9. Michael E. Vines, *The Problem of Markan Genre: The Gospel of Mark and the Jewish Novel* (Atlanta: Society of Biblical Literature, 2002), 153.

10. Ibid., 130.

11. Ibid.

12. Ibid., 146

13. Ibid.

14. Regarding chiasm in Jewish novels, Toni Craven says, "The sixteen chapters of Judith divide into two balanced and proportional parts," with each structured internally with a threefold chiastic pattern, according to her introduction to Judith in the *HarperCollins Study Bible,* 1460. See Carey A. Moore, "Book of Judith," *The Anchor Bible Dictionary* (vol. 3; ed. David Noel Freedman; New York: Doubleday, 1992), 117–25. For chiastic structures in Esther and Daniel 1–6, see David A. Dorsey, *The Literary Structure of the Old Testament: A Commentary on Genesis–Malachi* (Grand Rapids: Baker, 1999).

15. Theodore J. Weeden Sr., *Mark: Traditions in Conflict* (Philadelphia: Fortress, 1971), 25.

16. Werner H. Kelber, *Mark's Story of Jesus* (Philadelphia: Fortress, 1979), 90, 94.

17. Werner H. Kelber, *The Oral and the Written Gospel: The Hermeneutics of Speaking and Writing in the Synoptic Tradition, Mark, Paul, and Q* (Philadelphia: Fortress, 1983), 102, 114, 215.

18. Daryl D. Schmidt, *The Gospel of Mark* (Scholar's Bible; Sonoma, Calif.: Polebridge, 1990), 151.

19. Kermode, *The Genesis of Secrecy,* 67, 63. His note accompanying the photo-copied pages was dated June 20, 1983. The extended quotation is from pages 67–68.

20. Kermode's note accompanying the photocopied pages was dated June 20, 1983. While working on the final chapter, I ordered the paperback and quoted more from pp.112, 127, 137.

21. Ibid., 127.

22. Ibid., 137.

23. The extended quotation is from pages 67–68.

24. Ibid., 68.

25. Fowler, *Let the Reader Understand,* 262.

Mark's Rules, or Fun Finding Chiastic Patterns in the Gospel

BIBLICAL STUDIES NOTING CHIASMS usually treat them blandly—as if no fun is involved for the creator or reader. Rarely described as word puzzles or games, they are regarded as mnemonic aids for recitation or simply literary outlines. That dull approach dishonors our forebears for their humorous intelligence and creativity. If no one took pleasure in wordplays and puzzle patterns such as chiasms, then why are the Hebrew Scriptures replete with them?

The author of Original Mark formed so many intricate puzzles beneath the gospel story that it had to have been fun as well as arduous. Due to space constraints, this book contains only some of the chiasms that have been found.

You, too, can enjoy the difficult delights of deciphering Mark, but you have to know some of the rules set by the author. Join the fun! And don't forget to ignore the editor's alterations.

Pursuing the Pivot

As in chiasms generally, the midpoint usually is a "turning point." And it sometimes has a theme or catchword that resonates with the first and/or last step in the pattern.

Twin Centers?

Mark uses no double or matching midpoints. That is, you'll find, not ABCC'B'A', but ABCB'A'. Chiasms in some other ancient texts may have twin centers, but not in Original Mark.

Shorter Steps

The steps get shorter approaching the midpoint. The very center may be one word, part of a sentence, or one or two sentences. The A and A' steps of long chiasms often are fairly long. Because each episode has its internal chiasm, long chiasms may use that same tightly woven midpoint, but don't rule out a center arriving at another point in an episode.

Barriers

Do not let the chapters, verse numbers, paragraphs, and punctuation decisions by latter-era translators be unbreakable barriers for chiastic structures. Your chosen step may start or end in the middle of an episode, or two episodes may be grouped together for a single step.

Accumulated Evidence

Multiple Links

Chiastic patterns running over many episodes earn credibility from consistency and multiple hooks at each step. For example, steps A to J at the center should go back in reverse order to A' without exception. If steps E and E' are not as clever or well built as you'd like, look again. Are there similar or opposite actions? Catchwords you missed? Enlarge or shrink the E steps; is that better?

Types of Parallels

Rely mostly on actual word matches or catchphrases for parallels, but do not rule out motifs or themes that are striking. Corresponding words provide a more concrete proof than a possibly subjective interpretation of the author's intent. Yet some motifs or actions are so related that they are hardly accidental, especially if the two steps also have catchwords.

Give higher priority to words that have the same root in Greek than to different words with similar meanings or contrasts. But both instances are legitimate. English translations may be deceiving; for example, both "to make well" and "to save" are translations of *sozo* in Greek.

Double Duty

Any given episode in Mark serves at least a half-dozen different chiasms and thus contains some words that may link up with three other chiastic steps and some that might be employed once. Become suspicious about an odd word or a strange phrase in the story. It might be because a chiasm somewhere needed it.

Catchwords Rule

Don't assume that episodes very different in action/content would not yield matches in an otherwise successful chiastic pattern. A miracle story is different from a debate with religious opponents, but the gospel author supplies links when required. "Catchwords" may include numbers, place-names, Scripture allusions, sentence structures such as questions, family relations (father, mother, sons, daughters), or a profusion of negatives.

Chop-in-Half Principle

Lengthy stretches in Mark may be cut in half to produce two new chiasms, often each with its own storytelling character. Keep going. You will find boxes within boxes. Very important: Do not expect that the midpoint of one chiasm is the exact point where the next halves start and end. The author needed wiggle room so that at either end of a particular chiasm, for example, the same group of words would not serve full, half-, quarter-, and eighth-length chiasms. Some chiasms start a bit earlier or later so that the surface narrative does not suffer from excessive repetition.

Good luck.

Prologue, Acts 1–5, Conclusion, in Formal Chiastic Structure

FIVE MAIN ACTS, bordered by a prologue and conclusion, define the symmetrical, formal chiastic patterns of Original Mark. Except for Act 3, the theme of "messenger and/or message" begins and ends (A and A') each section, followed by the motif of "recognition or non-recognition" (B and B'). In Act 3, the middle section of Original Mark, the recognition theme takes the opening and closing bows (A and A'). I have listed the B themes as "messenger/discipleship" though the messenger theme is weak. It may not be the author's intent, wishing instead to save that motif until the very center of Act 3 with the word "messengers" *(aggelos)*. That spot, within an episode recovered from Luke, is also the pivot point for the formal chiastic structure of Original Mark.

To conserve space, passages are reduced to shorthand phrases. Some words were omitted if they do not provide substantial chiastic links. The Revised Standard Version (RSV) translation is used (unless otherwise noted) with the proviso that a gender-inclusive term might be put in brackets. Boldfaced words signify that the Greek word is the same (or has the same root), and if the English translation is different in these cases, the Greek word is in parentheses. Underlined words from Mark signify similar words, phrases, themes, or other links (numbers, place-names, grammar, Scripture allusion, et al.) that correspond to matching steps. Occasionally, if a key word occurs frequently in one step and its equivalent or opposite occurs the same number of times in its matching step, that will be noted in parentheses. Notice that 1:14 serves both the prologue and the start of Act 1. Mark allows this kind of "double duty" for adjacent chiasms.

Prologue: Mark 1:1–14

A (1:1–6) <u>Messengers/message</u>. Beginning, **gospel** of **Jesus** Christ, Son of **God;** Isaiah, I send my **messenger** *(aggelos)* before thy face, prepare thy way; voice crying in the wilderness; prepare way of <u>the Lord</u>, make his paths straight—**John** baptizer **in the wilderness,** preaching baptism of repentance, forgiveness of <u>sins</u>; went all of Judea, all of Jerusalem; baptized in Jordan, confessing <u>sins</u>; **John** clothed <u>camel's</u> hair, ate <u>locusts</u>, wild honey.

  B (1:7–9a) <u>Recognition</u>. Preached, after me comes <u>he who mightier than I</u>; not worthy; I baptized with **water;** he will baptize with Holy **Spirit.** In those days <u>came</u>[1]

    C (9b) Jesus from <u>Nazareth of Galilee</u>

      D (9c) and (he) was baptized

    C' (9d) in <u>the Jordan</u> by John

  B' (1:10–11) <u>Recognition</u>. <u>Came up</u> out of **water,** saw heavens opened, **Spirit** upon him like dove; voice from heaven, <u>Thou art my beloved Son</u>; with thee I am well pleased.

A' (1:12–14) <u>Messenger/message</u>. Spirit drove him into **the wilderness;** he was in **wilderness** forty days, <u>tempted by Satan</u>; was with wild <u>beasts</u>; and the **angels** *(aggelos)* ministered to him; after **John** was arrested, **Jesus** came into Galilee, preaching the **gospel** of **God,**

Act 1: Mark 1:14–4:12

A (1:14–22) <u>Messengers/message</u>. John **arrested** *(paradidomi)*, Jesus came into Galilee, <u>preaching gospel</u> of **God,** time fulfilled, **Kingdom of God** at hand, <u>repent</u>, believe gospel; passing by **the Sea,** saw Simon, Andrew <u>casting</u> net in **sea,** follow me; James, John in **boat;** called them; in **boat;** synaogogue, **taught, teaching, taught.**

---

1. In verse 9, I used the word order in Greek, which makes the symmetry more apparent.

B (1:23–28) <u>Recognition</u>. Man with **unclean spirit:** Jesus of Nazareth, **come** to destroy us? I know **who** you **are, Holy** one of **God;** rebuked him; **unclean spirit** came out. Amazed; commands **unclean spirits;** they obey. Fame spread throughout Galilee.

 C (1:29–34) **Left** *(exerchomai),* entered **house** <u>Simon, mother-in-law</u>, **took** *(krateo)* by hand, fever left. Brought him sick or <u>possessed with</u> **demons;** healed sick, diseases, **cast out** many **demons;** not permit **demons** to speak.

  D (1:35–39) **Simon,** others, **were with him,** sought Jesus; everyone is <u>searching for you</u>; go, that I may **preach;** why I came out, **preaching, cast out demons.**

   E (1:40–45) Leper **came to him;** make me **clean; touches,** makes him **clean,** <u>sternly charges secrecy</u>, See **you** say nothing, but talked **freely** *(polys).* He couldn't **openly** *(phaneros)* enter town; **came to him** <u>from every quarter</u>.

    F (2:1–13) **He returned again** *(eiserchomai palin),* paralytic, question in **hearts, rise** *(egeiro),* say this or that? Went out beside **sea.**

     G (2:14–17) Levi, follow me; in **house** (of tax collector), **eating; Pharisees:** why he **eat** with tax collectors and sinners? ("sinners" four times).

      H (2:18–19) <u>Old and new</u>. Three fasters: John's disciples, Pharisees, disciples of Pharisees; four non-fasters (disciples, Jesus, wedding guests, bridegroom).

       I (2:20a) The **days** <u>will come when</u> taken away

        J (2:20b) will be the bridegroom

       I' (2:20c) and <u>then they will</u> fast in that **day.**

      H' (2:21–22) <u>Old and new</u>. ("Old" three times; "new, fresh" four times)

     G' (2:23–28) On sabbath going through grain-fields; **Pharisees:** why doing not lawful? entered **house** of God, **ate** bread, to **eat.** ("sabbath" four times).

    F' (3:1–7a) **Again he entered** *(eiserchomai palin)* synagogue; man withered hand, hardness of **heart, come up** *(egeiro),* do this or that? Withdrew to the **sea.**

E' (3:7b–12) A **great** (*polys*) multitude from (four) regions, **great** multitude hearing all, **came to him,** healed **many,** to **touch** him, **unclean** spirits: **You** Son of God; he strictly ordered not to make him **known** (*phaneros*).

D' (3:13–19) Jesus called those he desired, appointed twelve to **be with him,** to be sent out to **preach, cast out demons: Simon** surnamed Peter, (rest of disciples).

C' (3:20–27) Family **went** (*exerchomai*) **seize** (*krateo*) him; say he possessed by Beelzebul, by prince of **demons** he **casts out demons;** Satan **cast out** Satan? If **house** divided, **house;** Satan; strong man's **house,** plunder **house.**

B' (3:28–3:35) Recognition. I say all sins forgiven, but whoever blasphemes **Holy Spirit,** never forgiveness; for said he had **unclean spirit.** Mother, brothers **came,** called. **Who are** my mother, brothers? Whoever does will of **God** is my brother, sister, mother.

A' (4:1–12) Messengers/message. **Teach** by **sea, boat,** on **sea, sea; taught** in parables, in **teaching,** listen, sower went out to sow; other seeds on rocky ground; seeds in good soil brought grain, yielding hundred-fold. Those about him with twelve: You **given** (*didomi*) secret of **Kingdom of God;** those outside, see not perceive, hear not understand, lest turn, be forgiven.

Act 2: Mark 4:13–6:46

A (4:13–34) Message metaphors. How will you understand **all** the parables? Sower sows word, (three failures), in good soil those who hear word, accept, bring forth grain 30-, 60- and 100-fold; to him who has will more be **given;** kingdom of God; seed grows, harvest; mustard seed, smallest of **all** seeds, greatest of **all** shrubs, **large** branches, birds of the **air** (*ouranos*); **many** parables, explained **everything.**

B (4:35–41) Non-recognition. In the **boat,** storm of wind, waves into **boat, boat** filling, [Jesus] asleep on cushion, **Teacher,** if we perish? Peace! ceased; great calm. Why afraid, no faith? awe; [disciples]: Who is this, that wind and sea obey him?

C (5:1–20) Out of **tombs,** man unclean spirit, **tombs, no one could bind** him, **bound** with chains; among **tombs,** cry out; saw Jesus; Son of Most High God, do not torment me; my name is Legion [Roman]; begged him ("beg" four times) not to **send**

them out; send us to swine, rushed into sea; people saw demoniac, **afraid.**

D (5:21–24) Synagogue <u>ruler</u>, Jairus by **name,** <u>falls at his
feet</u>, my daughter at point of death, lay <u>hands</u> on her, be
made well and <u>live</u>.

E (5:25–34) Woman with **twelve**-year blood flow, <u>spent
all she had</u>, **no** <u>better</u>; touch his <u>garment, garments,
healed</u> of disease; <u>told whole truth</u>, be <u>healed</u>.

F (5:35–40) <u>Daughter</u> is dead, why trouble Teacher?
Hearing, Jesus: Do not fear, only **believe;** came to
house, allowed none to follow except Peter, James,
John, **brother of James.** Weeping; child not dead,
but sleeping. <u>They laughed at him</u>. Took <u>father</u>,
<u>mother</u>, those with him, went where <u>child</u> was; tak-
ing her by **hand,** said:

G (5:41–42) Talitha cumi; which means, Little
girl, I say, <u>arise</u>; girl <u>got up, walked</u>; twelve years
old , they were <u>overcome with amazement</u>;

H (5:43) Charged no one should know this;
give her something to eat.

G' (6:1–2) Went away, came to his own country;
disciples followed. On sabbath, taught in synagogue; many who heard him were <u>astonished</u>,
Where this man get this? What wisdom given
him? What <u>mighty works</u> wrought by his hands?

F' (6:3–6) Is not this carpenter, <u>son</u> of Mary, **brother of
James,** Joses, Judas and Simon, are not his <u>sisters</u> with
us? <u>They took offense at him</u>. Jesus: Prophet is not
without honor, except in his own country, among own
<u>kin</u>, in own **house;** could do no mighty work there, laid
hands on a few, healed them; marveled at **unbelief.**

E' (6:7–13) Jesus sends out **twelve,** 2 by 2; <u>take nothing—</u>
no bread, **no** bag, **no** money; not put on 2 <u>tunics</u>; for <u>tes-
timony</u> against them; <u>preached</u>; <u>healed</u> them.

D' (6:14–16) <u>King</u> Herod, Jesus' **name** become known;
John Baptist <u>raised from dead</u>? Others, a prophet. Herod:
John, whom I <u>beheaded</u>, has been <u>raised</u>.

C' (6:17–29) Herod **sent,** seized John [Baptist], **bound** in <u>jail</u>,
Herodias wanted to kill him, but she **could not;** Herod **feared**

John, righteous and holy man; gave banquet daughter danced, pleased Herod and guests [Romans]: Ask for whatever wish ("ask" four times), head of John on platter; king **sent** soldier; his disciples took body, buried in **tomb.**

B' (6:30–33a) Recognition. Apostles returned, told all done, **taught;** Jesus: come away to lonely place, rest a while; had no leisure; went away in **boat** to lonely place. Many saw them, knew them.

A' (6:33b–46) Message metaphors. (feeding the multitude) They ran, from **all** towns, **great** throng, teach them **many** things. Jesus: **Give** them something to eat. Disciples: 200 denarii worth? How **many** loaves: five, two fish; groups of 100s and 50s; Taking five loaves, two fish, looked to **heaven** *(ouranos)* blessed; divided among **all;** they **all** ate; twelve baskets of pieces; those who ate 5,000.

Act 3: Mark 8:27–10:52

A (8:27–33) Recognition/non-recognition. **On the way,** he asked: Who people say I am? Who you say? Peter: You are Christ; **charged** *(epitimao)* tell no one. **Son of** man suffer **many** things, be rejected, killed, after three days **rise;** Peter **rebukes** him, Jesus **rebukes** Peter: **get** *(erchomai)* behind, Satan; not on side of God.

B (8:34–38) Discipleship/messengers. **Called to him** disciples; if anyone **would** come after me, deny self, take up cross; **whoever would** save **life,** lose it; **whoever** loses his **life,** saves it; gain world, forfeit **life?** What **give** in return for **life? Son of man** will be ashamed when **comes** in glory of Father with holy angels *(aggelos)*.

C (9:1–16) Initiation images. Some not taste death before **kingdom of God** come. **And after six days,** Jesus took Peter, **James and John** up mountain; garment became glistening white; appeared Elijah, Moses; Peter: **make** *(poieo)* three booths, **one** (for each); voice from cloud: **beloved Son, listen** *(akouo);* tell no one until **Son of** man **risen** from dead, question what **rising** meant; Elijah (John the Baptist) come first; **Son of** man suffer; Elijah, **did** to him what **pleased** *(thelo)*. They came to disciples; scribes arguing with them.

D (9:17–27) Man asks Jesus to cure mute son who goes rigid. Brought my **son; disciples** unable; faithless generation; spirit saw Jesus, boy fell, **rolled about.** He **rebuked** spirit; come out, never **enter** again; convulsing boy, like a corpse; most said **dead;** but Jesus **took** *(krateo)* **his hand, lifted him up** *(egeiro).*

E (9:28–35) In **house,** driven out by **anything** *(oudeis)* but prayer. Jesus taught: **Son of man will be delivered;** they will **kill** him; **after three days he will rise;** not understand, **afraid;** in **house,** what discuss **on the way; on the way** who greatest. Called **twelve.** If anyone **first, he** must **be last** of **all,** servant of **all.**

F (9:36–41) **Child, taking in his arms,** said, **whoever receives** one **such child** in my name **receives** me; **whoever receives** me, **receives** not me but <u>him who sent me</u>. **Teacher,** man casting out demons; we **forbade** *(kolyo);* not **following** us; **do not forbid** him; none do **mighty work** *(dynamis)* **able** speak evil; not against, for us. **Truly, I say to you, whoever** gives cup of water because you **belong** to Christ <u>will by no means lose reward</u>.

G (9:42–47a) **Whoever** <u>causes</u> little ones who believe in me <u>to sin</u>, millstone round <u>neck</u>. **If** <u>hand, cut off</u>, better enter life maimed, than with **two** <u>hands</u> to go hell. **If** <u>foot causes sin</u>, better lame than **two** <u>feet</u> in hell. **If** <u>eye causes sin, pluck out</u>; better enter kingdom of **God** with **one** <u>eye</u> than with **two,**

H (9:47b–50) be thrown <u>into hell</u>, worm not die, **fire** is <u>not quenched</u>. Everyone be salted with **fire;** salt is good; but if lost saltness, how season? Have salt in yourselves, <u>be at peace</u> one another.

(Mark10:1 inserted by editor, who cuts next six verses.)

I (Luke 9:51) Days near for him to be <u>received</u> up, he <u>set</u> his **face** *(prosopon)* to **go** *(poreuomai)* **to Jerusalem.**

J (Luke 9:52) He sent messengers ahead of him (lit., before his face), who went, entered village of Samaritans to make ready for him;

I' (Luke 9:53) but people would not <u>receive</u> him, because his **face** *(prosopon)* was **set toward** *(poreuomai)* **Jerusalem.**

H' (Luke 9:54–56) James, John saw it; Lord, want us to bid **fire** come down from heaven, consume them? He turned, rebuked them; went on.

G' (10:2–12) Lawful to divorce? Since creation, **God** made male, female; man joined to wife, **two** become **one** flesh; no longer **two, one** flesh; what **God** joined, not put asunder; **whoever** divorces, marries another, commits adultery; **if** she divorces, marries another, commits adultery.

F' (10:13–27) Bringing **children,** touch them; disciples rebuked; **do not hinder** *(kolyo),* to such **belongs** kingdom of God. **Truly, I say to you, whoever** not **receive** kingdom of God like **child** not enter. **Took in his arms; teacher,** eternal life? **Do not, do not; teacher,** from **childhood;** you will have treasure in heaven; **follow** me; Children, hard to enter kingdom of God; who **can** be saved? With men **impossible; possible** *(dynatos)* with God.

E' (10:28–34) Peter: We left **everything; no one** *(oudeis)* who left **house,** brothers, sisters; who will not receive hundredfold **houses,** brothers, sisters, in age to come eternal life. But many that **first** will **be last,** and **last first. On the road,** they **afraid.** Taking **the twelve,** told: **Son of man will be delivered** to chief priests, **deliver** to Gentiles, mock him, spit, **kill** him, and **after three days he will rise.**

D' (Secret Mark) Woman asks Jesus' mercy for deceased brother. Came to Bethany; brother had **died;** prostrating herself, **Son** of David, have mercy; **disciples rebuked** her. Angered, Jesus went to tomb; great cry; Jesus **rolled** stone, **going in,** stretched **hand, raised** *(egeiro)* **him, seizing** *(krateo)* **his hand.**

C' (Secret Mark+10:35–41) Initiation images. Young man **loved** him; **and after six days** Jesus told what to do, young man comes, linen cloth over naked; taught secret of **kingdom of God. Arising,** across Jordan. **James and John, sons of** Zebedee: **Want** *(thelo)* you **to do** *(poieo)* what we ask; what **want** me **to do?** Grant us sit **one** on right, **one** on left, in your glory; able drink cup I <u>drink, baptized</u> with <u>baptism I am baptized</u>; ten **heard** *(akouo),* indignant at **James and John.**

B' (10:42–45) <u>Discipleship/messenger</u>: Jesus **called** <u>them</u> **to him;** those who rule Gentiles, lord over, great men exercise authority; **whoever would** be great <u>must</u> be servant, **whoever would** first must be slave. **Son of man came** not to be served, but to serve, and to **give** his **life** <u>as ransom</u> for many.

A' (Secret Mark+10:46–52) <u>Non-recognition/recognition</u>. Came to Jericho; sister of young man Jesus loved, his mother, Salome there; <u>he did not receive them</u>; leaving, Bartimaeus, **son of** Timaeus, by **road-side.** Heard <u>Jesus of Nazareth</u>, cried, Jesus, **Son of** <u>David</u>, have mercy; many **rebuked** *(epitamao)* him; Jesus, **Son of** <u>David</u>; call him; **rise;** he sprang up, **came** *(erchomai)* to Jesus; <u>Master</u>, let me receive sight; faith made you well; he followed him **on the way.**

Act 4: Mark 11:1–14:9

A (11:1–6a) <u>Messengers/message</u>. Near Jerusalem, Jesus sent two disciples; go into village, find colt; bring it. If anyone says, why you **doing** this? say, the Lord **has** need, will send back. Went, found colt, untied it. What you **doing?** Told them what Jesus said;

B (11:6b–11) <u>Recognition</u>. they **let** them **go** *(aphiemi),* brought to Jesus; he <u>sat</u> upon it; garments on road; others spread branches; cried out, Hosanna! Blessed who comes in name of Lord! Blessed; Hosanna in highest! Entered Jerusalem, temple, late, went out to **Bethany** with twelve.

C (11:12–20) Jesus is <u>hungry</u>; sees <u>fig tree</u>, went to **find** anything, but **found** nothing; not **season** *(kairos)* for <u>figs</u>; not <u>eat fruit</u> again; entered temple, Drive out <u>those who sold, bought</u>; <u>overturned</u>, <u>money-changers</u>; not written? My **house** be called **house** of prayer. **Chief priests and scribes, sought way** to <u>destroy him</u>; feared, multitude, go in **evening,** in **morning** saw fig tree withered.

D (11:21–33) **Look, fig tree; have faith** in God; **Truly, I say to you,** <u>mountain</u>, **come to pass** *(ginomai);* so **Father,** in **heaven.** Came to Jerusalem; to him: By what <u>authority</u>, who gave you <u>authority</u>; **from heaven** or from **men,** if say **from heaven,** he will say, why **did not believe** him; shall we say from **men?** John <u>real</u> **prophet;** we do not **know** by what <u>authority</u> I do this.

    E   (12:1–12) Parables; man planted vineyard, **built** tower, into <u>another country</u>; tenants **beat, beat,** <u>kill, kill</u> servants sent <u>(in owner's name)</u>; still beloved son; send <u>son; killed him</u>; **give** vineyard; **read** scripture; **stone** which **builders** rejected, **Lord.**

      F (12:13–23) Teacher, you do <u>not regard position of men</u>; know you true, truly; <u>pay taxes</u>? their <u>hypocrisy; coin; render</u> to Caesar, to God. Teacher, <u>seven</u> brothers, died, woman (widow) also died, in resurrection whose wife will be; <u>seven</u> had her as wife.

        G (12:24–27) Jesus: know neither <u>scriptures</u> nor power of God? not read in book of Moses [Ex 3:6] I am God of Abraham, Isaac, Jacob? ("God" six times)

          H (12:28) A scribe comes as they dispute one another, **seeing he answered** <u>well</u>, **asked:** Which commandment first of all?

            I (12:29–31) Jesus: Lord **is one, love** your God **with all** your **heart,** soul, mind, **strength;** second, **love neighbor as yourself.** Is **no other** commandment <u>greater</u> than these.

              J (12:32a) Scribe said: You are right, Teacher;

            I' (12:32b–33) you truly said he **is one, no other** but he; to **love** him **with all** the **heart,** understanding, **strength,** and **love one's neighbor as oneself,** is <u>much more</u> than burnt offerings and sacrifices.

          H' (12:34) When Jesus **saw he answered** <u>wisely</u>, said, You are not far from kingdom of God. No one dared **ask** any **question.**

        G' (12:35–37) Jesus: How can <u>scribes</u> say Christ son of David? Inspired by Holy Spirit, David: [Ps 110:1]. David (three times) calls himself Lord (three times).

F' (12:38–44) In his **teaching,** said: Scribes <u>seek salutations, honor,</u> devour <u>widows'</u> house <u>pretense.</u> <u>Money in treasury, sums</u>; poor <u>widow</u> came, put in two <u>coins,</u> Truly, this poor widow put in more. *(ballo* put in, contribute, used seven times)

E' (13:1–20) Wonderful **stones, buildings;** not one **stone;** many <u>will come in my name; nation, nation</u>; **beaten,** say whatever **given;** brother will <u>deliver up</u> brother <u>to death, and father his child, hated</u> by all; let the **reader** understand, field, the **Lord.**

D' (13:21–32) **Look** here, **look** there. **Do not believe** it; **false prophets,** moon not give light; **from heaven,** <u>powers,</u> Son of **man,** <u>power.</u> From **fig tree, become** *(ginomai)* tender; **taking place** *(ginomai),* **Truly, I say to you,** these things **take place** *(ginomai),* **heaven,** <u>earth</u>; no one **knows,** not even angels in **heaven,** nor Son, only **Father.**

C' (13:33–14:2) Watch, when **time** *(kairos)* will come; man leaves home, <u>servants, each with his work, doorkeeper,</u> for master of **house** will come, in **evening** or **morning; find** you asleep. <u>Feast</u> of Unleavened <u>Bread</u>; **chief priests and scribes were seeking how** to arrest, <u>kill him,</u> not during <u>feast,</u> lest <u>tumult</u> of people.

B' (14:3–6) <u>Recognition.</u> At **Bethany,** he <u>sat at table,</u> woman came with flask of ointment, very costly, broke, poured over head. <u>Why</u> wasted? **Let** her **alone** *(aphiemi);* Why trouble her; she has done a beautiful thing to me.

A' (14:7–9) <u>Messengers/message.</u> You always **have** poor with you; you can **do** good to them; not always **have** me; she has **done** what she could, anointed my body beforehand. Truly, wherever gospel is preached in whole world, what she has **done** will be told in memory of her.

Act 5: Mark 14:10–15:33

A (14:10–18) <u>Messengers.</u> Judas Iscariot, one of <u>twelve,</u> went to chief priests to betray him; priests <u>promise</u> to give <u>money.</u> <u>First</u> day when <u>sacrificed</u> passover lamb; he sent <u>two</u> disciples, said, go, meet, wherever enter, say, Teacher says where room, to eat passover **with** disciples? Will show you room; disciples **went** *(erchomai),* found as he told them; prepared passover. When it **was** *(ginomai)* <u>evening</u>, he **came** *(erchomai)*

with the <u>twelve</u>; at table, Jesus: **Truly, I say to you,** one of **you will** betray me, one eating **with me.**

B (14:19–21) <u>Non-recognition</u>. Sorrowful, **one** another saying, <u>Is it I</u>? [Jesus]: **One** <u>of twelve</u>, dipping into dish **with** me. <u>Son of man</u> goes as **written;** woe by whom <u>Son of man</u> is betrayed; better if not born.

C (14:22–31) He **took** bread, blessed, broke it, **gave** *(didomi)* it to them; **take,** this my <u>body</u>; **took** cup, **gave** it to them, they all drank; my blood; I'll not <u>drink</u> again <u>fruit of vine</u> until I drink new in **kingdom;** Jesus: You will all fall away.

D (14:32–42) Gethsemane, pray; asks if hour might pass; remove cup from me; yet <u>not what I will, but what thou wilt</u>. [<u>three</u> disciples] not know what to **answer** ("watch" three times, but they fell asleep <u>three</u> times.) Son of man is **betrayed** *(paradidomi);* rise, my **betrayer** at hand.

E (14:43–54) Judas, one of the twelve, comes with chief priests, elders, scribes, armed crowd; given sign; when came up Judas kissed Jesus. They seize him. One who **stood by** *(paristemi)* struck <u>slave</u> of **high priest.** Let scriptures be fulfilled; all <u>forsook</u> him; young man followed, seized, ran away. **Peter** followed into **courtyard;** sitting with guards, **warming himself.**

F (14:55–59) <u>Whole</u> council sought testimony, put to **death;** we heard him say, <u>I will destroy this temple, in 3 days will build another</u>.

G (14:60–61) **High priest** <u>stood up</u>; what **testify** *(katamartyreo)* against you? Silent. Again **high priest** asked, Are you the Christ, **Son of** the <u>Blessed</u>?

H (14:62a) And Jesus said, I am;

G' (14:62–64a) You will see **Son of** man <u>seated</u> at right hand of <u>Power</u>; **high priest** tore garments; why need **witnesses?** *(martys)* You heard; what is decision?

F' (14:64b–65) They <u>all</u> condemned him as deserving **death.** Some spit on him, struck him, saying, <u>Prophesy</u>!

E' (14:66–72) **Peter** in **courtyard,** <u>maid</u> **of high priest,** seeing Peter **warming himself,** said you were with Nazarene; denied it; again to **bystanders** *(paristemi)*

denied it; she said, one of them; **bystanders** to Peter: you
one of them. (denied knowing Jesus third time); remembered (prophecy), broke down.

D' (15:1–15) Priests, council **delivered** *(paradidomi)* him to
Pilate, asked (three times about "King of the Jews"); accused,
Pilate asked: Have you no **answer** to make? Crowd asks Pilate
'to do as he was wont to do for them.' Pilate: What I do?
Crucify!, **delivered** Jesus to be crucified.

C' (15:16–24) Hail, **King** of Jews; strike his head; led out to
crucify; brought to place 'skull'; **offered** *(didomi)* him wine
mixed with myrrh, but did not **take** it; crucified him; divided
his garments among; casting lots for them.

B' (15:25–32a+Luke 23:39) Non-recognition: Third hour when
crucified **Inscription read:** King of the Jews; with him crucified
two robbers, **one, one;** You, who would rebuild temple in three
days; mocked: Let Christ, King of Israel, come down, that we may
see, believe. (Editor inserts 32b, deletes following.) **One** of criminals, railed, Are you not the Christ? Save yourself and us!

A' (Luke23:40–44) Messenger. Other rebuked him: Not fear God? You
under same sentence; we have due reward; this man nothing wrong.
Said: Jesus, remember me when you **come** *(erchomai)* into your kingdom. He (promises), **Truly, I say to you,** today **you will** be **with me**
in Paradise. (Mark 15:33=Luke 23:44) When sixth hour had **come**
(ginomai), darkness over earth until ninth hour.

Conclusion: Mark 15:34–16:8+1:3

A (15:34–36) Messenger forsaken? At ninth hour, Jesus cried with a loud
voice, *(phone),* Eloi, Eloi, lama . . . ? means My **God,** my **God,** why hast
thou forsaken me [Ps 22:1]? Some bystanders: **Behold** *(ide),* he **calling**
(phone), Elijah. One ran, filling sponge full of vinegar, gave to drink [Ps
69:21]. Let us see whether Elijah will come to take him down.

B (15:37–39) Recognition. Jesus uttered loud cry, breathed his last.
Curtain of temple torn in two top to bottom; when centurion, who
stood facing him, **saw** he breathed his last, said, Truly this man was
the Son of God!

C (15:40–42) Women looking from afar, among whom **Mary
Magdalene,** and **Mary the mother of James** the younger and
Joses, and **Salome,** who, when he was in Galilee, followed,

ministered to him; other women who came with him to Jerusalem. When evening had come, first day of Preparation, day before **the sabbath,**

    D (15:43) **Joseph** of Arimathea, respected member of council, looking for kingdom of God, took courage, went to Pilate, asked for **the body** of Jesus.

        E (15:44a) Pilate wondered if **he was** already **dead;** summoning **centurion,**

            F (15:44b) he asked whether he was already dead.

        E' (15:45a) When he learned from **centurion** that **he was dead,**

    D' (15:45b–46) he granted **the body** to **Joseph;** he bought linen shroud; taking him down, wrapped him in linen shroud, laid him in tomb hewn out of rock; rolled a stone against door of tomb.

C' (15:47–16:2) **Mary Magdalene and Mary the mother** of **Joses** saw where he was laid. When **the sabbath** was past, Mary Magdalene, **Mary mother of James,** and **Salome** bought spices, so might go, anoint him. Very early first day of week went to tomb when sun had risen.

B' (16:3–6a) Recognition. Saying to one another, Who will roll away stone from door of tomb? Looking up, saw stone rolled back—very large. Entering tomb, they **saw** young man sitting on right side, dressed in white robe; were amazed; do not be amazed; you seek Jesus of Nazareth, who was crucified. He has risen, he is not here;

A' (16:6b–8+1:1–3) Messenger forsaken. **See** *(ide)* place where laid him. But go, tell his disciples and Peter that he going before you to Galilee; there you will see him, as he told you. They went out, fled from tomb; trembling and astonishment came upon them; and they said nothing to anyone, for they were afraid. [The rest of A' probably jumps back to the opening.[1]] Beginning of Gospel of Jesus Christ, Son of **God.** As it is written; **behold** *(idou),* I send my messenger before thy face who shall prepare way [Mal 3:1, 4:5 Elijah]; **voice** *(phone)* of one crying in the wilderness; prepare way of Lord, make paths straight [Isa 40:3].

---

1. Mark allows borrowing from neighboring patterns (here, the prologue!) for additional catchwords or corresponding elements, such as two biblical allusions in each step here.

Secret Mark Episode in Act 3's Smaller Chiasms

THE LONG-MISSING "young man" episode—a two-part story once located between 10:34 and 35, and within 10:46 in the Gospel of Mark—fits well in the Act 3 chiasm seen in Appendix 2. Since the gospel author evidently created the chiastic puzzles in a way that any chiasm of some length could be split in half to produce two new chiasms, we demonstrate that thesis in the second half of Act 3 where it may be seen also that the episode known only from the Secret Gospel of Mark really belongs in Original Mark.

Second Half Chiasm in Act 3: Luke 9:51–Mark 11:2a

There was a "problem" with the second half of Act 3. It seemed that the gospel-length macrocode already presented a readymade chiastic pattern for that span. The "face set toward Jerusalem" episode from Luke 9:51–56 (along with Mark 10:2–9) and Mark 10:45–52 (+11:2a) were a chiastic pair in the macrocode. Could they also be the A and A' steps for the second half of Act 3, ending up at the same center verse? "So be it," I thought at first. At last, however, I remembered the rule for most chiasms in Mark is that the midpoint should reflect a theme and/or catchwords of that particular chiasm's beginning and end. The macrocode's center is the saying of Jesus at 10:31, the very idea behind chiasms and carried out here in the gospel's longest one. A different center would be suitable for the second half of Act 3, which begins with the ominous turn toward Jerusalem and ends with Jesus and followers arriving at the city's outskirts. The creative author used an alternate midpoint. The phrase "going up to Jerusalem" occurs in verses 32a and 33a; the tiny center is the phrase "what was to happen to him," referring to Jesus' last prediction of his fate.

A (Luke 9:51–56+Mark 10:2–9) Days <u>drew near</u> to <u>be received up</u>, set face to go to **Jerusalem;** he **sent** messengers, who went, entered **village;** they would **not receive** *(dechomai)* him, because face set toward **Jerusalem; his disciples** James, John: **Want** us to bid fire to come down *(katabaino),* consume them? He **rebuked** them; went to another **village.** Pharisees tested, if divorce lawful. <u>Moses, Moses;</u> for <u>hardness of heart</u>, he wrote, God **made** *(poieo)* them male, female; leave father, **mother; two** become one.

B (10:10–16) **Whoever** divorces wife; they were bringing children; disciples rebuked them; when Jesus saw it, was **indignant;** do not hinder; to such belongs <u>kingdom;</u> **whoever** not receive <u>kingdom</u> like child; blessed, laying his <u>hands</u> on them.

C (10:17–19) **Setting out** *(ekporeuomai),* man knelt before him, good **teacher, what** must I **do** to inherit <u>eternal life</u>; no one good but God **alone** *(heis);* you **know** commandments: do not kill, do not; honor <u>father</u>, mother.

D (10:20–28) **Teacher,** all these I observed from my <u>youth</u> *(neotes).* Jesus, **looking upon him, loved him;** sell, give to poor, come, follow me; at that saying, went sorrowful; Jesus **looked** around, said: hard for those with <u>riches</u> to **enter** *(eiserchomai)* **kingdom of God;** hard to **enter kingdom of God,** for **rich** man to **enter kingdom of God;** astonished, they said: Then who can be saved? Jesus **looked** at them: With men impossible, not with **God;** all things possible with **God.** Peter: Left everything, followed you.

E (10:29–31) Jesus: Truly, I say, no one who left house, **brothers,** <u>sisters</u>, mother, father, children or lands, <u>for my sake and for gospel</u>, who will not receive a hundredfold <u>now in this time</u>, houses, **brothers,** <u>sisters</u>, mothers, children and lands, <u>with persecutions</u>, and <u>in age</u> to **come** eternal life. But many that <u>first will be last, last first</u>.

F (10:32a) On the road *(hodos),* **going up** *(anabaino)* **to Jerusalem,** Jesus walking ahead; they were amazed;

those who followed were afraid. Taking the twelve again, he <u>began</u> *(archo)* to tell them

G (10:32b) what was to happen *(symbaino)* to him,

F' (10:33a) saying, Behold, we are **going up** *(anabaino)* **to Jerusalem;** and Son of man will be delivered to <u>chief priests</u> *(archiereus)* and scribes,

E' (10:33b–34+Secret Mark) and they will <u>condemn him to death, deliver him to the Gentiles; they will mock, spit on him, scourge, and kill him</u> (persecutions); <u>after three days he will rise</u> (gospel). They **come** into Bethany, a <u>woman</u> whose **brother** died; **coming,** prostrated herself before Jesus: Son of David, have mercy; disciples rebuked her; Jesus, angered, went off with her, tomb; straightway <u>great cry heard</u> from tomb; going near <u>Jesus rolled away stone from door of tomb;</u>

D' (Secret Mark) **Going in** *(eiserchomai)* where <u>young man</u> is, he stretched forth hand, raised him, seizing his hand; <u>young man</u>, **looking upon him, loved him;** they go out of tomb to house of <u>young man</u>; he was **rich;** and after six days, <u>young man</u> comes to him wearing linen cloth over naked body; **taught** secret of **kingdom of God.** Arising, he returned other side of Jordan (with God possible for rich man).

C' (10:35–38a) James, John, sons of <u>Zebedee</u>, **came forward** *(prosporeuomai):* **Teacher, do whatever** we ask; **what** want me **to do?** Grant us <u>sit</u>, **one** *(heis)* at <u>right hand</u>, **one** at <u>left, in your glory</u>; you do **not know what** you are asking.

B' (10:38b–44) Able drink cup I drink; be baptized with baptism I am baptized? we able; cup drink, baptism, baptized; to sit at my right <u>hand</u> or my left (<u>hand</u>) not mine to grant; when ten heard it, they **indignant;** those who <u>rule over the Gentiles lord it over</u>; **whoever** great must be servant; **whoever** first must be slave of all.

A' (10:45–46a+Secret Mark+46b–52; 11:1–2a) Son of man came to serve, <u>give his life as ransom</u>; Jericho, sister of young man Jesus loved, his **mother** and Salome there; Jesus did **not receive** *(apodechomai)* them. Bartimaeus, blind begger, by roadside: Son of <u>David</u>, have mercy; many **rebuked** him; cried: Son of <u>David</u>; <u>take heart</u>, he calling you; Jesus: What do you **want** me to **do** *(poieo)* for you? Blind man: My sight. Go, faith made you well; <u>drew near</u> to **Jerusalem;** he **sent two** of **his disciples;** go into **village** opposite you.

Fourth-Quarter, Act 3: Mark 10:31–34+Secret Mark+10:46–11:1

The final two people in Original Mark to benefit from Jesus' miraculous powers were the young man raised from the dead and a blind beggar. Their succinct stories of devotion to Jesus form the long A steps at start and finish of this last-quarter chiasm in Act 3. And the author apparently hints that they are as likely as anyone in the Gospel to be the (preordained?) choices to sit on Jesus' right and left in heaven, "those for whom it has been prepared" (10:40b), which is the evident midpoint of this chiasm. Jesus and the young man shared "agape" love; Jesus praised the persistent beggar for his faith and Bartimaeus began following Jesus. Though questioning whether the A step was this long, I felt that a parallel was intended between the linen cloth worn (literally, "thrown about") by the young man and the mantle the blind beggar "threw off" at the chance to meet Jesus. *Alas, a strong alternate chiasm is possible.* B may begin at "Going near, Jesus . . ." and end after the third use of "young man," which also means "servant." If so, three uses of "serve/servant" (10:41–45) form B'. For C and C', the Secret Mark words "after six days," naked [body], teaching the secret, "arising," and "Jordan" are initiation images resonating with six mentions of "baptize/baptism" (10:38–40), confirming the nature of the six-day rite. Thereafter, v. 35 is D, v. 36 is E, and v. 27 is D'.

A (10:31–34+Secret Mark) But many that are first will be last, and last first. They were **on the road,** going up **to Jerusalem,** Jesus walking ahead; were amazed, those who **followed** afraid. Taking the twelve, told what was to happen to him; we are going up **to Jerusalem; Son of** man will be delivered to priests and scribes, they will condemn him to death, deliver to Gentiles; mock, spit upon him, scourge, kill him; three days he will <u>rise</u>. **They come** to Bethany. <u>Woman whose brother</u> died **was there.** Coming, she prostrated herself before Jesus, **Son of David, have mercy;** disciples **rebuked** her. Jesus, angered, went with her to garden tomb; great **cry** *(phoneo)* was **heard** from tomb. Going near, Jesus rolled stone from door of tomb; going where young man was, stretched his hand, raised him, seizing hand. Young man, looking upon him, loved him, beseeched to be with him; came to house of young man, rich. After <u>six</u> days Jesus told him what; in evening, young man came, **wearing** *(periballo)* <u>linen cloth</u> over his naked body. Remained with him that

night, for Jesus taught him the secret of the kingdom of God. Arising,
returned to other side of <u>the Jordan</u>.

    B (10:35–3) James and John, **sons of** Zebedee, came forward to
him, said, Teacher, we want you to <u>do for us whatever we ask</u> of you.
He said, What do you want me to do <u>for you</u>? They said, **Grant**
(didomi) us to sit, one at your right hand and one at your left, in
your glory.

        C (10:38–39) Jesus: **You** do not **know** what you are asking. Are
you able to drink cup that I drink, or to be baptized with baptism with which I was baptized? They said: We are able. And
Jesus said to them, the cup that I drink you will drink; and with
the baptism with which I am baptized, you will be baptized;
(two sets of requirements)

            D (10:40a) but <u>to sit at my right hand or at my left</u> not mine
to grant,

                E (10:40b) but it is for those for whom it has been prepared.
            D' (10:41) When the ten heard it, they began to be indig-
nant at <u>James and John</u>;

        C' (10:42–44) Jesus called them, said, **You know** that those who
are supposed to rule over Gentiles lord it over them, and their
great men exercise authority over them. But it shall not be so
among you; whoever would be great among you must be your
<u>servant</u>; whoever would be first among you must be <u>slave</u> of all.
(two sets of requirements)

    B' (10:45) For **Son** of man also came not to be <u>served</u> but to <u>serve</u>,
to **give** *(didomi)* his life as a ransom <u>for many</u>.

A' (10:46–52, 11:1a) **They came** to Jericho; <u>sister of the young man</u>
whom Jesus loved, his mother and Salome **were there;** Jesus did not
receive them. As he was leaving Jericho with his disciples and great multitude, Bartimaeus, a blind beggar, **son of** Timaeus, was sitting by **roadside**. When he **heard** it was Jesus of Nazareth, began to cry out, Jesus,
Son of David, have mercy on me. Many **rebuked** him, telling him be
silent, but cried more, **Son of David, have mercy.** Jesus stopped: **Call**
(phoneo) him; they **called** blind man, saying, Take heart; <u>rise</u>, he is **calling** you; **throwing off** *(apoballo)* <u>his mantle</u>, sprang up, came to Jesus.
Jesus: What do you want me to do for you? Blind man said: Master, let
me receive my sight. Jesus: Go your way; your faith has made you well.
Immediately he received his sight, **followed** him **on the way.** When
they drew near **to Jerusalem.**

Eighths, 7th of 8 chiasms in Act 3:
Mark 10:32b–34+Secret Mark

Jesus told the fearful, unperceptive twelve of the awful things to befall him in Jerusalem as well as his resurrection after three days (A); but Jesus then instructed a new, devoted follower on steps toward learning the kingdom secrets (A'). This chiasm turns ironically on Jesus rolling away the stone from the tomb's entrance. After Jesus' body was laid to rest, this task that should have been done by the twelve but was done instead by the young man.

A (10:32b–34) Taking the twelve again, he began to tell them what was to happen to him; Behold, we are going up to Jerusalem; the Son of man will be delivered to the chief priests and scribes; they will condemn him to death, deliver him to the Gentiles; they will mock him, spit on him, scourge him, kill him; **and after** three **days** he will **rise.**

> B (Secret Mark) *sister's plea* And they **come** to Bethany. And a certain woman whose brother had died was there. Coming, she prostrated herself before Jesus and says to him, Son of David, have mercy on me. But the disciples rebuked her.

>> C (Secret Mark) And Jesus, being angered, **went off** *(aperchomai)* with her in the garden **where** the tomb **was,**

>>> D (Secret Mark) and **straightway** a great cry was heard from **the tomb.**

>>>> E (Secret Mark) And going near, Jesus rolled away the stone

>>> D' (Secret Mark) from the door of **the tomb,** and **straightway,**

>> C' (Secret Mark) **going in** *(eiserchomai)* **where** the young man **was,** he stretched forth his hand and raised him, seizing his hand.

> B' (Secret Mark) *brother's plea* But the young man, looking upon him, loved him and began to beseech him that he might be with him. And going out of the tomb, they **came** into the house of the young man, for he was rich.

A' (Secret Mark) **And after** six **days,** Jesus told him what to do, and in the evening the young man comes to him, wearing a linen cloth over his naked body. And he remained with him that night, for Jesus taught him the secret of the kingdom of God. And thence, **arising,** he returned to the other side of the Jordan.

Eighths, 8th of 8 chiasms, Act 3: Mark 10:35–52.

Jesus asked the identical question of the two brothers and of the blind Bartimaeus, and the point of the midpoint is that his followers should be faithful servants.

A (10:35–39) *demanding request* James and John, the **sons** of Zebedee, came forward: <u>Teacher</u>, we want you to do for us whatever we ask of you. <u>He said</u>, **What do you want me to do for you?** Grant us to sit, one at your right hand and one at your left, in your glory. Jesus: You do not know what you are asking. Are you able to drink cup that I drink, or to be baptized with baptism with which I am baptized? They said, We are able. Jesus: Cup that I drink you will drink; with the baptism with which I was baptized, you will be baptized.

   B (10:40–42a) but to sit at my right hand or at my left is not mine to **grant** *(didomi),* but it is <u>for those for whom it has been prepared</u> (as in the fourth quarter chiasm, the young man and Bartimaeus, both mentioned here in B') **When** the ten **heard it,** they **began** to be indignant at James and John. Jesus called to them and said,

      C (10:42b) You know that those who are supposed to <u>rule over</u> *(archo)* Gentiles <u>lord it over</u> them,

         D (10:42c) and their **great** men <u>exercise authority</u> over them.

           E (10:43a) But it shall not be so among you;

         D' (10:43b) but whoever would be **great** among you must be your <u>servant</u>;

      C' (10:44–44) whoever would be <u>first</u> *(protos)* among you must be <u>slave of all</u>.

   B' (10:45+Secret Mark+46–47a) For Son of man also came out not to be served but to serve, and to **give** *(didomi)* his life as ransom for many. They come to Jericho; sister of <u>young man whom Jesus loved</u>, his mother and Salome were there, and Jesus did not receive them; as he was leaving Jericho with his disciples and great multitude, <u>Bartimaeus, a blind beggar</u>, son of Timaeus, was **sitting** by the roadside. And **when** he **heard it** was Jesus of Nazareth, he **began** to cry out,

A' (10:47b–52) *plea for mercy* and say, Jesus, **Son** of David, have mercy on me! Many rebuked him, telling him be silent; but cried out all the more, **Son** of David, have mercy on me! Jesus stopped: Call him. Called blind man, saying, Take heart; rise, he is calling you. Throwing off his mantle he sprang up, came to Jesus. Jesus said, **What do you want me to do for you?** Blind man said, Master, let me receive sight. Jesus: Go your way; your faith has made you well. Immediately he received sight, followed him on the way.

If two more chiasms showed up after halving the quarter length chiasm, then why not split those two in half and find four more in Act 3's Round of Sixteen? The author, as seen repeatedly, does need some leeway on where each chiasm starts and ends, sometimes using the same passages for adjacent chiasms.

Sixteenths, 13th of 16, Act 3: Mark 10:32b–34+Secret Mark

This chiasm contrasts the personal characteristics of the young man and the twelve. The latter rebuked a woman seeking mercy, provoking Jesus briefly to anger. Complying with woman's appeal, Jesus resuscitated her brother, who will emerge as a model disciple.

> A (10:32b–34+Secret Mark) They were amazed, and those who followed were afraid. Taking the twelve again, he began to tell them what was to happen to him, saying, Behold, we are going up to Jerusalem; Son of man delivered to chief priests and scribes; condemn him to death, deliver him to Gentiles, mock, spit, scourge him and **kill** *(apokteino)* him; after three days he will rise.
>> B (Secret Mark) They **come** *(erchomai)* to Bethany. A certain woman whose brother had died was there. **And coming** *(erchomai)*, she prostrated herself before Jesus, says: Son of David, have mercy on me.
>>> C (Secret Mark) But the disciples rebuked her, and being angered,
>> B' (Secret Mark) Jesus **went off** *(aperchomai)* with her into garden where tomb was, and straightway a great cry was heard from the tomb. **And going near** *(proserchomai)*,
> A' (Secret Mark) Jesus rolled away the stone from door of the tomb, straightway going in where young man was, he **stretched forth** *(ekteino)* his hand and raised him, seizing his hand; young man, looking upon him, loved him.

Sixteenths, 14th of 16, Act 3: Secret Mark+10:35–37

Being raising from the dead and being with Jesus are themes that introduce and conclude this chiasm. Jesus rebuffed James and John, who demanded to be with Jesus in his (heavenly) glory, but the young man's loving request to be with him was promptly granted. The midpoint uses the verb "to rise," which can mean merely getting up in the morning, but another meaning of rising figuratively from the dead (a la baptism) is teased out by the reference to the River Jordan, site of Jesus' baptism. The word "hand" *(cheir)*, used twice in A, is underlined, not boldfaced, because the terms "at your right and left" are different words in which "hand" is understood but not stated.

> A (Secret Mark) And straightway, going in where the young man was, he stretched forth his <u>hand</u> and <u>raised</u> him, seizing his <u>hand</u>. But the young man, looking upon him, loved him and began to <u>beseech him that he might be with him</u>. And going out of the tomb, they came into house of young man, for he was rich. And after six days, <u>Jesus told him what to do,</u>
>> B (Secret Mark) and in evening the young man <u>comes to him</u>, wearing linen cloth over his naked body. And he remained with him that night, for Jesus **taught** him the secret of the kingdom of God.
>>> C (Secret Mark) Arising, he returned to the other side of the Jordan.
>> B' (10:35) James and John, the sons of Zebedee, <u>came forward to him</u>, said, **Teacher,** we want you to do for us whatever we ask of you.
> A' (10:36–38a) He said, <u>What do you want me to do</u> for you? They said, <u>Grant us</u> to sit, one at your <u>right hand</u> and one at your <u>left, in your glory</u>. But Jesus said to them, You do not know <u>what you are asking</u>.

Sixteenths, 15th of 16, Act 3: Mark 10:35–45

One of the Greek words for "not" *(ou)* appears once each in A and A', and B and B'. These negative admonitions from Jesus only reinforce the reason why the ten other disciples were upset with the favor-seeking James and John.

> A (10:35–38a) And James, John, the **sons of** Zebedee, came forward to him and said to him, Teacher, we **want** *(thelo)* you to do **whatever** *(hos)*

we ask of you; he said, What do you **want** *(thelo)* me to do for you?
Grant *(didomi)* us to <u>sit</u>, one at your right hand, one at your left, in
your glory. But Jesus said, you do **not** know what you are asking.

  B (10:38b–40) Are you able to drink cup I drink; or to be baptized
  with the baptism with which I am baptized? They said, we are able.
  And Jesus said to them, the cup that I drink you will drink, and
  with the baptism with which I am baptized, you will be baptized;
  but to sit at my right hand or my left is **not** mine to grant, but it is
  for those whom it has been prepared.

    C (10:41) When the ten heard it, they began to be indignant at
    James and John.

  B' (10:42–43a) Jesus called to him and said, you know that those
  who rule over the Gentiles lord it over them; and their great men
  exercise authority over them. But it shall **not** be so among you;

A' (10:43b–45) but **whoever** *(hos)* **would** *(thelo)* be great among you
must be your servant; **whoever** *(hos)* **would** *(thelo)* be first among you
must be slave of all. For **Son of** man also came **not** be served but to
serve, and to **give** *(didomi)* his life as ransom for many.

Sixteenths, 16th of 16, Act 3: Mark 10:46–11:1

Jesus is most often referred to as "he" in Mark, but in this chiasm the
author pointedly uses his name eight times (including twice in the
addendum to the Secret Mark episode). "Jesus" is used four times on
either side of the midpoint, which has the appelation cried out by the
blind beggar.

  A (10:46a+Secret Mark+46b) They came <u>to Jericho</u>; sister of <u>the young
  man</u> whom **Jesus** loved, his mother and Salome were there, and **Jesus**
  did not receive them. As he was leaving <u>Jericho</u> with **his disciples** and
  great multitude, Bartimaeus, a **blind** beggar, son of Timaeus, was sitting by **roadside** *(hodos)*.

    B (10:47–48a) When he heard it was **Jesus** of Nazareth, began to
    <u>cry out</u> *(krazo),* **Jesus,** Son of David, have mercy on me. <u>Many
    rebuked him</u>, telling him be silent, but he <u>cried out</u> all the more,

      C (10:48b) Son of David, have mercy on me.

    B' (10:49) **Jesus** stopped and said to them: <u>Call</u> *(phoneo)* him. And
    they <u>called</u> the blind man, <u>saying, Take heart</u>; rise, he is <u>calling</u> you.
    Throwing off his mantle, sprang up, and came to **Jesus.**

A' (10:51–11:1) And **Jesus** said to him: What do you want me to do for you? And the **blind** man said: Master, let me receive my sight. **Jesus** said to him: Go your way; your faith has made you well. Immediately he received his sight, and followed him **on the way** *(hodos);* when they drew near <u>to Jerusalem, to Bethpage and Bethany</u>, at the Mount of Olives, he sent two of **his disciples**.

Is it possible to divide further the second half of Act 3 into smaller-yet chiasms? Maybe. I had not tried by the time this book went to press. An excellent candidate is seen below.

Thirty-seconds, Act 3: Mark 10:35–41.

A (10:35–36) **James and John,** sons of Zebedee, came forward to him: Teacher, we want you to do for us whatever we ask of you. He said, What do you want me to do?
  B (10:37) They said to him, **Grant** us **to sit,** one at your **right hand** and one at your **left,** in your glory.
    C (10:38) But Jesus said, You do not know what you are asking. Are you able to **drink the cup that I drink,** or **to be baptized with the baptism with which I am baptized?**
      D (10:39) They said, We are able.
    C' (10:40) And Jesus said, **The cup that I drink** you **will drink;** and **with the baptism with which I am baptized,** you **will be baptized;**
  B' (10:41) but **to sit** at my **right hand** or at my **left** is not mine **to grant,** but is for those for whom it has been prepared.
A' (10:42) When ten heard it, began to be indignant at **James and John.**

The episode above is so obviously a chiasm that many students and scholars of Mark might have been lulled into thinking that the gospel author was content to compose only short and plainly visible puzzles. God forbid that a fine concentric episode such as this should be made to serve also chiasms to its right and left! Yet, that practice illustrates exactly the magnificent achievement of this first-century writer and puzzle-maker.

Establishing the Borders of the Editor's Insertion of 6:47–8:26

Mark 6:31–46

ONE OF MANY EPISODE CHIASMS in Original Mark, the feeding of the multitude shows that verses 45 and 46 in chapter 6 were written by the author, not the editor, because of the several catchwords linking steps A and A'.

A (31–34a) For many coming, **going** *(hypago),* had no leisure to **eat; went away** *(aperchomai)* in **boat** to lonely place by themselves. Many saw them **going** *(hypago),* and knew them, ran from all the towns; went ashore, saw a <u>great</u> **throng** *(ochlos).*

 B (34b) And he had compassion on them, because they were <u>like sheep without a shepherd</u>, began to teach many things. [Num 27:17]

  C (35–37a) Grew late, his **disciples** said, This is a lonely place; send them away, to go into country, villages round about, buy <u>something to eat</u>. Answered, You **give** them <u>something to eat</u>.

   D (37b) Shall we go and buy <u>two hundred</u> denarii worth of bread, and give it to them to eat?

    E (38a) How many loaves have you? <u>Go and see</u>.

     F (38b) And when they found out, they said, Five, and two fish.

    E' (39) <u>Commanded</u> all to sit down by companies upon grass.

D' (40) Sat down in groups, <u>hundreds</u> and <u>fifties</u>.

C' (41) Taking <u>the five loaves and the two fish</u> he looked up to heaven, blessed, broke <u>the loaves</u>, **gave** to **disciples** to set before people; divided <u>the two fish</u> among all.

B' (42) They <u>all ate and were satisfied</u>. [<u>Deut 8:10; 2 Kgs 4:42–44</u>]

A' (43–46) Took up twelve baskets full of broken pieces and fish. Those who **ate** the loaves were <u>five thousand men</u>. Made his disciples get into **boat, go before** *(proago)* him to other side, to Bethsaida, dismissed **crowd** *(ochlos)*. And after he had taken leave of them, he **went up** *(aper-chomai)* on mountain to pray.

Bridge Code: Mark 5:35–9:27

Chiastic patterns also spread across the seams between the acts (and also where they touch the prologue and conclusion). This bridge code spans the editor's inserted material from 6:47 through 8:26. One possible transition line from Original Mark may have been kept by the editor at 8:22, where Jesus and the disciples reached Bethsaida in separate boats.

A (5:35–41) Father is told, Your daughter **is dead.** Jesus **took her by the hand;** girl, I say <u>arise</u>.

B (6:1–6) Hometown among kin, **son** of Mary with brothers, sisters; <u>he could do no mighty works</u>; marveled at their **unbelief**.

C (6:7–13) Mission of the twelve **disciples;** authority over unclean **spirits;** they **cast out** many demons.

D (6:14–29) John the baptizer: **Elijah** raised **from the dead?** He was beheaded after Herodias's daughter danced and <u>pleased</u> Herod.

E (6:31–42) Jesus to disciples: Come away <u>by yourselves</u> to <u>lonely place</u>. He saw a great throng, taught them. Disciples: hour is late; send them away, to go <u>buy</u> something to eat. He answered, **You give** them something <u>to eat</u>. They said, Shall we buy two hundred denarii worth of bread, and give it to them to eat? [<u>Disciples ashamed of his words</u>.] How many loaves have you? Five, and two fish. So they <u>sat</u> down. Taking them he looked up to <u>heaven</u>, broke loaves, divided fish among them all. All <u>ate</u>, satisfied.

F (6:43–46/8:27–29a) They **took up** twelve baskets of broken pieces and the fish. And those who ate the loaves were <u>five thousand men</u>. He made his **disciples** get into boat and <u>go before</u> *(proago)* him to the other <u>side</u>, to Beth-saida, while he dismissed the **crowd** *(ochlos)*. Leaving them, he went up *(aperchomai)* mountain to pray. [8:22 And they **came** to Bethsaida. From Original Mark?] Jesus went on with his **disciples,** to villages of Caesarea Philippi; on the way he asked **disciples,** Who do **men** say that I am? Told him, John the Baptist; others say, Elijah; others one of prophets. Asked, But who do **you** say that I am?

> G (8:29b–30) **Peter** answered him, You are the Christ. And he **charged** *(epitimao)* them to <u>tell no one</u> about him.

> > H (8:31a) He began to teach them that the <u>Son of man</u> must <u>suffer</u> many things,

> > > I (8:31b) and be rejected by the elders and chief priests and scribes,

> > H' (831c) and <u>be killed</u>, and after three days <u>rise again</u>.

> G' (8:32) And he <u>said this plainly</u>. And **Peter** took him, and began to **rebuke** *(epitimao)* him.

F' (8:33–35) But turning and seeing his **disciples,** he rebuked Peter, and said, **Get** *(hypago)* <u>behind</u> me, Satan! For **you** are not on <u>the side</u> of God, but of **men.** And he called to him the **multitude** *(ochlos)* with his **disciples,** and said to them, If any [man] would come after me, let him deny himself and **take up** his cross and follow me. For whoever would save his life will lose it; whoever loses his life for my sake and the gospel's will save it.

E' (8:36–9:2a) For what does it <u>profit</u> a man, to <u>gain</u> the whole <u>world</u> and forfeit his life? For what can a man **give** in return for his life? For whoever is <u>ashamed of me</u> and <u>of my words</u>, of him will the Son of man also be ashamed, when he comes in the <u>glory of his Father</u>. Truly, I say to **you,** some <u>standing</u> who will not <u>taste</u> death before they see kingdom of God. Jesus took Peter, James, and John <u>up a mountain apart by themselves</u>.

D' (9:2b–13) **Elijah** and Moses appeared talking to Jesus; charged them to tell no one until Son of man should have <u>risen</u> **from the dead;** <u>rising</u> **from the dead.** First **Elijah** must come; did to him what they <u>pleased</u>.

    C' (9:14–20) A father brought to Jesus his son who has a dumb **spirit.** I asked your **disciples** to **cast** it **out,** and they were not able.

    B' (9:21–25) The **son** had affliction <u>from childhood</u>. Father cried out, I believe; help my **unbelief.** Jesus <u>commanded spirit to come out, healed boy</u>.

A' (9:26–27) Boy, lying still after spirit left, prompted crowd to say, He **is dead.** But Jesus **took him by the hand** and lifted him up, and he <u>arose</u>.

First-Quarter, Act 3: Mark 6:45–46+8:27–9:29

Private moments appear in the start, midpoint, and finish of Act 3's first-quarter chiasm, which borrowed two verses from the end of Act 2. There Jesus had sent the disciples off in a boat, dismissed the crowd, and went up a mountain to pray. The midpoint also takes place on a mountain when only Jesus was seen by the disciples after Elijah and Moses vanished from that vision. The ending has the disciples asking Jesus a question privately. The full A and A' steps have another thematic parallel: Both Jesus and the boy with the dumb spirit will appear to have been vanquished by death but both arise.

A (6:45–46) **Disciples** get in boat to Bethsaida; dismiss **crowd;** up mountain, **pray.** (8:27–33) Jesus **went on** *(exerchomai)* with **disciples** to Caesarea Philippi; on way, **asked** disciples, Who do people say **I** am? Said, John Baptist; others, Elijah; one of prophets; **asked** them, Who **you** say that **I** am? Peter: **You** are Christ. **Charged** *(epitimao)* tell none. Son of man suffer **many** *(polys)* things, <u>be killed</u>, after three days <u>rise</u>; said plainly. Peter rebuked him; **seeing** disciples, **rebuked** him, behind me, Satan, not on side of God.

    B (8:34–37) Multitude with disciples, **if** anyone come after me, deny self, take up cross, follow me; whoever save life would **lose** *(apollymi)* it; who **loses** life will save it; what profits to gain world, forfeit life? What give for life?

        C (8:38–9:1) <u>Ashamed of me, my words</u> in <u>adulterous and sinful</u> **generation**, will **Son** of man ashamed, in glory of Father with holy angels. Truly, some standing here not taste death before see kingdom of God come with power.

D (9:2–5) Jesus took Peter, James, John, led up high mountain; transfigured, garments glistening, intensely white, no fuller on earth could bleach. Appeared **Elijah** with Moses, talking with Jesus. Peter: Master, let's **make** *(poieo)* three booths, one for you, Moses, **Elijah.**

> E (9:6–7) He <u>did not know what to say</u>; were exceedingly <u>afraid</u>. A cloud overshadowed them, voice, This is my beloved **Son;** listen to him.

>> F (9:8a) Looking around, <u>no</u> longer **saw** <u>anyone</u>
>> G (9:8b) but Jesus only.
>> F' (9:9a) As came down mountain, charged tell <u>no</u> <u>one</u> what had **seen,**

> E' (9:9b–10) until the **Son** of man should have risen from the dead. So they <u>kept matter to themselves, questioning</u> what rising from dead meant.

D' (9:11–13) Asked, Why scribes say first **Elijah** must come? Said, **Elijah** comes restore all things; how is written Son of man suffer many things, contempt? **Elijah** has come, **did** *(poieo)* to him what pleased, as written.

C' (9:14–19) Came to disciples, saw great crowd, scribes arguing; greeted him. What you discussing? Teacher, brought **son;** dumb spirit, seizes him, grinds teeth, becomes rigid; <u>asked your</u> <u>disciples</u> to cast out; <u>they not able</u>. O <u>faithless</u> **generation,** <u>how</u> <u>long I with you, bear with you</u>?

B' (9:20–24) Brought boy to him and spirit convulsed boy who fell on ground. How long had this? From childhood. <u>Cast into fire</u>, water, to **destroy** *(apollymi)* him; **if** you can do anything. Jesus: **If** you can! <u>All things possible to</u> one <u>who believes</u>. Father of child cried out, <u>I believe</u>; help my unbelief!

A' (9:25–29) When Jesus **saw crowd,** he **rebuked** *(epitimao)* unclean spirit, **You** deaf, dumb spirit, **I** command, **come** out, never enter again. Crying, convulsing **terribly** *(polys),* **came** out; boy was <u>like corpse</u>, so **most** said, He is <u>dead</u>. Jesus took him, he <u>arose</u>. In house, **disciples** **asked** *(eperotao)* privately, Why could we not cast it out? This kind not **driven out** *(exerchomai)* by anything but **prayer.**

Macrocode

Starting at Prologue (1:1–14) and Epilogue (15:34–16:8)

I HAD ARRANGED the opening and closing of Mark this way, eventually prompting me to go further into the Gospel. If, however, the two sections were considered two giant steps (A and A') for the rest of this gospel-length macrocode, then "ministered to" *(diakoneo)* at 1:13 and 15:41 would be added catchwords.

Prologue
Messenger: John the Baptist. **Behold** *(idou)*, send messenger **before** thy face.
John the Baptist, appeared, preaching.
   Setting: wilderness
      John the Baptist baptizes Jesus
         Saw heavens **open** *(schizo)*, Spirit enters Jesus; Godly **voice** *(phone)* calls Jesus beloved **Son.**
            Jesus, sorely tested in wilderness, aided by angels

---

Conclusion
            Jesus, nearing death, feared that God forsook him.
         Jesus breathes last, utters **cry** *(phone)*; temple curtain **torn** *(schizo)*; centurion: this man **Son** of God.

Joseph of Arimathea buries Jesus
Setting: the tomb
Messenger: Young man: Risen, **see** *(ide)* place they laid him; tell disciples and Peter he going **before** <u>you</u> to Galilee; but (women) said nothing to anyone (failed messengers).

The great distance between the ensuing pairs of chiastic steps requires this style of presentation until the smaller, more manageable midpoint is reached.

(1:14–15) After John arrested, Jesus **came** into Galilee, preaching gospel of **God:** The <u>time</u> is fulfilled; **kingdom** of **God** is at hand; <u>repent</u>, **believe** in the gospel.

> (15:32–33+Luke 23:39–43+15:33) Let Christ, King of Israel, come down <u>now</u> from cross, see, **believe.** One of criminals railed, You not Christ? Save yourself and us! Other rebuked, Do not fear **God;** under same condemnation, we justly; receiving due reward of deeds; this man done nothing wrong; Jesus, remember me when you **come** into **kingdom;** truly, <u>today</u> you be with me in Paradise. When <u>sixth hour</u> had come, darkness over whole land until <u>ninth hour</u>.

(1:16–20) **Passing along** *(parago)* Sea of Galilee, **Simon,** Andrew, **casting** *(amphiballo)* net; make you <u>fishers of [people]</u>; they followed; little farther, <u>James</u>, son of Zebedee, <u>John, brother</u>, mending nets; left **father** in boat.

> (15:21–31) **Passerby** *(parago)* **Simon** of Cyrene; **father** (of two <u>brothers</u>), carry cross; brought to Golgotha; garments, **casting** *(ballo)* lots; crucified two robbers, <u>one on his right, one on his left</u>; mocked, <u>saved others</u>.

(1:21–28) Synagogue; taught as one who had authority, not as **scribes;** spirit **cried:** Jesus, <u>I know you, Holy One of God</u>. Be <u>silent</u>. People: <u>New teaching, with authority, commands spirits, they obey him</u>. Fame through **all** Galilee. (four signs of power)

> (15:1–20) **Whole** council, **scribes,** led him to Pilate. Pilate asked: <u>Are you King of the Jews</u>? Jesus: You said so; asked again; <u>made no further answer</u>. Pilate: Release King of the Jews? Crowd, **cried, shouted:** Crucify him. Soldiers led him away, **whole** battalion; mocked him. (four times "King of the Jews")

(1:29–39) Jesus lifted up Simon's mother-in-law, fever left; healed many, cast out many demons; would not permit demons to speak, because they **knew** him. In morning, a great while before day, he rose, went to pray. Simon pursued, (reminded Jesus of mission); went throughout **Galilee,** preaching, casting out demons.

(14:66–72) Maid: You were with Nazarene, Jesus. Peter denied, neither **know** or understand; again denied it; after a little while, bystanders: you are **Galilean.** He began to invoke a curse on himself: I do not **know** this man of whom you speak. Cock crowed second time; Peter remembered Jesus said, Before cock crows twice, you will deny me three times; he broke down, wept.

(1:40–2:12) Leper, make me clean; **I** will, be clean; **see** that you say nothing, but show to **priest,** as **proof** *(martyrion);* **reported** *(akouo)* he was home; to paralytic, your sins forgiven; scribes, **sitting,** questioning in hearts: **Why** does this man speak thus? It is **blasphemy! Who** can forgive sins but God alone? Jesus: **Son of man** has authority on earth to forgive; **I** say to you, rise.

(14:55–65) **Testimony** (twice) *(martyria),* **false witness** (twice) *(pseudomartyreo),* **testify against** *(katamartyreo);* **heard** *(akouo)* to say, **I** will destroy; high **priest:** You **Son** of the Blessed? **I** am, will **see Son of man seated** at right hand of Power, clouds heaven; high **priest: Why** we still need **witnesses** *(martys)?* You have **heard** *(akouo)* his **blasphemy! What** is your decision?

(2:13–17) **All** crowd **gathered** *(erchomai),* he taught; saw Levi **sitting** at tax office; **follow** me, he **followed** him; tax collectors and sinners were sitting with Jesus; many **followed; scribes:** Why? Jesus: I came not to call righteous but sinners.

(14:51–54) Young man **followed** him; ran away naked; **all** the chief priests, elders, **scribes** were **assembed** *(synerchomai).* Peter had **followed** at distance, **sitting with** guards, warming himself.

(2:18–22) Your disciples do not fast; can wedding guests fast while bridegroom with them? **Days** will come when bridegroom is taken away from them, then will fast in that **day.** (Teaching:) No one sews piece unshrunk cloth on old garment; if does, the **patch** *(pleroma)* tears away from it, worse tear is made.

(14:43–50) Judas came, <u>one of the twelve</u>, with him crowd, clubs, swords. Sign, <u>one I kiss</u> is the man; <u>kissed him</u>; seized him; Jesus: **Day** after **day** I was with you in temple <u>teaching</u>, you did not seize me. Let scriptures be **fulfilled.** *(pleroo)* They all forsook him, fled.

(2:23–3:12) One sabbath, disciples plucking grain. **Look** *(ide),* why doing what not lawful on sabbath? **Son of man** is lord even of sabbath; man with a withered **hand, hand; Come** here *(egeiro);* **hand, hand.** Whenever unclean **spirits** beheld, **fell down before** *(prospipto)* him: <u>You are the Son of God</u>.

   (14:32–42) While I pray; watch (lit., keep awake); going further, he **fell** *(prospipto)* <u>on ground</u>, prayed, <u>Abba, Father</u>, remove cup; found them sleeping; Simon, you asleep? **Spirit** willing; again sleeping, third time; sleeping, taking rest? **Son of man** betrayed into **hands** of sinners. **Rise** *(egeiro),* **see** *(idou),* my betrayer.

(3:13–19) On **mountain,** he appointed <u>twelve</u> to be with him; Simon whom he surnamed **Peter;** James, son of Zebedee . . . and Judas Iscariot, who <u>betrayed</u> him.

   (14:26–31) **Mount** of Olives; You <u>will all fall away</u>. Peter: I will not. Jesus: You will deny me <u>three</u> times. If I die, I will not, all said same.

(3:20–35) Crowd, could not **eat;** family went to seize him, said he possessed. If **kingdom** divided, **kingdom** cannot stand; house divided cannot stand. **Truly, I say to you,** all sins forgiven **sons of men,** but whoever blasphemes Holy Spirit, never has forgiveness, guilty of eternal sin; whoever does will **of God** my mother, brother, sister.

   (14:17–25) As **eating,** Jesus: **Truly, I say to you,** one of you will betray me, one **eating;** one after another: Is it **I?** One of twelve; **Son of man** goes as written, woe to man by whom Son of man is betrayed; better not born. Blessed bread, all drank. **Truly, I say to you;** drink it new in **kingdom of God.**

(4:1–8) **Teach** beside the <u>sea</u>, sat in boat on <u>sea</u>, beside the sea. **Taught** in parables, in **teaching,** said: Sower sows; other seeds yielded <u>grain</u> hundred-fold. (ground <u>not prepared</u> for three plantings, growth in good soil)

(14:12–16) <u>Day of Unleavened Bread</u>, passover; where <u>prepare</u> to eat? Man carrying jar of <u>water</u> meet you; say to householder: **Teacher** says, where is guest room? Show you room <u>ready</u>; there <u>prepare</u> for us; prepared passover. (<u>to "prepare"</u> meal three times; success when find furnished room ready).

(4:9–12) He who has ears to **hear,** let him **hear.** Those about him with **the twelve** asked about parables. To you **given** *(didomi)* secret of kingdom of God; those outside, not perceive; **hear,** do not understand, lest turn, be forgiven.

(14:10–11) Judas Iscariot, one of **the twelve,** went to chief priests to **betray** *(paradidomi)* him; when **heard** it, were glad. Sought to **betray** him.

(4:13–20) Not understand parable? Sower sows the <u>word</u>. Others sown among thorns, hear the <u>word</u>, but <u>cares of world, delight in riches, desire for other things</u>, choke the <u>word</u>. Those sown in good soil <u>hear word and accept it</u>, bear fruit.

(14:3–9) Woman with <u>alabaster flask, ointment of pure nard, very costly</u>; broke it, poured it over his head. <u>Why was ointment wasted? Might have sold for three hundred denarii</u>, given to poor. Done beautiful thing, anointed my body beforehand; whenever <u>gospel is preached</u>, memory of her.

(4:21–29) <u>Nothing hid, nor anything secret</u>, except to come to light. **Take heed.** If man should scatter seed, **sleep** and rise <u>night and day</u>; sprout and grow, **knows not** how.

(13:33–14:2) **Take heed,** watch (lit., keep awake); you do **not know** when; watch; you do **not know** when master will come, <u>evening, midnight, cockcrow</u> or <u>morning</u>—lest he find you **asleep.** Chief priests, scribes seeking to arrest Jesus <u>by stealth</u>, kill him; not during feast.

(4:30–34) Kingdom of <u>God</u>, what **parable** *(parabole)* shall we use? It is like mustard seed, smallest of all seeds on **earth;** grows up, **puts forth** large **branches,** so birds of the **air** *(ouranos)* can make nests. With many **parables** he spoke **the word** to them; not without a **parable.**

(13:28–32) From fig tree learn its **lesson** *(parabole);* soon as its **branch** becomes tender, **puts forth** leaves; **heaven** *(ouranos)* and

earth shall pass away, but my **words** will not. Of that day, hour, no one knows, not angels in **heaven,** nor the Son, but only the Father.

(4:35–5:4) On that **day,** in the boat, storm of **wind** arose, waves beat into boat; he rebuked the **wind:** Be still; **wind** ceased; even **wind** obeys. ("wind" four times)

> (13:24–27) In those **days,** sun darkened, stars falling, powers in heaven shaken; Son of man; send angels, gather his elect from the four **winds.**

(5:5–19) Night and **day** among tombs and **mountains** *(oros)* [demoniac] cried out. Saw Jesus, worshiped him: Jesus, Son of Most High God, by God, do not torment; swine on **hillside** *(oros),* let us **enter** them; **entered** swine, into sea, herdsmen **fled.** People came to see what **happened** *(ginomai);* told what **happened;** Jesus: Go home, tell how much **the Lord** has done for you.

> (13:14–23) Let those in Judea **flee** to **mountains,** [not] **enter** house; alas, for those who give suck in those **days.** Pray it not **happen** in winter; those **days** will be such tribulation, not **been** *(ginomai)* since creation, never will **be** *(ginomai).* If **the Lord** not shortened **days;** he shortened **days.**

(5:20–34) Began to **proclaim** *(kerysso)* how much Jesus had done; Jairus: My little daughter is at point of death *(eschatos);* lay hands on her, be **made well** *(sozo).* Woman, flow of blood, if I touch garments, I shall be **made well;** Daughter, your faith has **made you well;** go in peace.

> (13:9–13) Gospel must be **preached** *(kerysso)* to all nations; brother deliver up brother to death, father his child, children rise against parents, put to death; But who[ever] endures to the end *(telos)* will be **saved** *(sozo).*

(5:35–43) Jesus: Do not fear, only believe; allowed no one to follow but **Peter, James** and **John,** brother of James; why you make tumult and weep? Little girl, **arise** *(egeiro);* ordered, no one should know this.

> (13:3–8) **Peter, James, John** and Andrew asked him privately; what will be sign, all to be accomplished; do not be alarmed; nation will **rise** against nation.

(6:1–6) Began to **teach** in synagogue, many astonished: Where did this man get this? What is wisdom given to him? What mighty works wrought by his hands? Is not this the carpenter; are not sisters **here** with us? Jesus: <u>Prophet</u> not without honor except in own house; <u>marveled</u> at unbelief.

(13:1–2) As came out of <u>temple</u>, one disciple said, Look, **Teacher,** <u>what wonderful</u> stones and <u>what wonderful</u> buildings! Jesus said: See these great buildings? (<u>Prophesied</u>:) Will not be left **here** one stone upon another, that will not be thrown down.

(6:7–13) **He called to him** <u>the twelve</u>, sent them **two** by **two,** no **money,** not to **put** on **two** tunics. They **cast out** *(ekballo)* many demons.

(12:41–44) Multitude **put** *(ballo)* **money** in treasury. Rich **put** in big sums. Poor widow **put** in **two** coins. **He called to him** <u>his disciples,</u> said widow **put** in more.

(6:14–29) <u>Is Jesus Elijah</u>? King Herod, **heard, heard, heard him gladly,** gave **banquet** for court. Head of John the Baptist on platter. Disciples **heard** it.

(12:35–40) <u>Is Christ son of David</u>? Lord, lord; put enemies under thy feet; throng **heard him gladly;** scribes like places of honor at **feasts,** devour widows' houses.

(6:30–46) <u>Three scriptural allusions</u>. Shall we buy with <u>two hundred</u> denarii? <u>Commanded</u> crowd sit on grass; looked to <u>heaven</u>; fed all with <u>five</u> loaves and <u>two</u> fish.

(12:28–34) <u>Three scriptural citations</u>. Which <u>commandment</u> is <u>first</u> of all? Love God as <u>one; second</u>, love neighbor; more than burnt offerings; <u>kingdom of God</u>.

(Skip over 6:47–8:26, which was added later to the Gospel.)

(8:27–33) Who do people say **I am?** John the Baptist, <u>Elijah</u>, prophet? You say **I am?** Christ. **Taught** them Son of man killed, **rise** again; Peter rebuked him; Satan, you not on side of **God.**

(12:18–27) **Teacher,** <u>Moses</u> wrote. Questions on widow who married seven brothers who died. Whose wife in heaven when rise from dead? **God** said, **I am God** of <u>Abraham, Isaac, Jacob</u>. He is not **God** of dead.

(8:34–9:1) Deny self, follow me. Whoever loses life <u>for my sake</u> will save it. What <u>profit to gain world</u>, forfeit life? What can **give** *(didomi)* for life? Glory of <u>Father</u>. Some will **see** *(eidon)* kingdom of **God.**

(12:13–17) We know you do not regard positions of men. Should **pay** *(didomi)* taxes to Caesar; should we **pay** them? **Look** *(eidon)* at a coin; Whose likeness? **Render** *(apodidomi)* things of Caesar to Caesar; to **God** things that are **God's.**

(9:2–10) Transfiguration; garments **became** *(ginomai)* <u>glistening</u>, <u>intensely white</u>; **exceedingly afraid** *(ekphobos);* voice **came** *(ginomai)* out of cloud: **my beloved Son,** listen; **kept** *(krateo)* to themselves.

(12:1–12) Vineyard owner sends **beloved son,** tenants kill him; stone rejected has **become** head; Lord's **doing** *(ginomai);* <u>marvelous in our eyes</u>; tried to **arrest** *(krateo)* him but **feared** *(phobeo)* multitude.

(9:11–13) Why **scribes** say first <u>Elijah</u> must come? <u>Elijah</u> does come first to restore all things. Son of man suffer many things. I tell you <u>Elijah (John the Baptist)</u> has come; **did** with him as they pleased.

(11:27–33) Priests, **scribes,** elders said, By what authority you **do** these things? <u>Baptism</u> of <u>John</u> from heaven? All held <u>John</u> was prophet; we do not know; neither will I tell you by what authority I **do** these things.

(9:14–32) **Teacher,** brought my son; asked disciples to **cast** it **out; faithless** generation; (spirit) often **cast** <u>into water</u> **to destroy him;** who **believes;** help **unbelief;** I <u>command</u> you, come out, **never** enter **again;** in **house,** disciples: why could not **cast out** *(ekballo);* by **prayer; passed through** Galilee; **teaching** Son of man killed; **afraid** to ask.

(11:12–25) Went to **see** if fig tree had fruit; not season; (<u>command</u>) may **no one ever again** eat fruit from you; **drove out** *(ekballo)* merchants temple; **taught** my **house** called **house** of **prayer;** priests sought **to destroy him; feared;** astonished at **teaching; passed by** fig tree withered; **faith** in God; mountain **cast** <u>into sea</u>; whoever **believes;** ask in **prayer, believe** received; when **praying.**

(9:33–50) **On the way;** silent, **on the way** discussed who greatest; Jesus **sat down,** called **twelve;** if **anyone** first; last of **all, all;** whoever <u>receives</u>

one such child **in** my **name,** <u>receives not me but him who</u> **sent** me; we
saw man **casting out** demons **in** your **name, forbade** *(kolyo)* him, not
following us; Jesus: do not **forbid; no one** who does mighty work **in**
my **name** be able to speak evil; bear the **name** of <u>Christ</u>; if cause to sin,
thrown, thrown, thrown, cut off, cut off.

    (11:2b–11) Find colt **tied** *(lyo),* **no one** has **sat; untie** it; if **anyone**
says why, say Lord has <u>need</u>, will **send** it back; found colt **tied;
untied** it. Brought colt to Jesus, **threw** garments on it, he **sat** on it;
spread garments **on the road;** spread branches cut from fields; those
followed cried, <u>Hosanna! Blessed he who comes</u> **in the name** of
<u>Lord</u>! Blessed <u>kingdom of father David</u>; entered Jerusalem; looked
at **everything,** out with **twelve.**

(Luke 9:51–56+10:2–9) Days <u>drew near to be received up</u>, set face go
to **Jerusalem, sent** messengers, went **village** Samaritans; they would
not receive *(dechomai)* him; set toward **Jerusalem;** James, John: **want**
fire consume them? **rebuked** them; **village.** <u>Pharisees</u> test; <u>Moses,
Moses</u>; for <u>hardness of heart</u>; God **made** *(poieo)* male, female; shall leave
father, **mother; two** become one.

    (10:45–46a+Secret Mark+46b–52,11:2a) Son of man came, <u>give
life as ransom</u>; Jericho, sister, **mother,** Salome; Jesus did **not receive**
(apodechomai); blind beggar: Jesus, Son of David, have mercy, many
rebuked; Son of <u>David</u>; call him, <u>take heart</u>; to Jesus; what **want** me
do *(poieo);* <u>Master</u>, receive sight; faith made well; <u>drew near</u> to
Jerusalem, sent two disciples; go to **village.**

(10:10–16) **Whoever** divorces wife; they were bringing children; <u>disci-
ples</u> rebuked them; when Jesus saw it, was **indignant;** do not hinder; to
such belongs kingdom of God; **whoever** not receive <u>kingdom</u> of God
like child; blessed, laying his <u>hands</u> on them.

    (10:38b–44) Able drink cup I drink; be baptized with baptism I am
baptized? we able; cup drink, baptism, baptized; to sit at my <u>right</u>
<u>hand</u> or at my <u>left (hand)</u> not to grant; when <u>ten</u> heard it, **indig-
nant** at <u>James and John</u>; those who <u>rule</u> Gentiles; not you; **whoever**
would be great; **whoever** would be first, must be slave of all.

(10:17–19) **Setting out** *(ekporeuomai),* man <u>knelt</u> before him, good
teacher, what must I **do** to inherit <u>eternal life</u>? No one good but God
alone; know commandments: Do not; honor <u>father</u>/mother.

(10:35–38a) James, John, sons of Zebedee, **came forward** *(prosporeuomai)*, **Teacher, do whatever** we ask; **what** want me to **do?** Grant us sit, one at right, one at left <u>in your glory</u>; "You **not know what** you are asking."

Midpoint of Macrocode

A (10:20–27) **Teacher,** all these I observed from my <u>youth</u> *(neotes).* Jesus, **looking upon him, loved him;** sell, give to poor, come, follow me; at that saying, went sorrowful; Jesus **looked** around, hard for those with **riches** to **enter** *(eiserchomai)* **kingdom of God; enter kingdom of God;** amazed at words; for **rich** man to **enter kingdom of God;** who can be saved? Jesus **looked at** them, with men impossible, not with **God,** all possible with **God.**

B (10:28–31a) Peter **began to say** *(archo lego):* **Lo** *(idou),* we left everything, **followed** you; no one who left house, **brothers,** <u>sisters</u>, mother, father, <u>children</u> or lands, for <u>my sake and for the gospel</u>, who will not **receive** *(lambano)* hundredfold in this time houses, **brothers,** <u>sisters</u>, mothers, children, lands <u>with persecutions</u>, and in age to **come** <u>eternal life. Many that are will be</u>[1]

C (10:31b–f) first

last

and

last

first.[2]

B' (10:32–34+Secret Mark) <u>They were</u> on road, going to Jerusalem, Jesus ahead; amazed, those **followed** afraid; **taking** *(paralambano)* <u>twelve</u>, he **began to tell** *(archo lego)* what going to happen to him, **Behold** *(idou),* going up to Jerusalem; **Son of** man <u>delivered</u> to chief priest, scribes; will <u>condemn</u> him to <u>death, mock, spit upon him, scourge, kill</u> him; <u>three</u> days <u>he will rise</u>; **come** into Bethany, <u>woman</u> whose **brother** had died there;

A' (Secret Mark) Coming, she prostrated before Jesus: Son of David, have mercy; disciples rebuked her. Jesus, angered, went with her to garden, tomb was; cry heard; Jesus rolled stone from tomb, **going in** *(eiserchomai)* where <u>young man</u> *(neaniskos);* raised him, seizing his hand;

---

1. Word order in Greek.
2. Word order in Greek.

young man, **looking on him, loved him,** began to beseech to be with him; going out of tomb, came to **house** young man; he was **rich;** after six days, what to do; young man wearing linen cloth over naked body; remained night; Jesus **taught** secret of **kingdom of God**. Arising, returned to other side of Jordan.

Suggested Reading

Secret Gospel of Mark and Other Gospels

Brown, Scott G. "On Composition History of the Longer ('Secret') Gospel of Mark." *Journal of Biblical Literature* 122 (Spring 2003): 89–110.

Cameron, Ron, ed. *Semeia 49: The Apocryphal Jesus and Christian Origins.* Atlanta: Scholars Press, 1990.

Dart, John. *The Jesus of Heresy and History: The Discovery and Meaning of the Nag Hammadi Gnostic Library.* San Francisco: Harper & Row, 1988.

Gundry, Robert H. *Mark: A Commentary on His Apology for the Cross,* esp. "Excursus on the Secret Gospel of Mark," pp. 603–23. Grand Rapids: Eerdmans, 1993.

Hedrick, Charles W., with Nikolaos Olympiou. "Secret Mark: New Photographs, New Witnesses." *The Fourth R* 13 (September/October 2000): 3–11 and 14–16.

Iersel, Bas M. F. van. *Mark: A Reader-Response Commentary.* Journal for the Study of the New Testament: Supplement Series 164. Sheffield: Sheffield Academic Press, 1998.

Kelber, Werner H. *Mark's Story of Jesus.* Philadelphia: Fortress, 1979.

Kermode, Frank. *The Genesis of Secrecy: On the Interpretation of Narrative.* Cambridge: Harvard University Press, 1979.

Koester, Helmut. *Ancient Christian Gospels: Their History and Development.* Harrisburg, Pa.: Trinity Press International, 1990.

———. "History and Development of Mark's Gospel (From Mark to Secret Mark and 'Canonical' Mark)." Pages 35–57 in *Colloquy on New Testament Studies: A Time for Reappraisal and Fresh Approaches.* Edited by Bruce C. Corley. Macon, Ga.: Mercer University Press, 1983.

———. *History and Literature of Early Christianity.* Vol. 2 of *Introduction to the New Testament.* Philadelphia: Fortress, 1982.

Meyer, Marvin. *Secret Gospels: Essays on Thomas and the Secret Gospel of Mark.* Harrisburg, Pa.: Trinity Press International, 2003.

Sellew, Philip. "Secret Mark and the History of Canonical Mark." Pages 242–57 in *The Future of Early Christianity: Essays in Honor of Helmut Koester.* Edited by Birger A. Pearson. Minneapolis: Fortress, 1991.

Smith, Morton. *Clement of Alexandria and a Secret Gospel of Mark.* Cambridge: Harvard University Press, 1973.

———. *The Secret Gospel: The Discovery and Interpretation of the Secret Gospel according to Mark.* New York: Harper & Row, 1973.

Tolbert, Mary Ann. *Sowing the Gospel: Mark's World in Literary-Historical Perspective.* Minneapolis: Fortress, 1989.

Chiasms

Breck, John. *The Shape of Biblical Language: Chiasmus in the Scriptures and Beyond.* Crestwood, N.Y.: St. Vladimir's Seminary Press, 1994.

Dewey, Joanna. "The Literary Structure of the Controversy Stories in Mark 2:1–3:6." Pages 109–18 in *The Interpretation of Mark.* Edited by William Telford. Issues in Religion and Theology 7. Philadelphia: Fortress, 1985.

Dorsey, David A. *The Literary Structure of the Old Testament: A Commentary on Genesis–Malachi.* Grand Rapids: Baker, 1999.

Scott, M. Philip. "Chiastic Structure: A Key to the Interpretation of Mark's Gospel." *Biblical Theology Bulletin* 15 (January 1985): 17–26.

Stock, Augustine, "Chiastic Awareness and Education in Antiquity." *Biblical Theology Bulletin* 14 (January 1984): 23–27.

Thomson, Ian H. *Chiasmus in the Pauline Letters.* Journal for the Study of the New Testament: Supplement Series 111. Sheffield: Sheffield Academic Press, 1995.

Welch, John W., and Daniel B. McKinley, eds. *Chiasmus Bibliography.* Provo, Utah: Research Press, 1999.

Biblical Reference

Aland, Kurt. *Synopsis of the Four Gospels.* English ed. New York: United Bible Societies, 1982.

Cameron, Ron. *The Other Gospels: Non-Canonical Gospel Texts.* Philadelphia: Westminster, 1982.

Funk, Robert W., ed. *New Gospel Parallels.* Vol. 1 of *The Synoptic Gospels.* Philadelphia: Fortress, 1985.

Miller, Robert J., ed. *The Complete Gospels: Annotated Scholars Version.* Polebridge Press Book. San Francisco: HarperSanFrancisco, 1994.

Morrison, Clinton. *An Analytical Concordance to the Revised Standard Version of the New Testament.* Philadelphia: Westminster, 1979

Index